D0918441

EMPIRE IMAGINED

EMPIRE IMAGINED

THE PERSONALITY OF AMERICAN POWER

VOLUME ONE

GISELLE FRANCES DONNELLY

SUNY
PRESS

Cover art: "The Armada Portrait" by John Gower, courtesy of the Bedford Estates.

Published by State University of New York Press, Albany

© 2022 State University of New York

All rights reserved

Printed in the United States of America

No part of this book may be used or reproduced in any manner whatsoever without written permission. No part of this book may be stored in a retrieval system or transmitted in any form or by any means including electronic, electrostatic, magnetic tape, mechanical, photocopying, recording, or otherwise without the prior permission in writing of the publisher.

For information, contact State University of New York Press, Albany, NY
www.sunypress.edu

Library of Congress Cataloging-in-Publication Data

Name: Donnelly, Giselle Frances, author.
Title: Empire imagined : the personality of American power, volume one /
   Giselle Frances Donnelly.
Description: Albany : State University of New York Press, [2022] | Includes
   bibliographical references and index.
Identifiers: ISBN 9781438489858 (hardcover : alk. paper) | ISBN 9781438489865
   (ebook)
Further information is available at the Library of Congress.

10 9 8 7 6 5 4 3 2 1

For Bethie

The Spaniards govern in the Indies with all pride and tyranny, and like as when people of contrary nature at the sea enter into galleys, where men are tied as slaves, all yell and cry with once voice *liberta, liberta*, as desirous of liberty or freedom, so no doubt whensoever the Queen of England, a prince of such clemency, shall sit upon that firm of America, and shall be reported throughout all that tract to use the natural people there with all humanity, courtesy, and freedom, they will yield themselves to her government and revolt clean from the Spaniard.

—Richard Hakluyt, *Discourse of Western Planting, 1584**

---

*Richard Hakluyt, "A particular discourse concerning the great necessity and manifold commodities that are like to grow to this Realm of England by Western discoveries lately attempted, Written in the year 1584," http://explorehistory.ou.edu/wp-content/uploads/2018/01/Hakluyt-Discourse-of-Western-Planting.pdf.

CONTENTS

ILLUSTRATIONS

PREFACE

This book is the first in a series intended to plumb what might be called the "unconscious mind of American strategy-making," to perform a sort of "strategic psychoanalysis." Frequently, a nation's strategy is imagined as the product of a highly rational, organized, and material process: an objective weighing of material national interests, an assessment of threats, a balancing of means, ways, and ends culminating in a formal document or memorandum that guides government policy and the use of military force. What follows is rather different. Patterns emerge from the chaos, but they originate from the ways that kings and queens, princes, generals, the people at large—the "political nation"—view the world, what in it is worth fighting for, and how best to do it. Formal strategy decisions and documents tend to ratify preexisting prejudices and habits of thought. The series tells a long, winding, complex, and occasionally contradictory tale, a kaleidoscope of contingency, individual character, battlefield chance, confessional and ideological struggle, unforeseen technological consequence, clashing cultures, humanity in all its shapes and colors.

I first began to wonder about America's attitudes to such questions during my service as a staff member of the House Armed Services Committee in the late 1990s. In these early post-Cold-War years, and in particular as the former Yugoslavia broke into savage ethnic conflict, the senior committee members—of both political parties—felt adrift, unmoored from the certainties that came with decades of opposition to the Soviet Union. These post-Cold-War conflicts were "teacup wars," according to some analysis, which meant, to President Bill Clinton as well as to Congress, that the United States should stay out of the tiny tempest.[1] I wrote statements and speeches for the committee chairman and passages in legislation to such effect. Yet even for conservative

Republicans, as for the president they loathed and mistrusted, this distanced stance was hard to hold. Perhaps it was hard to tell a Serb from a Croat from a Bosniac, but it wasn't hard to tell good guys from bad guys, nor to grasp that, if America remained unwilling to do anything, no one else was really able to. Soon the complaint became not Clinton's recklessness, but his fecklessness; when, through the agency of NATO, he committed US forces to the region, he enjoyed the hearty support of Newt Gingrich's caucus. I wrote more statements and speeches and legislative language, now to that opposite effect.

Why the change? It was not the product of a measured reevaluation of interests, costs, or material benefits, not the manifestation of a "new world order." It was—as many who counseled against involvement feared—the reemergence of old habits, moral as well directly strategic. Beyond partisanship, beyond policy debate, the course ahead for the politicians for whom and against whom I worked was defined principally by their inherited past and by their understanding of what that past meant.

And so I began to read backward to the American founding and the Revolution. Surely, as an intentionally constructed and naturally fractious state rather than a blood-and-soil nation, with a written constitution, this was the key moment. But then I read backward some more, and as I did so it became increasingly clear that 1776 was a revolution within a strategic tradition, not against it; the colonists' complaint against George III stemmed first from his imperial timidity more than his tyranny. Like the 1990s, the late 1760s and early 1770s were very much a "unipolar moment," with Britain the "sole superpower" upon whose domain the sun did not set. In seeking a "peace dividend" and to avoid breaking china in continental Europe, it was the king—and the parliament he dominated—who failed to fulfill what Americans believed to be the longstanding imperial proposition.

The end of the backward trail and the origins of the imperial proposition seemed to me to be in the Elizabethan era, in the events sketched in this volume. That is when Englishmen—who were "British" in mind if not yet in form—first came to North America to stay. In mind they were also men and women (their queen especially) of the Reformation, not yet the Enlightenment, and this habit is one more deeply ingrained and less appreciated than the "1776" version of America has it; it is also very much at odds with the present "1619" version of America. As statesmen and strategists, the British of North America were "globalists" with a nuanced assessment of the worldwide balance of power, the very opposite of "Little Englanders" sheltering behind the wooden walls of their navy. They felt their geopolitical and military weakness keenly and that the only security lay in imperial expansion. And finally, they made a fundamental connection between their security and their liberty; the only safe world was a just and free world. One might, of necessity, make pacts with devils, even with Catholics, but they could not last. To grant Philip II of Spain his desired sphere of influence was to commit national and confessional suicide. Philip's coinage captured his visage on one face and his strategic vision on the other: "*Non sufficit orbis*"—The world is not enough." While the Spanish king's eyes may have been looking to heaven, Elizabeth and her advisors feared it was in fact fixed upon them.

My gaze, too, has been more or less unblinking in trying to stalk these deep American strategic habits to their lair and bring them to light. Family, friends, and colleagues have tolerated—enabled?—this monomania with love, kindness, and forbearing. These gifts demand acknowledgement. The traditional order of these things is to conclude with one's family, but I need to start there; my beloved bride Bethie is the source of an ever-fair sea and following wind. Family was also the font of my professional life. I come from a newspaper clan and my journalism career at the Army Times Publishing Company was following the family trade, in my father William Donnelly's footsteps and those of his stepfather and alongside my brother John and sister Ann. That was also the source of my lasting interest and education in military affairs. I owe a continuing debt of gratitude to former Army Chief of Staff General Carl Vuono and his personal staff, including Raoul Alcala, Jim Fetig, Bob Killebrew, Dave Petraeus, and Doug Lute, all of whom took me places I would never have otherwise been and taught me things I might never have otherwise learned. My transmogrification from scribbler to scholar would not have been possible but for Eliot Cohen, until lately dean of Johns Hopkins School of Advanced International Studies and the power behind its superb strategic studies program; Eliot has been a teacher, debating partner, business partner, and friend ever since. He also introduced me to a group of like-minded students of strategy and civil-military affairs, who have patiently provided a sensible sounding board as I've worked through this study: Dick Kohn, Peter Feaver, Tom Ricks, Tom Keaney, Andy Bacevich, and the aforementioned Bob Killebrew. A fourth source of inspiration and insight I have derived from my former comrades on the House Armed Services Committee staff: Andy Ellis, Robert Rangel, Maureen Cragin, Dino Aviles, Phil Grone, and especially Dave Trachtenberg shared the congressional trenches, where we struggled hand to hand to understand how politicians think about war and the use of armed force; the experience gave me a kind of extra empathy for the princes and parliaments of the distant past. I also learned to appreciate the critical role that staff—"clerks" in Elizabethan terms—must play in support of such leaders. Deep states are durable states; Philip II squandered riches, lives, and Spain's moment of preeminence for the want of sufficient support staff. Fifth: I have been privileged to work in the uniquely American world of the Washington "think tank" for two decades and in particular for institutions whose funding comes from private donations rather the government largesse. My time at the Project for a New American Century was a formative experience and a wonderful opportunity, a product of the energy, patriotism, and kindness of Bill Kristol. Gary Schmitt has been a partner in crime since those years, a source of deep knowledge on the American founding and common baseball traditionalism for two decades. Gary also joined me at the American Enterprise Institute, which has been my home for nearly two decades. I say without boast that AEI is in the front rank of private research institutes; its presidents—Chris DeMuth, Arthur Brooks, and Robert Doar during my tenure—have been unwavering in their commitment to the support and intellectual independence of AEI scholars. And this without-fear-or-favor ethos has been most vividly embodied in the two women who have been my direct bosses: Danielle Pletka and Kori Schake, lionesses in protecting us cubs. I owe a callout to Michael Rinella, Susan Geraghty, Eileen Nizer, Ryan Morris, Alicia Brady at the State University of New York press for their help and patience. And Barry Hudock is powerful reminder of why authors are so obsequiously grateful to those who edit their copy. His touch has been gentle, but his gaze severe; if errors in the text or citations remain, the fault is entirely mine. Readers will appreciate Danielle Curran's elegant maps as this tale follows the tracks of military forces across the globe.

But this author's greatest gratitude goes to those rarely met: the scholars and historians who have come before me and upon whose shoulders I rest, and the readers, present and future, whom I hope to engage, enlighten, and, above all, entertain. This is a work of synthesis, an argument built because others were willing to dig through archives, private collections of papers, and a mountain of primary sources that no individual could climb. Repaying this debt can only be partial, in the form of citations as meticulous as I can make them and, in perhaps larger return, by transmitting this knowledge to those who read this volume and this series.

Giselle Donnelly
Takoma Park, Maryland
March 2022

INTRODUCTION

In July 1947, the journal *Foreign Affairs* published "The Sources of Soviet Conduct," perhaps the seminal contribution to the Cold War strategy of the United States. Writing as "X," State Department official George Kennan intended the article—which reprised points he had made in several official memoranda, including the so-called "Long Telegram" the previous year—to be an explanation and guide to understanding Soviet strategy and behavior. He aimed to describe the "political personality of Soviet power," an effort he called a "task of psychological analysis" to discern a "pattern of thought" and the "nature of the mental world of the Soviet leaders." If Soviet "conduct is to be understood"—and, as a matter of American strategy, "effectively countered"—it required not only a grasp of the principles of Soviet ideology but the effects of "the powerful hands of Russian history and tradition."[1] Kennan thus argued that Josef Stalin and other Soviet leaders saw international politics and the struggle for power through a unique set of lenses, lenses that might filter and distort even nature's purest colors and shapes. It mattered less what wavelengths objects reflected than what wavelengths appeared to Russian eyes.

This book is the first in an intended series that is an attempt to employ Kennan's approach to understand the sources of American conduct and in particular to uncover the origins of a political personality of power conceived in the Anglo-American colonial experience, but recognizable even in the United States of the twenty-first century. This story will end at 1776 rather than begin there, as Americans mostly have been taught to do. While American independence most definitely marked a geopolitical discontinuity and a revolutionary rupture in the British Empire, the argument here is that it was George III who sought a new direction in strategy. To American minds, the English after 1763 increasingly seemed determined to turn away from the past path of social, economic, and political progress and imperial growth. As if spooked by their spectacular and surprising successes in the Seven Years' War, the king and his counselors wanted to at least halt in place if nothing more; their colonists wanted nothing more than to pick up the pace of imperial expansion while earning for themselves a stronger hand in guiding the effort. They believed that, inevitably, the direction of the "British empire for liberty" would be set in North America. Americans are still hurrying, though we occasionally collapse in exhaustion, along a similar path.

This search for strategic motivations and direction in deep history is, in the parlance of modern political science, the study of "strategic culture," which became a fully theoretical field of inquiry in the later years of the Cold War. Indeed, there is a large and occasionally impenetrable body of scholarly literature on the subject, and it's hardly a concept without flaws, including logical flaws. The idea is itself a conjunction of two notoriously inexact terms: what constitutes *strategy* and what *culture* are questions that have themselves provoked centuries of debate. This book will confine itself to a view of strategy derived from Clausewitz: herein, as in *On War*, *strategy* means "the use of engagements for the object of the war."[2] That is, strategy stands at the intersection of military affairs and politics. The traditional complaint about this definition is its emphasis on military force as the tool of the strategist; even the US Department of Defense favors a broader understanding. The official dictionary of military doctrine defines *strategy* as "a prudent idea or set of ideas for employing the instruments of national power in a synchronized and integrated fashion to achieve theater, national, and/or multinational objectives."[3] The phrase *the instruments of national power* is supposed to encompass diplomatic, informational, and economic means, as well as military power. And it is an indication of the current military understanding of American strategic culture that strategic ideas must be "prudent." Historically, strategic culture can lead to error and defeat as often as insight and victory, and it can be both successful and imprudent. Yet Clausewitz's insight that military power is the essential tool of strategy and statecraft not only still stands, but imparts a clarity and discipline in usage that is critical for the purposes of this study. This work will expand slightly on the great Prussian colonel's definitions—the "uses" of force, for example, will include preparation for potential engagements and thus touch on a range of issues from military finance to doctrine to technology—but preserve the original meaning. The term *strategic* will describe essentially military matters.

The argument will equally insist that strategy-making emanates from a larger culture, shared across the political nation, meaning not just kings and courtiers, ministers and parliamentarians, but also society more broadly—which may wield a decisive weight. The definition of *culture* is, then, necessarily gelatinous. Culture comprises, says Merriam-Webster, "the customary beliefs, social forms, and material traits of a racial, religious, or social group; *also*: the characteristic features of everyday existence (as diversions or a way of life) shared by people in a place and time; the set of shared attitudes, values, goals, and practices that characterizes an institution or organization; the set of values, conventions, or social practices associated with a particular field, activity, or societal characteristic."[4] The root of the word is the Latin *cultura*, itself derived from the participle of the verb *to cultivate*, as in the development of agriculture, and thus it contains the idea of a process and progress through time, of slow change but also of possible improvement.

But if the idea of strategic culture is perhaps inherently imprecise, it is nonetheless a powerful one, for it attempts to account for domestic political, social, and intellectual trends that may shape international behavior; it is less deterministic than the varieties of "realism" favored by its theoretical and academic opponents. The key idea behind the notion of strategic culture is that a nation—or, more broadly, any "actor" on the international stage—defines its security goals and strategy in a way that reflects its political culture, that political culture is, if not perfectly constant, then at least relatively so and has a measurable effect on the ways in which decisions are made and wars waged. Alastair Iain Johnston's summary definition of strategic culture is plain: "Those who use it tend to mean that there are consistent and persistent historical patterns in the way particular states think about the use of force for political ends."[5] Or, conversely, two different "actors" facing roughly similar challenges of international politics or security might well act in entirely different ways, reflecting different strategic cultures.

The concept of strategic culture rose in interest during the 1970s and 1980s, when it began to seem that the Soviet Union and the Red Army regarded the use of nuclear weapons very differently than US and Western European statesmen and soldiers. In particular, the Soviets sounded, in their military doctrines, as though they were far more willing to employ nuclear weapons, especially "tactical" nuclear weapons, on the battlefield and during an invasion of Germany or a war against NATO. A short 1977 RAND monograph by Jack Snyder, *The Soviet Strategic Culture: Implications for Limited Nuclear Operations*, might be said to be the spark that ignited a wider interest in the idea of strategic culture.[6]

Snyder made relatively narrow claims about Soviet strategy-making; his purpose was primarily to contrast Soviet writings with what Americans understood to be the universal logic of nuclear weaponry, war, and escalation.[7] Yet far from liberating strategists from the excessively deterministic interpretations of realist theory, those taken with Snyder's work tended simply to substitute another, equally rigid system: strategic culture was as ironclad as structural realism. Rather than simply shaping Soviet thought about nuclear war, Soviet strategic culture, as it came to be interpreted, was viewed as a kind of straitjacket of Russian history that not only guided but tightly bound Soviet doctrine. In the work of Colin Gray, for example, the Cold War appeared as an inevitable confrontation between the United States and the Soviet Union, with each side driven by a deeply ingrained strategic culture.[8] Gray and like-minded scholars struck a chord during the turbulent times of the late 1970s and early 1980s, when it appeared to many that the United States was ill-prepared for the challenges of Soviet expansionism.

In recent years, the theory of strategic culture has become more nuanced—and perhaps sacrificed some clarity and power—by subsuming more factors in its analysis. Strategic culture is now considered as less rigidly determining national behavior but rather more generally informing, shaping, or coloring strategic choices. Also, strategic culture can be measured not simply by observable behavior but by attitudes and domestic political debate, ideas expressed in military doctrine, the writings of elite and popular commentators—almost any cultural "representation" or "text." Others have noted the interaction of organizational issues and culture, most particularly the peculiarities of professional armies, in shaping strategy-making. But in some cases, what counts as an element in strategic culture becomes so vague as to lose meaning; while it makes sense to allow that culture can change, it ought to represent more than passing fashion. The danger is that, in skilled hands, the concept of strategic culture can be so malleable as to lose any form at all.

Perhaps the most durable definition of strategic culture is that of Forrest E. Morgan: "Strategic culture is an integrated system of shared symbols, values, and customs that, working through perceptions, preferences and governmental processes, impose a degree of order on the ways that policy makers conceive and respond to the strategic environment."[9] This is an attempt to constrain the "cultural" element of theory to those habits and shared values most relevant to actual strategic behavior and decision-making. Thus "strategic culture" becomes, in the terminology of political science, an "intervening variable" that stands between the "independent variables" that the world presents to political leaders and military commanders, and the "dependent variables," their responses. It acts as the filter, the lens that Kennan described. Broadly speaking, a culture consists in a wide variety of symbols, customs, and sets of values which do not necessarily or directly drive strategic decision-making— although political values may have such effects by strongly shaping what Morgan calls "strategic preferences." And, particularly with the development of increasingly modern and complex bureaucracies, both civilian and military, organizational processes and preferences take root that become elements of a larger strategic culture.

But this book is not a case study intended to illuminate or advance theory. It is rather an attempt to borrow from theory to understand the origins of American strategic behavior. In this regard, the strategic culture school at least offers a promise that the various schools of "realism" do not. Indeed, it has almost become a litmus test of professional realism to wonder at the many imbecilities of American leaders, regardless of party, who seem impervious to the wisdom of realist theory. Ironically, George Kennan might be said to have had more empathy for the sources of Soviet and Russian conduct than he did for that of the United States. As he lost the struggle over Cold War policy within the Truman administration, Kennan began to see Americans as hopelessly ideological, as a kind of strategic brontosaurus: an American politician "lies there in his comfortable primeval mud and pays little attention to his environment; he is slow to wrath—in fact, you have to whack his tail off to make him aware that his interests are being disturbed; but, once he grasps this he lays about him with such blind determination that he not only destroys his adversary but largely wrecks his native habitat."[10]

Kennan's contemporary Hans Morgenthau thought the ideological impulse in American strategy needed to be not only bridled but destroyed. It was a "nefarious trend of thought." He lamented the fact that the American political establishment had a "bias against a realistic approach" to power.[11] Modern realists remain despairingly detached, quite unable to fathom why such a powerful nation over-militarizes its approach to the world, resorts to excessive secrecy, and infringes on domestic liberty in ways that endanger the republic. "Why," wonders Harvard political scientist Stephen Walt, "is a distinguished and well-known approach to foreign policy confined to the margins of public discourse, especially in the pages of our leading newspapers, when its recent track record is arguably superior to the main alternatives?" Chalmers Johnson concludes his long lament on *The Sorrows of Empire*: "From the moment [the United States] took on a role that included the permanent military domination of the world, we were on our own—feared, hated, corrupt and corrupting, maintaining 'order' through state terrorism and bribery, and given to megalomaniac rhetoric and sophistries that virtually invited the rest of the world to unite against us. We had mounted the Napoleonic tiger. The question was, would we—and could we—ever dismount?"[12]

The question for this study is not whether the United States ought to behave differently, but why it began to behave as it still does. If America indeed rides an imperial tiger, why did we choose to saddle such a beast in the first place? If realists are perplexed, the past professional literature on American strategic culture does not seem to have a compelling answer either. One academically significant analysis in the field was Reginald C. Stuart's 1982 study *War and American Thought*.[13] Stuart begins his book with an essentially sound observation:

> Armed conflict litters the American past, even though Americans believe themselves to have been historically pacific. Viewed through a patriotic lens, all American wars have been justified struggles in self-defense, initiated only after unprovoked aggression. But the record reveals that Americans have fought both offensive and defensive wars, and that many can only be labeled aggressive, and even expansionist. Further probing suggests that in all cases, these conflicts arose from the ambitions of politicians and leaders who conceived of themselves as thinking and acting in the national interest. War, like peace or trade, has always been used as an instrument of policy, although American mythology has maintained that Americans always rejected Carl von Clausewitz's dictum to that effect.[14]

Stuart also correctly roots early American strategy-making within the European tradition of the times. Indeed, he suggests, "Because they remained Englishmen in so many ways, it is difficult to determine what was distinctively American about American attitudes toward war."[15] In Stuart's view, American strategic culture reflected a "limited-war mentality," rooted in the politics and political philosophy of the eighteenth and early nineteenth centuries. Importantly, he allows that "crusading impulses interwove through the period of this generation's political domination of American affairs," but, in his analysis, this is a much-subordinated strain. Stuart insists that crusading "ideals never breached the barricades when it came to war," that Americans of the time "distinguished sharply between 'civilized' and 'savage' warfare" and that the limited-war paradigm was recognizable even in Civil War times.[16]

The argument of this book will be almost completely contrary. To begin with, it is essential to look farther back than the eighteenth century, past the Enlightenment to the Reformation, especially if we are to discover the roots of the ideology of politics and war that realists find so distorting and toxic. Indeed, "crusading" impulses are not merely "interwoven" in the fabric of American strategy-making; they are the loom that gives it design and shape. No less than Cold Warriors, English colonists in North America fought not only to create a more favorable balance of power but also to secure a more just international order. If, for Clausewitz, strategy stood at the crossing point of military tactics and secular politics, for Anglo-Americans, the international politics of the colonial era was inseparable from the fortunes of a kind of "Protestant International," a diverse and decentralized but global confessional community. Even in its most virulent manifestations, however, the distinctions between religious faith and political liberty, or "liberties," became blurred. The Valois French or, later, the Austrian Hapsburgs might attend Mass, but their strategic behavior could align them with the "Good Old" Protestant cause, which even occasionally, as the Bourbons wrenched the French church away from Rome, enlisted the pope. Likewise, the distinction between "civilized" and "savage" war was no barricade, but a gossamer tissue that might be ripped at any time, not only in conflicts between Europeans and indigenous tribes or whites and nonwhites, but among Europeans, between Anglo-Americans, and, by the mid-1860s, between fellow Americans. A white man named "Tecumseh" promised to "make Georgia howl," to the great delight and with the enthusiastic agreement of his soldiers.

This book seeks the deep roots of American strategic culture by examining the attitudes that shaped attempts to establish "New English" plantations in the American hemisphere, basing them on the model used in Ireland. This is to stand against the popular prejudice to regard the American experience as springing ex nihilo in 1776 or during the founding generation. This is central to the myth of American exceptionalism. It is also to reject the alternative "1619" narrative lately promulgated by the *New York Times*, now published in book form as "a new origin story," timing the American founding to the arrival at Point Comfort, Virginia, of the privateer *White Lion*, the first ship bearing African slaves and recasting the American experience as, first and foremost, an empire for slavery.[17] This book offers a third narrative, in which the "empire for liberty" which Thomas Jefferson described to James Madison will be seen gestating among the English, then the British, then across the Atlantic world, and the narrative will cast the American wars of liberation as a conflict about the nature and course of this first British empire, concluding that it was left to the newly born United States to pursue the original ideals in the traditional manner while Great Britain went her own way to found another empire in the nineteenth century.[18]

The term *empire* will also be used liberally through this work and the series. In current usage, the word carries an immense weight of baggage and will no doubt harden some hearts against the narrative. But whatever the modern connotations, there can be no doubt that Anglo-Americans lived in a world of empires and believed that to forge their own was necessary for survival, both national and confessional, let alone for prosperity. Greater Britain was not the only "composite monarchy" of the era, and by comparison to the polities they subsumed and replaced, they were nothing if not empires. "How else is one to describe these giants?" asks Fernand Braudel.[19] This first British empire was intended, as William Cecil, chief counsellor to Elizabeth, put it in the late 1550s, as a quasi-contractual "regime"—one that bound the monarch as well as the subject—in a mixed government meant to secure political "amity" and the basic Protestant religious affinity that transcended the English church to provide a bond among the many British nations and protect them against existential external dangers while securing the "liberties" that defined a just and stable international order.[20] Scots and Irish and North American colonists were to be partners in this enterprise, and indeed the Scottish Reformation that was contemporaneous with Elizabeth's crowning helped to inspire Cecil's imperial vision. It was these larger confessional and ideological purposes that justified the exercise and expansion of imperial power and elevated the regime's interests above those of than any individual ruler or dynasty. Two centuries onward, Jefferson, Madison, and the American founders inherited this elemental imperial idea and sought to reform it—for a second time—in order to sustain, expand, and improve it.

Several other terms deserve definition. The adjective *British* is employed in a way some would claim is anachronistic. But the idea of *Britain* well predated the establishment of the United Kingdom, and it is to this that the book refers: the concept of an imperial polity centered on England—and indeed, principally southern England—and its interests but encompassing a range of peoples as participants in a common enterprise. Yet another is the term *Puritan*, meant not only to describe a sect but to distinguish the idea of strict Protestant observance—a felt faith that began well before there was a Puritan or Separatist movement. Many of Puritan tendencies remained communicants within the Church of England, but only because they believed deeper reforms were possible.

In telling the story of Anglo-American strategy-making through a series of pulse-taking vignettes, this book and this series also attempt to give due regard to circumstance, contingency, and personality in the development of strategic culture. A culture represents an accretion of habits over time, a way of understanding and filtering experience, not a rigid doctrine or system. In part, it is this imprecision that gives the culture its durability and strength; as Kennan lamented, the Anglo-American dinosaur requires a ferocious beating before it begins to rouse itself.

Finally, this analysis is not, unlike that of Kennan or subsequent realists, intended as an immediate measure of current US policy or strategy, except insofar as it makes Americans more self-aware. That in itself might be a step forward; since the end of the Cold War, strategy-makers in Washington have looked either relentlessly outward, assessing "threats" or "global trends," or obsessively inwards, hoping to promote "nation-building at home" while leaving the rest of the world to rot. Indeed, American policymakers often seem possessed of an almost willful ignorance both about American strategy-making in history and about military matters. An empire that sought security through constant expansion is said to have a strong "isolationist" streak. When dazzled by new technologies, military power appears to many as a cure-all; when disoriented by the fog of war, military power is disparaged as "solving nothing." In addition to reminding Americans of their deep-rooted strategic culture and long-standing strategic preferences, these stories might serve as case studies in both the enduring uses and purposes of the *ultima ratio regis*.

1

A WORLD ENCOMPASSED

On September 26, 1580, Sir Francis Drake and his crew of fifty-nine brought the *Golden Hind* into harbor at Plymouth in Devon, in southwest England, from whence it had sailed three years before. The galleon, a mere 120 feet long—eighteen feet at the beam and drawing but nine feet—must have been riding low in the water, for she was carrying an immense weight of gold, silver, spices, and other plunder seized from Spanish and Portuguese colonies and treasure ships in the Pacific; Queen Elizabeth's half-share of the revenue exceeded the rest of the royal income for the year. But Drake's circumnavigation of the world was more than a famous voyage of exploration or exploitation. It was also a statement of geopolitical and strategic intent. Drake had declared that English-speaking peoples would be global, great-power players, seeking to order the world not only to advance their material interests but to craft international politics to be more congenial to what they regarded as their political and religious liberties.

Drake brought problems as well as plunder home to his sovereign. When word of the buccaneer's return arrived in London, Elizabeth immediately summoned the body of advisers known as her privy council. Her longtime principal adviser, William Cecil, Lord Burghley, suggested that the loot might have to be returned, lest it exacerbate tensions with Spain's King Philip II or, worse still, provoke a war for which England was unprepared. Burghley ordered that the treasure be brought to the Tower of London and inventoried. Yet the order was suspended when Sir Francis Walsingham, the principal secretary of state for foreign affairs and a backer of the Drake voyage—he had colluded with Elizabeth to keep Burghley in the dark, or at least to give him a shred of deniability, about Drake's purpose—refused to sign it. Burghley may have shared Walsingham's fears of Catholic Counter-Reformation, but he worried about the wisdom of provoking the powerful Philip while Walsingham welcomed it. Playing for time, the queen ordered that official word would be that Drake had brought back little profit. She also summoned Drake to the capital with a sampling of his treasures.

The truth of the Drake story quickly leaked; the corsair was an immediate sensation and national hero. The Spanish ambassador to London, Don Bernadino de Mendoza, soon began to register complaints. Neither the ambassador nor Philip knew exactly the amount of Drake's take, but they knew it was a lot—one prize he captured, a ship called the *Cacafuego*, had carried twenty-six tons of bullion. The ambitious Drake cut a dashing figure at court, dispensing gifts and entertaining lavishly. But it was only gall and wormwood to Mendoza, who complained to Philip:

> Drake is squandering more money than any man in England. . . . He gave to the Queen the crown which I described in a former letter as having been made here. She wore it on New Year's Day. It has five emeralds, three almost as long as a little finger, whilst the two round ones are valued at 20,000 crowns, coming, as they do, from Peru. . . . He offered to Burghley ten bars of fine gold worth 300 crowns each, which, however, he refused, saying that he did not know how his conscience would allow him to accept a present from Drake, who had stolen all he had.[1]

To add insult to injury, Elizabeth announced on New Year's Day of 1581 that in the spring she would board the *Golden Hind*, knight Drake, and afterward create a special dry dock in the Thames to display the ship. Domestic propaganda imperatives trumped diplomatic discretion.

In fact, Elizabeth's domestic concerns were inseparable from the larger European balance of power, and here the situation was as bad or worse; English morale and prestige needed a boost. No sooner had she mounted the throne in 1558 than she was forced to cede the port of Calais, England's last toehold on the European continent, to the French. Yet France, the traditional English enemy, was by 1580 a kind of "frenemy"; her civil wars of religion made sometime strategic partner of Protestant Huguenots, and keeping the Guise family faction either away from the throne or at least mired in the contest for it was a key ploy in the attempt to turn back Spain's "bid for mastery" of Europe.[2] For a decade, Philip II's armies had been a constant menace to the Netherlands, threatening not only England and France but Germany's Protestant principalities, and Philip's goals included not just political hegemony but a Catholic Counter-Reformation. Elizabeth had been in an escalating quasi-war with Philip that depended heavily on piratical practices. And as queen of an increasingly ideological political nation, one that saw English interests as part of an international "Protestant interest," disavowing Drake was not really an option.[3]

But more than an emotionally satisfying and profitable effort to annoy the Spanish king, Drake's voyage was a reflection of the rapidly expanding horizons of English elites and, in particular, of a changing perspective that put England less at the margins of the European world and more to the center of an Atlantic world, which might supply the power London needed to balance Catholic empires. In fact, with his raids along the Pacific coast of South and Central America and his return via the Moluccas, Drake had introduced a fully global calculus into London's strategic reckoning. In particular, the safety of the English "homeland"—the British Isles, the surrounding waters and the lowlands of northwest Europe—was inseparable from the balance of power in the New World. These new horizons also correlated with an increasing anti-Spanish cast to English policy; substantial portions of the royal share of Drake's booty would go to finance anti-Spanish and anti-Catholic causes, such as the Dutch Protestant rebellion and the suppression of incursions in Ireland by mercenaries working for Pope Gregory XIII.

The idea that the answer to England's most pressing strategic problems—the rise of Spain and in particular its increasing dominance of the Netherlands—might lie in transatlantic adventure was a commonplace well before Drake sailed; the connection between New-World gold and silver and Old-World power was hard to miss. Spanish imports of bullion had been rising steadily for decades and would peak in the 1590s at an average of about £3 million per year, about a quarter of which went straight into Philip's coffers; by contrast, Elizabeth's annual "ordinary" revenue was about £250,000 (to pay for "extraordinary" expenses such as major military campaigns, she had to convene her parliament and ask them for new grants or taxes).[4] While there might not have been other Aztec or Inca empires to plunder, there might well have been other sources of mineral wealth, like the enormously productive silver mines at Potosí

Figure 1.1. Spain's American Empire.

in Peru. Or, as seafaring Englishmen knew, there was the alluring target of the annual Spanish treasure fleet. Without American riches, Philip would not be able to sustain his military power in northwest Europe or fuel his policy of Catholic Counter-Reformation.

Drake and other English "adventurers" had long been raiding in the Caribbean, as had French Huguenots. Drake had spent the spring of 1571 cruising the coast of the "Spanish Main,"—that is, eastern Central America—coming away with plunder the Spanish claimed was worth about £66,000; even if, as is likely, the Spanish claim is exaggerated, Drake had put himself on the path to wealth.[5] Perhaps more significantly, he had reconnoitered the area around Nombre de Dios, the Central American port where the annual eastbound treasure fleets were loaded. Thus, two years later, Drake had led an even more daring raid that made common cause with local bands of *cimarrones*—escaped slaves, probably both African and indigenous—to intercept a mule train headed for Nombre de Dios. In haste, about fifteen tons of silver were buried and lost, but Drake made it home with another £40,000 worth of gold.[6] In sum, Drake had demonstrated that the Spanish position in America was vulnerable, not just at sea but ashore, where the prospect of cooperation with local allies could multiply both financial and strategic rewards.

Finding the limits of Spanish power in the South Atlantic and even into the Pacific was a tremendous temptation, not only to Drake but other corsairs. But in the mid-1570s, Elizabeth and her privy council confronted a host of complex strategic problems at home and in Europe. At home, the Elizabethan religious settlement was unraveling; the queen's Protestantism was not nearly strong enough to satisfy the Calvinist sympathies of her parliament; the queen remained devoted to ritual and even more to a hierarchical church order to buttress English social and political order. There was also the matter of Elizabeth's successor and the future of the regime; this inherently difficult issue divided the queen from the larger political nation. At the same time, Mary Stuart, the queen of Scots and immediate heir to the English throne, remained a rallying point for Catholic dissent and focus for Scottish, French and Spanish intrigue. France was racked by intermittent but very violent religious civil war. In the Netherlands, the Spanish Duke of Alba's savage attempt to repress revolt and suppress Calvinism had failed, and Philip looked to moderate his policies there, even restoring English trading privileges in the Low Countries.[7] For the moment, the queen was not looking for another fight and so halted a planned expedition by Richard

Grenville, a West Country neighbor and rival of Drake, and sent Drake himself off to Ireland. Yet there was no lasting peace to be had. Elizabeth could not control such an inherently complex and violent situation. By 1576, the chances of an accommodation with Philip had already all but vanished; as Walsingham's intelligence network revealed, the Spanish monarch was already coming to believe that he could not conquer the Netherlands without first attacking England. In July 1577, Philip sent the methodical Duke of Parma, Alexander Farnese, to the Netherlands to prepare a slow but inexorable squeeze on the Dutch rebels. A break in the French civil wars left the Catholic Guise family—Mary Stuart had been born a Guise—free to resume its intrigues on a weak-willed French king. This, in turn, raised again the specter of a Spanish-French Catholic coalition, the ultimate English nightmare and present danger throughout Elizabeth's reign. The queen needed to take some initiative, despite the many weaknesses of the British position.

The planning for Drake's voyage is shrouded in mystery—much was done in secret and many papers, including those of Walsingham, have been lost—and thus surrounded by historical controversy.[8] The principal sponsors of the project were Walsingham and the Earl of Leicester, Robert Dudley, the queen's longtime favorite; these were the strongest advocates of an aggressive strategy of "geopolitical Protestantism," not only at sea but on the European continent. They were anti-Catholic, anti-Spanish, and pro-intervention both in France and the Netherlands, and they made a powerful and popular faction at court, in parliament, and among a broader public. Great effort was expended, and ultimately wasted, to keep the Drake deliberations secret from Burghley who, though a devout Protestant and a militant anti-Catholic, favored a policy of caution and husbanding of limited English resources. But these were differences over means, not ends, and, had Cecil so objected to the Drake adventure, he almost certainly could have prevented it. The ambiguities and sketchy records of planning as well as the public demonstrations of regret after Drake's return should not disguise the depth of Elizabethan strategic agreement.

Though only fragments of Drake's instructions survive, his voyage was extremely well chronicled and subsequently litigated and lionized. It is most likely that the intent of the voyage was to feel for the limits of Spanish and Portuguese power in South America, both in the South Atlantic and along the "South Sea" or Pacific coast of "Peru" as far north as thirty degrees south latitude, where Drake "should spend 5 months in tarrying upon the coast to get knowle[dge] of the princes and countries there."[9] This strongly suggests that Drake's purpose was to recruit local allies; as in continental Europe, Elizabethans looked for local partners in the struggle against Philip. And as the Spanish looked at Ireland and the French at Scotland as unlocked backdoors—or in Burghley's phrase, "posterior gates"—to England, so might the Pacific coast or the Central American isthmus provide points of entry into Spanish America. Although unstated, it was surely expected that Drake would finance his voyage and, if his past luck held, turn a handsome profit by plundering Spanish shipping and settlements along the way. The silver of Peru had begun to replace that of Mexico in Spanish finances, and the sea line of communication from the viceregal capital of Callao to Panama was sheltered from English Caribbean raiders.[10] Elizabeth contributed substantially to the venture. Still, although it is more accurate to think of Drake as a privateer than an outright pirate, the queen was not anxious to escalate her quasi-war into an outright confrontation; there was no written commission, but neither is there doubt of her interest. Drake later contended that, in their meeting to discuss the expedition, Elizabeth had declared that she "would gladly be revenged on the King of Spain for divers injuries that I have received."[11] Drake's recollection

Drake's Circumnavigation 1577-1580

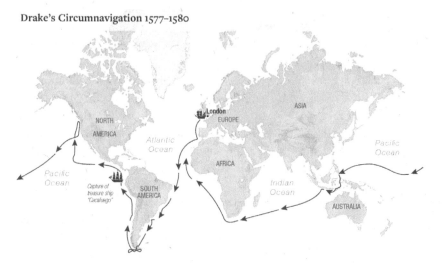

Figure 1.2. Drake's Circumnavigation, 1577–1580.

was self-serving but probably accurate. Elizabeth may have feared a wider war with Philip, but she also feared that the devotion to the Protestant cause of her own Puritan-minded seamen—like Drake—and advisers—like Walsingham and Leicester—might cloud their strategic and military judgments. Nonetheless, the queen and Cecil were convinced that the threat was real and growing; Spain had replaced France as the greatest worry. She could and would be pushed, but only so far and so fast. Elizabeth needed to preserve a film of deniability and England was not ready for open war.

Drake's small flotilla of five ships made its way out of Plymouth harbor on December 13, 1577, sailing southward.[12] Keeping well clear of Spain, Drake coasted along northwest Africa through January 1578, hopping westward through the Canary Islands. By February he broke west for the open Atlantic, reaching the Brazilian coast on April 5. The crossing was fairly straightforward sailing, but it marked a deterioration of relations with Thomas Doughty, Drake's social superior and the personal secretary to Sir Christopher Hatton, who was another of Elizabeth's court favorites, one of her principal spokesmen in parliament, and a sponsor of the expedition. Drake continued southward to the estuary of the River Plate over the next few weeks, took on water, and prepared to enter the South Atlantic.

The weather turned foul, as did Drake's relations with Doughty, who seemed to be fomenting a dissenting and potentially mutinous party within the expedition. Under the compound strains, Drake chose to consolidate both his fleet and his command prior to entering the Straits of Magellan: Doughty was charged, tried, and executed on July 2; only three ships continued southward. On August 23, at the Atlantic end of the Strait, Drake lowered his sails in honor of his queen, simultaneously renaming his flagship, the *Pelican*, as the *Golden Hind*, taking the name from Hatton's crest.

The *Golden Hind*, the *Elizabeth*, and the *Marigold* reached the Pacific end of the Strait and entered the Great South Sea on September 6, 1578, and there encountered truly vicious storms and towering seas. The fleet struggled into early October, scattered and battered. The *Marigold* was lost. Out of contact with Drake, George Wynter took *Elizabeth* back into the relatively calm waters of the Strait, where she rested until early November and then reversed course homeward, reaching England in July 1579. On November 8, Wynter, brother of Admiral William Wynter, another noble backer of the expedition, "call[ed] my whole company together . . . [and] made my determination generally known, which was for the east parts of the world, using what persuasion I could. . . . But all was in vain for the [sailing] Master did utterly dislike of it, saying that he would fling himself overboard rather than consent to any such voyage. . . . He said Mr. Drake hired him for Alexandria [Egypt], but if he had known that this had been the Alexandria, he would have been hanged in England rather than have come on this voyage."[13]

Despite the loss of his escorts and one of the *Golden Hind's* pinnaces with eight men aboard, Drake resumed sailing northward along the Chilean coast, reaching the island of Mocha on November 25. There his watering party was ambushed by local Indians, leaving two men killed and Drake himself wounded. But it was an Indian encountered back at sea, fishing in a canoe, who turned the expedition's fortunes by directing Drake to the port of Valparaiso, where on December 5, the *Golden Hind* took its first plunder.

Drake continued to raid ever farther northward through early 1579, striking Callao, the port of Lima, in mid-February. Drake harvested no booty in Callao, but did come away with tantalizing news of a fully loaded treasure ship, the *Nuestra Senora de la Concepcion*, better known as the *Cacafuego* ("fire-shitter"), that had recently left Callao for Panama. Drake's presence stirred the Spanish viceroy, Don Fransciso Alvarez de Toledo, to action. Drake set sail for the treasure ship and Toledo sent ships in pursuit of Drake.

Drake gained his prize first. On the evening of March 1, 1579, he caught the *Cacafuego*, took her, and the next day went aboard to reckon the haul. The registered treasure alone was worth nearly £150,000, and the unofficial take might have been double that; this was by far the ripest fruit Drake had ever plucked. But by now Drake had worked his way well north, perhaps even past the equator. And with his ship now riding low in the water with the weight of bullion the question was: how to get it home? To reverse course back to the Straits of Magellan would be to run a gauntlet of the now-aroused Spanish settlements. There were two other alternatives: seek the hoped-for "Northwest Passage" above North America or strike out across the Pacific and thus home by the Indian Ocean and around Africa. Drake split the difference, sailing north along the coast until reaching what is California today. With no sign of any northern passage home, he then struck west across the Pacific.

The transpacific route held great promise, even for crews that had been away from home for nearly eighteen months and had already made themselves wealthy men. They well knew that the Portuguese trade in the Spice Islands of the South Pacific and in India was as lucrative or more than the Spanish bullion; some spices were worth more per unit of weight than gold. And given that Philip of Spain was on the cusp of inheriting the Portuguese crown, the Spice Islands were rising in strategic importance; the wealthier Philip was, the more dangerous he would be. Indeed, in planning the expedition, there had always been an option for sailing for the Moluccas, the archipelago at the center of the Southeast Asian spice trade, and Wynter had made reference to a rendezvous there in his explanation of his decision to turn homeward when the fleet was scattered after passing through the Strait of Magellan. The *Golden Hind* needed more than sixty days to cross the open Pacific and got a hostile reception upon making landfall in the Carolinas, but the reception in the Moluccas more than met expectation. Drake was warmly received by the King of Ternate, named Babu, then fighting to free his kingdom from Portuguese rule. As the Spanish agent in the islands reported, Babu opened negotiations with Drake by saying that he was not a friend of the Portuguese but an independent king, and that as "Captain Francis had said that he was a vassal of the Queen of England, if the Queen desired to favor and help him to expel the Portuguese from that region, he would concede to her the trade in cloves, which up to that time the Portuguese had had. Captain Francis, on the part of the Queen of England, promised that within two years he would decorate that sea with ships for whatever purpose might be necessary."[14]

Drake's promise would not be fulfilled for a long time to come— much to Babu's distress; in 1605 his son wrote to King James I of England begging help against Spain, which had inherited and then expanded Portugal's East Indian empire. But in addition to six tons of cloves, Drake would return home with a trove of strategic information about East Indian politics—and particularly the locals' desire for a European counterweight against Iberian power—that promptly insinuated itself into English minds. The import of Drake's raids in the South Seas was deeply planted in Spanish minds as well. Before Drake made landfall in Micronesia, a tide of correspondence had begun to break on Philip II's desk; one of the king's counselors pronounced himself "terrified" by the "boldness of this low man."[15]

And so it is quite believable that when the *Golden Hind* pulled into Plymouth harbor, the first question on the crew's mind was "Is the Queen still alive?" Drake might be returning home a hero, but without political cover from Elizabeth and his friends on the privy council, everything might be forfeit. As it happened, the quasi-war between England and Spain had again begun to escalate. In 1579 a papal military expedition had landed in southern Ireland, in Munster, to foment rebellion. Philip protested that the scheme was entirely that of Pope Gregory XIII, but whatever credibility that story had was diminished when mostly Spanish reinforcements arrived in Ireland the same month that Drake arrived in England. The Ireland expedition also gave Elizabeth a good excuse to hold onto the proceeds of the Drake expedition.

But the Drake story is not just a tale of sea-dog daring. As even this truncated telling suggests, it reflects the habits of mind that characterized the strategic calculations of Elizabeth, her principal strategic advisers, and, importantly, of an amorphous but growing and increasingly important—and extremely well-informed—body of public opinion on such matters. As will be argued below, Elizabeth's long reign proved a formative period in English strategy-making, the parent of a larger British strategic culture which in turn produced an American offspring.

2

ELIZABETHAN SECURITY ARCHITECTURE

The political elites of the Elizabethan age were profoundly aware that England was a "fallen imperial power,"[1] riven by domestic dissent and disorder, driven from its last toehold on the European continent, with an impoverished and arthritic government, a miniscule and antiquated military, and uncertainty about which of the two continental great powers, Spain or France, was the larger threat; England feared it was "a bone thrown between two dogs."[2] The comfortable dynastic framework of late medieval and early modern European politics was being torn apart by the passions of Protestant Reformation and Catholic Counter-Reformation. Drake's plunder, welcome as it was, also underscored that England was decades behind Spain and Portugal in translating New-World exploration into Old-World wealth, military might, and political influence. England's very independence rested upon its ability to play a game of global power.

Isolation was not an option. During the first half of the sixteenth century and throughout Henry VIII's reign, the focus of the struggle for European mastery between the French Valois dynasty and the Hapsburgs under Charles V had been in Italy, but in the 1540s it shifted to north-west Europe, and in particular to the Rhineland and Flanders. This made the English Channel less an east-west barrier between England and the European mainland than a critical north-south line of communication between Hapsburg Spain and the Netherlands. Because France had long been the most proximate threat, traditional English strategy had been to maintain the "Burgundian alliance" with the Hapsburgs to keep the

French out of the Low Countries. But now the danger was that England's interest—which really was to keep either power from dominating the northwest European coastline and thus posing a threat of invasion—would be subordinated to those of the greater powers.

Elizabeth's two predecessors had indeed been bones for dogs. The brief reigns of Edward VI and Mary Tudor had lurched from one extreme to the other. Edward, just nine when Henry VIII died in 1547, had been a figurehead for regent Edward Seymour, the Duke of Somerset, and then John Dudley, the Duke of Northumberland, both of whom had transformed the Church of England into a fully Protestant, though still episcopal and hierarchical, institution. Hoping to exclude Catholic Mary Tudor from following the sickly Edward, Northumberland also sought an alliance with Henry II of France to secure the Protestant succession—through his daughter, Lady Jane Grey—and his own power. Northumberland's gambit failed, but his fears proved valid. Mary came to power determined to restore the Catholic faith, ruthlessly suppressing heresy and political faction. Thus she made an alliance with Spain, marrying Philip II, son and heir to the Spanish portion of the Hapsburg Empire. But when Philip took the Spanish throne in 1556 (and assumed rule in the Netherlands), he sought to involve England in further wars with France. In sum, Elizabeth inherited a crown caught in a vortex of personal, dynastic, confessional, domestic, and international political and military currents that she could not control and had little means to influence.

She also inherited an empty purse. Henry VIII had financed the wars of the 1540s against Scotland and France in large measure out of the revenues gained by nationalizing the English church and confiscating lands and wealth from the monasteries. And although some of Henry's defense investments, such as his shipbuilding and coastal fortifications program, had residual benefits that lasted into Elizabeth's time, a good deal of the money went to pay for the wars of the "Rough Wooing" of Scotland—the object of the wooing was the then-infant Mary Queen of Scots, whom Henry wooed for his son Edward, but it was a strategic union with Scotland that he desired and that made the wooing rough—and the massive invasion of France in 1544. When the Hapsburg Emperor Charles V cut a deal with the French, Henry found himself living the nightmare of English kings, alone in a two-front war in both Scotland and France. Over the last three years of his reign, Henry had spent more than £2 million, about three-quarters of which was squandered. And indeed, the two wars continued through the reigns of Edward VI and

Mary Tudor, at least in part in Mary's case under the influence of her Spanish husband, Philip II. Elizabeth's England was exhausted militarily. The ultimate humiliation was the loss of Calais: "England had lost its most heavily fortified base, which had served as both its gateway into France and its chief bastion against French aggression. . . . Henry's wars had demonstrated that England was not strong enough to expand its beachhead in France, but Mary's war had lost that beachhead altogether. For the first time in centuries, the sovereign of England now held no territory in Continental Europe."[3]

But perhaps even more important, Elizabeth came to power just as the Catholic Counter-Reformation was gathering steam. This had direct implications for every aspect of Elizabethan strategy. To begin with, the Elizabethan religious settlement not only cast the confessional die domestically but inevitably—and much to Elizabeth's discomfort—pulled England into the role of leader of the Protestant cause throughout Europe. Protestantism by its very nature tended to dissent; beyond the break with Rome, the doctrinal differences between Lutherans and Calvinists were already making the international "Protestant interest" a herd of cats, and that herd would grow more feral, fractious, and fissiparous as the reformed faith put down roots across northern Europe and throughout the British Isles. Protestantism also carried with it a whiff of republicanism, or at least anti-authoritarianism, particularly on the part of the Dutch; indeed, for more than a century, the English and Dutch would be locked in a strategic love-hate embrace. The Anglican *via media* was a political compromise that reflected the queen's own religious views (and she had well-reasoned and well-informed ideas). That made it a wobbly platform for strategy, both domestically and internationally. Broadly speaking, Elizabeth was tugged toward a more radical and aggressive Protestant posture, in response to pressure from a variety of directions: her privy councilors, the parliament, the nascent political nation, the poorly organized but energetic and potentially powerful European Protestant community, and a stream of events well beyond her control. The result was that there was an ineluctable ideological overlay to Elizabethan strategy, despite the queen's conservative instincts, and she would enjoy no strategic pause to rebuild England's strength. She was forever running a Red Queen's race.

Consequently, neither a traditional dynastic framework nor any sort of proto-nationalist one alone suffices to explain Elizabeth's strategic behavior. The best that can be done, given that Elizabeth ruled through five decades of nearly endless tumult, is to try to outline a very rough architecture of security priorities that underlay the queen's responses to the many crises she faced, trace its development over time, and focus upon a handful of actions that illustrate England's dilemmas. The following chapters reveal how long-term strategic goals and habits of strategy-making worked themselves out in particular circumstances. These vignettes have been chosen, in part, as a contrast to much past writing, scholarship, and myth on the subject, particularly the navalist and nativist conception of "Little England" as an isolated island "set in a silver sea" relying on its "wooden walls" for security and the accompanying idea that Elizabethan strategy was fundamentally defensive. The sketch that follows below will portray late sixteenth-century England as opportunistically but relentlessly expansionist and ideological, seeking to expand its security perimeter and to project power, to build a "British" empire even when this was an apparently risky or foolish endeavor. In sum, the many operational, financial, and bureaucratic constraints of Elizabethan means did not diminish the intended ends of Elizabethan strategy. That said, Elizabeth and her advisers had no intrinsic interest in direct conquest or rule; greatness was not a self-justifying purpose. The Dutch, whenever the rebellion against Spain was going badly, would offer to make her their queen, too, but her response was invariably hostile. Scotland was to be a strategic partner—junior, to be sure, but a partner whose interests, particularly those of the lowland Protestants, were to be weighed in the account. Even in Ireland, extreme measures were a matter of last resort and repeated failure of lesser methods. Too often for Elizabeth's liking, she found herself compelled to engage, commit, and intervene; surrounded and outnumbered, the wisest course often was limited attack. Late Tudor England may have seen itself as a fallen empire, but it was devoted to recovering its position as a European—indeed, a global—great power, and to carving out a sphere safe for the practice of the Protestant faith.

But if the Elizabethans had global ambitions, their first concerns were about the durability and legitimacy of the regime at home. Thus the primary principle of English strategy was to secure the queen's ability to govern domestically. Even in the late sixteenth century, this was a question of asserting London's writ throughout England and Wales. As the chapter on the Northern Rebellion of the late 1560s will show, it was also a matter of assuring a Protestant (if not necessarily a Tudor) succession. This was a question of stability—the Henrician break from Rome, the full-blown and aggressive Protestantism of Edward VI, and the fiery Catholic *revanche* under Mary had progressively ripped the English social and political fabric quite badly—but also of sect. A growing majority of the nobility, the emerging merchant class, and the English public were seriously committed to Protestant religious reforms and, over the course of Elizabeth's reign, a set of aggressive anti-Catholic policies at home and abroad. And what, in Elizabeth's early years, was an English Catholicism marked by traditionalism and devotion to "old ways," became itself more aggressive and, in later years, a focus of Counter-Reformation intrigue. Pope Paul IV, with financial backing from Philip II, founded a university for the training of English Catholic clerics at Douai in northern France that soon was smuggling in missionaries to try to revive the English Catholic community and rally it against Elizabeth. Indeed, at least until the 1580s—when Elizabeth was clearly past childbearing capacity, war with Spain was unavoidable, and Mary Queen of Scots was finally eliminated—succession was perhaps the central strategic issue of the era; the safety of the regime surpassed that of the ruler. That also made the queen's marriage a matter of public, even parliamentary, debate and concern; no decision could be Elizabeth's alone.

The second set of strategic priorities for Elizabeth and her privy council were Scotland and Ireland. Unless these postern gates were closed to French, Spanish, and Popish influence and friendly, Protestant local regimes were put in place, England faced an existential threat. These two theaters not only were central to two of the military campaigns discussed below but also remained a constant concern throughout the period. Scotland was and had long been the dominant danger, but beyond geography alone there was a strong desire to sever the "auld alliance" between Scotland and France—brought to particularly troublesome and vivid life in the person of Mary Stuart—and prevent the further fracturing of Scots domestic politics brought about by the take-no-prisoners Calvinism of John Knox and the grip of Presbyterianism on the Scots Protestant imagination. Like the Dutch, the Scots seemed dangerously republican to English eyes, insufficiently deferential to monarchy and traditional order. Elizabeth's successors would come to see Protestant dissent in Scotland to be as threatening as Catholicism, and even in the queen's time the Scottish Kirk was a constant irritant as well as essential partner; she needed them inside the tent, but they were full of piss and vinegar. From the start of her reign, what William Cecil memorialized as a "*coniuntione Anglie Scotie*," a "perpetual peace" between England and Scotland, based upon a common Protestant ideology and Elizabeth's imperial right, was a principal strategic concern.[4]

The Irish were just as troublesome. English kings had been the *soi-disant* and nominal lords of Ireland since the Norman Henry II received the blessing of Pope Adrian IV in 1155, landed a large fleet at Waterford in 1171, and took the vassalage of the Irish chieftain Ruaidhrí four years later. But the English "Pale"—the Anglicized corruption of *an pháil*, as the Irish called the boundary around Dublin and the surrounding counties—that slowly spread westward across the Irish lowlands was inherently vulnerable. English policy had more often relied on deal-making with Irish clan leaders than on direct military coercion. Under the many pressures of late sixteenth-century international politics, this rather rickety approach collapsed. Despite the strain in the 1590s from the continuing and global war with Spain and varying but constant and substantial commitments in France or the Netherlands, Elizabeth responded to her Irish crisis with a further huge and sustained mobilization that would, for the first time, demonstrate England's ability to project power to all corners of Ireland. Moreover, the Irish experience and particularly the campaigns of Elizabeth's late years in response to the sustained rebellion led by the Earl of Tyrone reveal the expansionist nature of English strategic culture. This continued in Ireland after Elizabeth, beginning with the "plantation" of the Scots in Ulster undertaken in 1606, but Ireland also would provide a laboratory of colonial expansion for centuries to come.

Elizabeth, like her predecessors and successors, preferred to fight her great-power battles not at home but away. The saga of the *Gran Armada* of 1588 highlights the role of rising English naval power during the period, but it is better to see this third element in Elizabethan security architecture as encompassing not just the Channel, the "Narrow Seas," but the entire eastern Atlantic, from the North Sea through the Bay of Biscay and the related coastal parts of Europe from Holland to northern Spain and Portugal. Indeed, although Elizabeth did her best to avoid and to limit English land-force engagements in continental Europe, the need for commitments of men and money proved constant. As Brendan Simms has convincingly argued, a clearer picture of England's strategic and operational reasoning emerges when the region is taken as a whole, a "moat-and-counterscarp" system intended to add some strategic depth to an exposed England.[5] Simms's construct is an elaboration of Elizabethan rhetoric; it was Cecil who advanced the idea of the continental counterscarp. Over the course of Elizabeth's time, England's perception of threats to its great-power ambitions shifted profoundly, beginning an eastward shift that would continue through centuries to come. Paris had been the traditional enemy, but the many civil wars of religion that roiled France in the late 1500s and the rise of the Protestant "Huguenot" faction confounded that clear calculation. Conversely, Englishmen previously thought of the Hapsburg Empire as a counterweight to France, but Philip II eventually convinced even Elizabeth of his inveterate hatred of all things Protestant and English. And, periodically, there was a fear that the two Catholic powers would unite in a crusade against England. In sum, the situation proved too volatile and violent for diplomatic balancing alone. This larger western European theater of operations, both maritime and continental, was where England's status as a great power would be measured. The queen's reign was punctuated by periodic interventions, but the "counter-armada" of 1589 described below provides unique insight into the process of Elizabethan strategy-making.

As suggested in the above account of Francis Drake's epic voyage, the Elizabethans' nucleus of strategic concerns—domestic regime durability, stability throughout the British Isles, and a favorable balance of power in littoral northwestern Europe—was nested within a truly globe-spanning appreciation of power. Drake's reports of the opportunities in Southeast Asia would do much to create an East India lobby among London's merchant class. And Englishmen already understood the role the Mediterranean and the greater Middle East played in European politics and trade; preparing for the 1589 expedition, Elizabeth sought the help of Sultan Mulay Ahmed of Morocco in evicting the Spanish and restoring the Portuguese pretender Don Antonio to the throne in Lisbon: "Nothing could happen more in accordance with our wish than that so good a path should be opened with your"—the Sultan's—"favour and assistance to regain him"—Don Antonio—"his estate."[6] But the most important element in the rest-of-the-world calculus was "the Americas," and in particular that part of the Americas—a kind of "greater Caribbean Basin," which included Peru (whose treasure was transferred through Panama)—that produced and returned to Europe the resources that propelled Spain's bid for European hegemony and drive for Counter-Reformation.

Thus, Elizabethan expansionism included, on a small but still important scale, the first English attempts at a permanent lodgment in this New World. Like Drake's voyage, this was a strategic endeavor first and foremost, rather than an exploration primarily intended to increase the store of human knowledge; as the concluding vignette will make clear, the Roanoke colony was intended as a base of operations for piracy, a sally port from which English sea dogs might sail in search of Spanish treasure ships. Indeed, the bulk of this series will be a chronicle of the rising importance of the Americas theater, if one may collectively term it so, in what would become an Anglo-American set of strategic views shared across an Atlantic world. The Americas also would be seen by Elizabethans as an important theater in the ideological struggle. They understood that the Spanish had a head start not only in exploiting the riches of the New World but also in Catholicizing it. Bringing the reformed faith to the indigenous "Indian" peoples in the Americas may have been more moral justification than motivation, but it was a constant theme of the Elizabethan strategic conversation. As Richard Hakluyt put the case to the queen in the "executive summary" of his *A Particuler Discourse Concerning the Great Necessitie and Manifolde Commodyties That Are Likely to Growe to This Realme of Englande by the Western Discoveries Lately Attempted* of 1584, commonly known as the *Discourse of Western Planting:* "The Spaniards govern in the Indies with all pride and tyranny; and like as when people of contrary nature at the sea enter into gallies, where men are tied as slaves, all yell and cry with one voice, *Liberta, liberta,* as desirous of liberty and freedom, so no doubt whensoever the Queen of England, a prince of such clemency, shall seat upon that firm of America, and shall be reported throughout all that tract to use the natural people there with all humanity, curtesy, and freedom, they will yield themselves to her government, and revolt clean from the Spaniard."[7]

Considering the ambitions and architecture of Elizabethan strategic thinking, the calculus of ends and ways, also helps to understand the development of the means, that is, of what eventually would be described as the fiscal-military state that included Elizabeth as ruler or executive, her privy council, her naval and land-force technical advisers, a "professional" bureaucracy, government finance, relations with the parliament and the larger political nation, and more. There is an immense amount of superb scholarship on each of these subjects that cannot be fairly summarized here but must be taken into account. Not only was Elizabeth a monarch by divine right, who ruled and reigned, she was a woman of strong character, extremely quick mind, enlightened education, and complex personality. She was an astute politician who was much beloved by her people, a love expressed in a willingness to suffer taxes and impositions from her that they would not tolerate from her Stuart successors; only in the aftermath of the Glorious Revolution of 1688 would the English countenance consistent financial support. But she was a woman in an era that regarded female rule as inherently suspect, as can be seen in John Knox's *The First Blast of the Trumpet Against the Monstrous Regiment of Women*, published just as Elizabeth ascended the throne: "To promote a woman to bear rule, superiority, dominion or empire above any realm, nation or city is repugnant to nature, contumely to God, a thing most contrarious to his revealed will and approved order and finally it is the subversion of good order, of all equity and justice."[8] Elizabeth loathed Knox, the driving force behind the Scots Presbyterian Reformation, who for his part remained unapologetic, adding yet a new source of English-Scottish tension to a relationship troubled for centuries. And in England itself, under the terms of the revived Act of Supremacy that was the first element in the Elizabethan religious settlement, the queen could not be, as was Henry VIII, the "head" of the English church, only its "governor." Nor, of course, could she take the field as Henry had done. She could inspire her troops, as she did her army at Tilbury as it readied itself to repel the armada: claiming the "heart and stomach of a king" ready to heap "scorn that Parma or Spain, or any Prince of Europe, should dare to invade the borders of my realm." But she had also to acknowledge that she "had the body of a weak and feeble woman" forced to "place my chief strength and safeguard in the loyal hearts and goodwill of my subjects."[9] Elizabeth preferred diplomacy, where her influence was greatest; in war, she had to rely on others, her male advisers and commanders. She was forever torn between the need to trust and reasons to fear.

THE QUEEN'S COUNSELLORS

In particular, the queen relied upon William Cecil, who was already an experienced bureaucrat, having served under Edward VI as an aide to the lord protector and de facto ruler, the Duke of Somerset. If there was a chief architect of Elizabethan strategy, it was Cecil, who served initially as secretary of state, was raised to the peerage as Baron Burghley in 1571, and continued to serve as treasurer; Burghley remained Elizabeth's closest adviser until his death in 1598. Burghley had an uncanny ability to put himself in the queen's mind but also a subtle sense of how to lead her to unpleasant but necessary conclusions. His state papers are thick with pro-and-con assessments of the many policy problems that Elizabeth faced, but fewer direct recommendations. In particular, though deeply Protestant himself and more than willing to deal harshly with

Catholics in the British Isles, Burghley was adept at downplaying—or disguising—the confessional or ideological dimension of international affairs that the queen never liked.

Burghley is often portrayed by his biographers or historians of the Elizabethan age as a realist, practical, a *politique*, but that assessment is relative. Three other men played large roles in advising the queen, and they were unapologetic, aggressive Protestants. Burghley's successor as secretary of state was Francis Walsingham, like Burghley a middling member of the English elite, a bureaucrat and the son of bureaucrats; part of Elizabeth's way of maximizing her domestic power was to promote men from outside the very top ranks of the nobility, men who lacked large, landed estates and thus substantial bases of power outside of the queen's patronage. Walsingham lacked Burghley's ability to channel the queen's thoughts—God came before queen in his reckoning—but his talents of intelligence-gathering and espionage, particularly counterintelligence against Mary Queen of Scots and the Spanish and domestic plotters against the regime, made him not only tolerable but invaluable to Elizabeth. Walsingham's antipathy toward Catholics became an implacable hatred in 1572, when, serving as the English ambassador in Paris, he was caught up in the St. Bartholomew's Day Massacre, the frenzied spree that claimed the lives of Admiral Gaspard de Coligny, the leading Huguenot noble, another three thousand French Protestants in Paris, and perhaps as many as ten thousand across France.[10] The massacre shocked all in England, but particularly the devout among the Protestant elite, many of whom had close connections to leading Huguenots. Walsingham concluded, "I think [it] less peril to live with [the French] as enemies than as friends."[11] This summarized his attitude toward Spain and Catholics in general.

Walsingham was a confidant of Burghley, but over the course of his career he moved closer to Burghley's supposed rival, Robert Dudley, from 1564 the Earl of Leicester. "Robin" was the first and greatest of Elizabeth's favorites. Dudley was the fifth son of the Earl of Northumberland who, on the death of Edward VI, had attempted a coup by backing Lady Jane Grey, a Protestant, over the Catholic Mary Tudor for the succession. Northumberland's failure cost him his head and his son his inheritance. Elizabeth, smitten with the dashing, clever young man who was also a master of the courtier's arts, raised him, rapidly, to the highest station. Once so elevated, Leicester become a political force in his own right. He developed a following, a faction that has sometimes been seen as a political party in the making. Leicester was a close student of international and military affairs and a strong advocate for a forward strategy and intervention in the Netherlands. He might have married Elizabeth had she not been queen. But with Elizabeth's favor came a very short leash, and it was not until the late 1580s that the earl was given the military responsibilities he craved and which compromised his special relationship with Elizabeth. But, as Wallace MacCaffrey has observed, Leicester had banked limitless credit with the queen: "She could scold, bully and humiliate him, but to the end of his life he never forfeited her deepest trust in him."[12]

With Leicester's death, just months after the scattering of the Spanish armada in 1588, the queen's favor fell to Robert Devereux, the young Earl of Essex. In contrast to Burghley, Walsingham, and the young Leicester, Essex came from the front rank of the English nobility, one of the dozen or so earls. Essex was determined to win martial glory and stole away from court to partake the Portugal expedition of 1589, much to Elizabeth's displeasure, but two years later and though he was but twenty-four years old, she trusted him with command of the English force sent to help Henri IV in Normandy. Essex, whether because of pedigree, the age difference, or plain personality, was far readier to challenge the queen than Leicester had been. The high-water mark of his glory was the 1596 Cadiz expedition, which almost immediately became a major part of Elizabethan myth. Though an advocate of continental war, Essex was sent to Ireland in 1599 to suppress the growing rebellion. His failures there and distance from court—and court intrigue by Burghley's son, Robert Cecil, and the Cecil faction—made him increasingly erratic, to the point of paranoia. The end result was banishment, degradation, and a half-cocked coup attempt that ended on the executioner's block.[13] In simple terms, Essex stepped into the leadership of the more aggressive Protestant and anti-Spanish faction, into the void created by the deaths of Leicester in 1588 and Walsingham in 1590 and by the aging of Burghley. Elizabeth, too, had aged, and her subjects were tiring of fighting and paying for what seemed to be unending wars. Essex may have had a fundamentally weaker hand to play, and though he played it boldly, he ultimately played it badly.

Yet, of Elizabeth's advisors, Cecil stood alone, not just for his longevity and his ability to channel the queen's mind, but for his organization, mastery of contemporary political thought, and his well-articulated conception of empire and an imperial state. Perhaps more than Elizabeth herself, Cecil was the architect of the British imperial regime, crafting a design that could be adapted and reformed and expanded according to circumstance. It served England well for two centuries and as a legacy for an independent America.

It can be said that the essential Cecil often lurked behind the curtain. His many memoranda were often written in the classical rhetorical mode in *utramque partem*—arguing both sides of the case. And his political goals—building an imperial monarchy that was powerful yet still constrained by conciliar advice, parliament, and the larger political nation—were in tension if not openly contradictory. The memoranda represent the working out of specific problems in relation to larger strategic and political principles.

First among these was the promotion of Protestant faith and practice. From his days at Cambridge, Cecil had been at the heart of a Protestant family and patronage network.[14] This formed a nucleus of Edwardian government and its modernizing programs; Cecil was not yet thirty years of age when he became secretary to the king, and even as power over the young monarch shifted from the Duke of Somerset to Northumberland, the mandates of political power and religious reform were inextricably intertwined; likewise were the handicaps created by a questionably legitimate boy king and the occasions for the exercise of rule through council. As Stephen Alford puts it, these experiences shaped Cecil's "early Protestantism and the providential edge it gave to his early Elizabethan political analysis." Behind the Ciceronian façade lay a man with almost Puritan beliefs, and indeed in his later career he did his best to shield the nascent Puritan movement from Elizabeth's wrath and the scourgings of Archbishop John Whitgift. Even as he yoked himself to the new queen's tightly held bridle, he lamented to Sir Thomas Smith that his "public actions" were "most comenly in publicke things of the world, yet I thank God, I doo submit all my conceptes and thughts as mere folly, to the wisdom and piete of the Gospell."[15] As we shall see in subsequent chapters, Cecil was always at pains to improve the quality of preachers and preaching; he regarded both as critical to cementing not just true faith but the political cohesion of a diverse and growing regime. With age, advancing position and property, and a deepening appreciation of the limits of English power—and with other energetic Protestants at court full of fervor—Cecil's piety was less apparent yet still his principal motivation. He may have been Elizabeth's first minister, but Baron Burghley forever placed the regime above the monarch and the dynasty.

This mental framework carried over to Cecil's view of international affairs and strategy; the confluence of "Daungers within the realme, or from forrayn partes, or from both" was inseparable, he noted in 1559. The Treaty of Cateau-Cambresis, Cecil worried, was a conspiracy among France, Spain, and the Catholic Church against the new regime in England, and his fears were reinforced by dispatches from the new ambassador in Paris, Sir Nicholas Throckmorton. These indicated that the vehicle of conspiracy was Mary Stuart, Queen of Scots. The resulting "memorial of certain pointes meete for restoring the Realme of Scotland to the Auncient Weale" was prototype Cecil, "demonstrat[ing] the power of a British imperialist rhetoric and the apocalyptic terms in which early Elizabethan governors interpreted and made sense of continental and British political affairs."[16] Establishing Mary—by birth a member of the powerful Guise family, the leaders of the Catholic faction in France's religious wars—in Scotland would, Cecil argued, "pav[e] the way for an invasion of England . . . [and] the removal of Elizabeth," as well as the return of Catholicism.[17] His answer was military intervention in support of the Protestant party in Scotland and the *"coniuntione Anglie Scotie"* mentioned above.

Many accounts of the era make too much of personality and faction, though the personalities were very large ones. Not only was there broad harmony of outlook among the queen's leading advisors, but the Elizabethan public sphere or political nation was a growing factor in strategic decision-making, particularly in the longer run, than the magisterial studies based upon state papers imagine. Peter Lake and Steve Pincus have argued for an English "post-Reformation public sphere" created from the 1530s through the 1630s—with the Elizabethan era as the "formative period"—that was remarkably complex. "The most spectacular examples of such behavior," they write, "were often overtly oppositional, the work of Protestant opponents of a Catholic regime and then of Catholic opponents of a Protestant ones, or of Puritan critics of a national church. However . . . many of the first and most sophisticated efforts to appeal to and mobilize various publics emanated from the center of the regime itself. These appeals were intended either to induce the queen to take actions she did not wish to take or to prevent her from doings things she wanted to do."[18]

And because the distinctions between what was religious or confessional and what was political were blurred—any issue or crisis appeared in a number of lights—these appeals were intended to and did have effects on strategy. As J. E. Neale's voluminous accounts make plain, the major actions and concerns of Elizabeth's parliaments involved much debate—even when it did not directly affect policy—about the direction of English strategy.[19] This is most obviously apparent when the queen, whose "ordinary" revenues and "chested treasure" savings could not sustain even the limited military forces she required, came to the parliament for additional funds. Strategic concerns informed the nature and limited extent of Elizabeth's initial religious reforms, and subsequent parliaments constantly pushed for more; this was a debate Elizabeth eventually won, but was nevertheless one in which she had to engage. And parliament never stopped nagging her to marry or to somehow settle a Protestant succession. K. J. Kesselring's meticulous account of the Northern Rebellion of 1569, which informs much of the chapter to follow, charts the propaganda efforts and puts a large frame around what was militarily a small affair. The queen and Cecil were intimately involved in the "spinning" of the rebellion, and notably in ways that promoted—once the initial rebellion had been successfully suppressed—the ideological and confessional character of the revolt.[20] This was not a step they had to take in order to suppress the uprising itself. But it was important to put the regime in synch with its base of popular support.

One final consideration: the ends and ways of Elizabethan strategy were forever constrained by the means. As hinted above, the queen's finances were shaky. So is much of the scholarship on the early modern economy, but a fair estimate would put the king of France's income at perhaps three or four times greater than Elizabeth's, and Philip II's at eight times as much.[21] Achieving the goal of returning to the front rank of great powers, of strategic independence, was beyond any realistic planning horizon. And if Elizabeth could change tack with the slightest breeze, she largely kept her bearings—though, to repeat, she did have to sail before the wind of a broader political nation. The number of principal strategic advisers remained small, with Burghley, Walsingham, and even the melodramatic Leicester released from duty only in death and Essex in his abortive revolt. The stability extended to a larger ring of trusted and experienced diplomats, generals, and advisors, some of whom will appear in the chapters to come. Perhaps most tellingly, the era saw a consistent pattern of military modernization that reflected an underlying consistency in strategy-making.

But it was in the art and science of force planning and force design that the patterns of Elizabethan long-term strategy are to be seen. Force designs and weapons systems—warships or artillery pieces—are expensive, require long-term investments, and inevitably involve trade-offs in capability; the demands of speed or cost often cancel out the desire for firepower, durability, or protection. Under Elizabeth, both the royal navy and England's land forces underwent a profound transformation, professionalization—mixed with a kind of privatization—and expansion, all to create a force more capable of projecting power abroad. English soldiers fought on many battlefields, season after season, and, as the Ireland chapter will make plain, in increasing numbers. English sailors began to chart the course that would one day allow them to claim that they ruled the waves.

The late Tudor navy is, in particular, a testament to the global ambition and expansionist and aggressive intent of Elizabethan strategy. The two fleets of the "armada year" of 1588 reveal the differences in strategic orientation between Elizabeth's England and Philip's Spain. The English had begun to build warships that maximized firepower and sailing qualities better suited to the open waters of the Atlantic. They were sleeker, rode lower in the water, and carried fewer troops to be used for boarding, and they were intended not just to defend the home waters but to operate globally, to project power. Philip's armada was largely built around galleys that could be rowed as well as sailed, and they had high "castles" fore and aft to create "high ground" from which to shoot down on opposing decks when it came to grappling and boarding. These Spanish ships were optimized for the Mediterranean, and the stout, sturdy, and slow designs had been proven against the Turks at Lepanto in 1571. They had to huddle together for protection, be it in transatlantic convoys, in the famous crescent moon formation the English first encountered off Eddystone Rocks, or as they did off Gravelines when they could not avoid English fireships. If the English modernized their army along continental lines, after the disaster of 1588 Spain rebuilt its navy more along English lines.

By Elizabeth's death, the queen's strategic ambitions—despite her shallow purse and cautious intentions—had o'erleaped themselves. England suffered from a moment of "imperial overstretch" that left her Stuart successors with a conundrum: imperial ambitions that were both very popular and prohibitively expensive. Yet she had set goals that could not be easily renounced; when the Stuart clan was restored to power, they had o'erlearned the lessons of the early seventeenth century and would be o'erthrown for good. Englishmen extolled Elizabeth as "Gloriana" not because they remembered her reign as peaceful—it was not at all peaceful—but because they remembered their aspiration to greatness in the securing of the "liberties," both at home and abroad, which they held dear. Her subjects might grumble about failure or the cost in blood or taxes, or divide themselves into faction, but they could not accept a lowering of sights. This was a puzzle the Stuarts could not solve.

Elizabeth had also led Englishmen into North America and oriented the colonizers there squarely within the strategic zeitgeist. It is not hyperbole to say that England's colonies in America were a product of the Elizabethan tradition. Nor should it come as a surprise that the colonists would take this strategic culture to heart; it gave them a cohesion that was otherwise hard to come by. It also gave them a larger purpose that saw them through many failures and gave meaning to the struggle and loss of lives. American colonies were but a tiny part of the story of Elizabethan strategy, but the Elizabethan experience played a giant role in shaping how the colonists would think about war and power.

3

THE NORTHERN REBELLION

As a military event, the Northern Rebellion of 1569 merits nothing more than the tiniest mention. The largest engagement, the "battle" near Naworth Castle of February 20, 1570, was little more than a small and apparently poorly planned and executed ambush of royal forces by the followers and tenants of Lord Leonard Dacre, a "warlord" of the borderlands between Scotland and England who was not even the leading rebel. Precipitously attacking the troops of Henry Carey, Baron Hunsdon, cousin to Queen Elizabeth, Dacre's footmen charged and were crushed, with perhaps three hundred killed. Dacre was particularly rash in that a reinforcing force of fifteen hundred Scots—as many troops as Hunsdon had—was about a day's march away.[1]

At the same time, the larger story of the rebellion—the conditions and the conspiring that led to the revolt, the government's response and the rebellion's consequences—is a kind of microcosm of Elizabethan strategy-making, touching on almost every aspect of the regime's strategic architecture: the political effects of the confessional divides occasioned by the Reformation; the stability, durability, and legitimacy of the queen's rule in England itself, particularly in its northern "marches"; the unending need for action in the British "near abroad," particularly in Scotland; England's position in the European balance of power; and the profound shift in priorities that saw Spain, for a century, displace France as the primary great-power threat. The inherently complex crisis was further complicated by the intrigues and entanglements of the queen's council, court, and most powerful nobles; policy was intertwined with personality, not least including that of Elizabeth herself.

Much of the contest and crisis revolved around religion and how faith intertwined with politics, be it personal, domestic, or international. Elizabethan Protestantism was a quicksilver phenomenon, a doctrinal mishmash, institutionally weak and a subject of continuous definition and debate across all classes of Englishmen, many of whom were well informed about the European religious debates of the previous fifty years. As Patrick Collinson has written, the Elizabethan era was one of "abortive reform. In the event the renewal of religious life, the formation of a 'godly preaching ministry' and a profoundly moral transformation of society was to come not through legislation and the overhaul of institutions but by the religious force of Protestantism itself in its apostolate at the grass roots."[2] And where this kind of bottom-up reform collided with the top-down predilections of the Elizabethan hierarchy, there, too, was conflict. Nevertheless, because Protestantism had to provide social and political cohesion across a disparate set of kingdoms—the glue of an imperial regime—the queen and her advisers had a strategic interest in matters of religion equal to their confessional, doctrinal, and intellectual interests, which were themselves not inconsiderable.

In 1569, this process was barely underway. Protestants may have been a slight majority of the population, but in many areas—most importantly, in the north—Catholicism and the "old ways" remained well entrenched, as did the local power structures intertwined with them. Moreover, London was its own biggest obstacle. The formal religious settlement of the previous decade fully satisfied almost no one, probably least of all the most forward-looking and articulate Protestant reformers; the English church was neither Lutheran nor Calvinist, though it shared elements of both, and it retained, in large measure thanks to Elizabeth's effort, many of the hierarchical and ceremonial trappings of Catholicism. Elizabeth insisted upon priestly vestments—thereby creating years of controversy—and kept a crucifix in her private chapel. The ambiguity could be a strength—many of the reform-minded could find a home, even if it was a "fixer-upper," in the national church—but also a weakness—it was a challenge to translate confused confessional principles into an ideology that would bind together both British peoples and European political allies; there was something for everyone but not quite enough for anyone. For her part, Elizabeth clung not only to conservative theological ideas but a belief in a divine-right, dynastic basis for political order. She was wary of "hot gospellers" at court and even of the firm faith of her first, closest, and longest-serving strategic confidant, William Cecil. Even less did she desire to lead a Protestant crusade or to see England as the champion of a confederation of Protestant European states and principalities. At the same time, such a position was hard to avoid, abroad as well as in Britain. It was a necessary commitment for England internationally. Protestants on the continent were either oppressed minorities under Catholic sovereigns or, in the case of the Dutch, rebels against them. Moreover, the areas of northwest Europe where Protestantism was most advanced were also the parts of the continent that mattered most to English security. But Elizabeth had little patience for those of any faith who would overthrow a monarch ordained by God. In sum, Tudor strategy-making was deeply imbued with a sense of a national and international "Protestant interest" which was never dispositive but always present. Just as church reform was a bottom-up, hearts-and-minds affair, so were, in many ways, strategic habits. Elizabethan policies produced the greatest cohesion and had the most measurable influence when defined most broadly, as patriotic anti-Catholicism. When it was defined most aggressively and Calvinistically or, conversely, narrowly Anglican, it tended to produce dissent and divisiveness. The quasi-Puritans of the Elizabethan era had influence and were an enduring and powerful element, but they never enjoyed the kind of dominant control they prayed for. The same limits applied to the most conservative Anglicans, even in the last decade of Elizabeth's rule. And, of course, English Catholics, diminishing in number but overly represented among the older gentry and with periodic support from the European continent, lived in the shadows. The Northern Rebellion thrust these confessional controversies out from the dark—where Elizabeth preferred them to remain—into the open. It was the rebels who forced her hand, in good measure because their leaders hid their narrower feudal, family, and political interests behind the banner of the Old Religion. In response, the queen and her councilors exploited the opportunity to link Catholicism with treason, tapping into popular opinion while also shaping and exciting it in ways that had later consequences. In sum, this was the moment when the Elizabethan regime defined, and began to implement, its imperial vision.

THE PROBLEM OF THE NORTH

The north of England had long been a problem for its southern-based rulers, the Tudor family in particular. The centralizing efforts of the

Tudor regime—modernizing reforms necessary to defend England's security interests in a shifting international environment marked by the rise of Spain—and their concomitant promotion of Protestantism exacerbated these long-standing tensions and were immediately threatening to the prestige, power, and traditional autonomy of the northern nobility, especially that of Yorkshire and the "marches" along the Scottish border. Nor did the barons of the North care for economic and commercial modernization, the growth of trade and industry, or the enclosure of common lands, which seemed to be at the expense of local and agrarian interests. In reaction to Henry VIII's break with Rome and Thomas Cromwell's reforms, the old noble families—the Percys, Nevilles, and Dacres, along with tens of thousands of lesser northern Catholics—had in 1536 joined in the "Pilgrimage of Grace," demanding a return to the papal fold and a parliament free from Henry's influence. Though the crisis was defused by vague promises of pardon before it erupted into open hostilities, several hundred of the movement's leaders were executed. Henry Percy, the Earl of Northumberland, was deprived of his title even though he remained loyal to the crown. Writing in the early 1960s, Conyers Read characterized northern society as "reactionary"; there is something to this idea, even if it simplifies and caricatures in a way later historians have been loath to do.[3] Taken altogether, northern England was "quite a brutal place," and its nobility had long been antipathetic to the consolidating power or to modernizing social and religious tradition.[4] If the Elizabethan religious settlement was too tepid for the purer Protestants of southern England, it was too hot for the more Catholic north. The nobility of the North, many of them "Yorkists" during the Wars of the Roses while the Tudors were "Lancastrians," had enjoyed a huge measure of freedom and local control; now London demanded a more controlling role.

The county of Durham was an especially tough nut to crack. Its distinctive palatinate jurisdiction reserved to local magnates powers normally exercised by the crown, and in Durham and its eponymous cathedral city, that meant the bishop. In Christopher Kitching's summary: "In Durham writs ran in the Bishop's name. It was *his* peace, not the King's which might be broken."[5] To Elizabethans, the northern church—even when nominally Protestant—had to be remade from an obstacle to regime authority into a tool for centralization. The bishopric was also the second wealthiest in the kingdom, giving it a large measure of temporal as well as spiritual influence; its holdings including highly profitable coal mines whose ores were shipped through Newcastle to London. Henry

VIII's Franchises Act of 1535 had begun a process of yoking this "last principality" and its episcopal structure to the rest of his nascent empire, a move that may well have contributed to the uprising the following year. Alas Henry, whose heart's desire was to reestablish himself as a continental European power, made but modest progress on his northern frontiers, not only in Scotland, where his war of "rough wooing" failed to produce a dynastic match for his son, but in the English marches. Henry had neither the time nor the money to fulfill his strategic designs. The Bishop of Durham, Cuthbert Tunstall, even though a close advisor to the cast-off Catherine of Aragon, managed to survive Henry and a term of imprisonment in the Tower of London under Edward VI—the boy king's lord protector, Edward Seymour, was unable to prove charges of treason—to be restored as bishop and president of the Council of the North, at age seventy-nine, upon the reign of Mary Tudor. Tunstall was deprived finally in September 1559 after he refused the Elizabethan Oath of Supremacy and held prisoner until his death a few weeks later. The queen, preoccupied with matters closer to home and happy to pocket the bishopric's revenues, took her time about naming a replacement. In 1561 she chose James Pilkington to take the seat at Durham. He had been a Marian exile in Geneva and, upon his return, Regius—that is, royally sponsored—Professor of Divinity at Cambridge. Upon his return to London, he quickly earned a reputation for his charismatic preaching, which impressed the queen, though, given Elizabeth's attitude toward Puritan piety, shipping the razor-tongued Pilkington out of London to the wilds of Yorkshire may also have appealed. Once ensconced in 1561, Pilkington toured the bishopric, administering the Oath of Supremacy to his churchmen and magistrates. This helped weed out the oligarchs who had run the region under Tunstall—the bishop's corrupt temporal chancellor, Robert Meynell, had "ruled this country alone above twenty years and with the evil report of all men," moaned Pilkington.[6] The new bishop brought with him a new team of administrators. Even these first steps in yoking the northern church to London's purposes were not without second-order consequences. They lowered the level of graft somewhat and pushed the cause of reform, but they also introduced new political complexities. Pilkington was himself prone to be covetous and contentious, but beyond that, and in lieu of material support from London, he needed the bishopric's revenues to fund his reforms; the Elizabethan proclivity for self-funded policies was nearly universal. Pilkington intended to unsettle the regional ancien regime but understood that reform might spark resistance. The bishop reported ominously to Cecil, "I am afraid to think what may follow if it be not foreseen. The worshipful of the shire is set and of small power, the people rude and heady and by these occasions most bold."[7] Pilkington's prickly personality aside, this was an accurate assessment. He needed reinforcement.

To stiffen his program, Pilkington in 1563 brought in William Whittingham as Durham's dean. Like Pilkington, he was the nominee of Robert Dudley, Elizabeth's favorite and soon to become Earl of Leicester. During his exile, Whittingham had worked on the English-language Geneva Bible, and succeeded John Knox as pastor of the English community in the city that gave the work its name. Indeed, he worked directly under Calvin himself, whose sister he married. Mrs. Pilkington's zealousness enraged the traditionalists of Durham, particularly when she burned the banner of St. Cuthbert, the patron saint of the county. The bishop and dean understood their mission to drag the north of England into line with London and the south. They set about their tasks with systematic vigor and little regard for the old oligarchs. They ruthlessly searched for and destroyed remnants of the old faith—images and altars and rood screens from parish churches and even, despite Elizabeth's express orders, funeral monuments. "Our poor papists weep to see our churches so bare," Pilkington boasted. '[T]here is nothing in them to make curtsy unto, neither saints nor yet their old little god."[8] The bishop also reported regularly to Cecil not just about the persistence of Catholic traditions but the efforts of Catholics abroad to establish covert networks in the area; Spain, embarking on its Counter-Reformation, was ever probing for English weaknesses, and the North was one. Pilkington and Whittingham topped what David Marcombe has described as "a clerical hierarchy which was probably unique in its indiscretion."[9] The pair also cast the mold for a similar program in York under new bishop Thomas Young. Yet for all the new clergy's prodding, those of the old faith dug their heels in more deeply, hiding banned books and icons not only in church nooks but in their homes. Their efforts to reform church services enjoyed only slightly better results, suffering both from die-hard attitudes and the dearth of well-educated clerics, despite Pilkington's recruiting drives and the government's backing. "By the mid-1560s," concludes Marcombe, "it seemed plain that the new Protestant elite was attempting to establish a permanent niche for itself in country society on the strength of episcopal and capitular patronage and that this rapid expansion of the 'church interest' was at the expense of . . . some of the established families of the shire. . . . The law of diminishing returns had begun to apply to such a degree that the new Elizabethan hierarchy could only establish its own fortunes by seeking to deprive others."[10]

THE SCOTLAND PROBLEM

The situation in the north of England problem was inseparable from England's long-running Scotland problem. England's northern border was a sieve; from a strategic perspective, lowland Scotland and the north of England made what amounted to a single theater. Border "rievers"— derived from the Old English word for "rob"—raided in both directions, often conspiring with and against one another. And when not plundering one another, local nobles were intermarrying; the sociopolitical order was, as we shall see, not unlike that of Ireland. Indeed, Elizabeth's first step, after the religious settlement in Parliament of 1559, had been to back the Protestant party in Scotland in ejecting the French and establishing an English-leaning regency. But that solution was beginning to unravel. Mary Queen of Scots, though now in protective custody at Bolton Castle in North Yorkshire, had constantly pushed this bubbling cross-border pot toward the boiling point. The Scots had deposed her, but she had escaped across the border and schemed not only to return to power in Edinburgh but to advance her claim to Elizabeth's crown. She was also an irresistible attraction to Elizabeth's French and Spanish enemies. This volatile combination of factors in the North and Scotland set the conditions for the Northern Rebellion, as well as for a break in the strategic collegiality of Elizabeth's senior advisers, for a power struggle within the privy council, and, in particular, for at least momentary opposition to Cecil's increasing dominance at court. But once provoked, the regime responded to all these provocations with vigor, not only terminating the rebellion itself with extreme prejudice but embarking on an energetic campaign to suppress faction and dissent that ended with the execution of Thomas Howard, the Duke of Norfolk and perhaps the leading peer of the realm; with a renewed pro-English government in Edinburgh; with a systematic drive to push church reform measures in the north; and, in the end, with the elevation of Cecil to be Lord Burghley, ennobling Elizabeth's de facto first minister and securing his influence for the rest of his life. In short, the rebellion set in motion a consolidation of the Elizabethan regime, a more precise definition of English strategy, and the ideology of "the Protestant interest." It marked a critical step in the making of an empire and an imperial mode of strategic thought.

In his many works on Elizabethan policy, Wallace MacCaffrey described the late 1560s and early 1570s as the "testing-time of the regime."[11] This summary still stands; the test sprang initially from concerns about the questions of succession and Elizabeth's marriage, which drove the queen to fury and her councilors, courtiers, and people to frustration. These issues had been much discussed in the Parliament of 1563, forcing the queen to prorogue it—that is, to suspend the session without dissolving the legislative or requiring new elections—until 1566, when the need for money outweighed the risks of renewed debate. In part to allay domestic anxieties, Elizabeth had been flirting with both French Valois and Austrian Habsburg suitors, so the queen might insist that the situation would soon enough be resolved and that there was no need for either private or public prodding. The queen also feared that, once either married or having named a successor, her rule and life would be in jeopardy.

The volatile situation in Scotland and the even more volatile actions of its queen also complicated the succession question. Mary was the daughter of James V of Scotland, scion of the Stuart family and husband to Margaret Tudor, sister of Henry VIII of England; this established Mary's claim to the English crown, even though Henry's last will and testament—a document of contested provenance—excluded the Stuart family from succession. Mary's mother was Mary of Guise, a powerful French noble family and leaders of the Catholic faction in France's wars of religion. Henry had hoped to eliminate French influence in Scotland by betrothing the infant Mary to his son, the future Edward VI of England, but Mary was instead raised in France and contracted to marry the dauphin. Francis II had died in 1560 and, although Mary returned to Scotland, she did not directly challenge the Protestant ascendancy created by the Reformation crisis of the preceding years.

Instead, she shopped for a new husband on the continent, increasing her attractiveness by reasserting her claim to the English crown should Elizabeth die without an heir. For a time, her main target was Philip of Spain's unstable son, Carlos. When that failed, Mary began to scheme more actively in Britain, and even Elizabeth briefly thought that a Leicester match might remove the danger. In 1565, Mary rather abruptly, probably out of passion more than political calculation, married James Stuart, Lord Darnley—a match furthered, paradoxically, by

Burghley and Leicester—who was a Catholic; thus did the fate of the Stuart clan entwine itself in English politics for nearly two centuries. Mary compounded this offense by quickly bearing a son in June 1566, the prince who eventually would become James VI of Scotland and James I of England. This not only threatened and enraged Elizabeth but drove the Scots Protestants to rebel, though unsuccessfully at first. But the marriage did not last; Darnley was an arrogant man and Mary an ambitious woman. She met with her leading nobles in November 1566 to discuss "the Darnley problem." The following February, Darnley was dead under mysterious circumstances, and the Earl of Bothwell suspected in the case. The pace of events continued to accelerate. Bothwell was tried and acquitted—he had arranged a sham proceeding—on April 19. He abducted Mary on April 24 and married her on May 15. This was too much for the Scottish nobility, and a broad association of lords, both Catholic and Protestant, confronted Bothwell's forces on June 15; Bothwell and his troops fled the field. The following day Mary was imprisoned at Loch Leven Castle. On July 23 she miscarried twin sons, and on July 24 she abdicated the throne. On May 2, 1568, she escaped confinement and fled to northern England. By May 13 she crossed back into Scotland with six thousand troops but was defeated. Then on May 16 she slipped back into England by fishing boat. Elizabeth, like the Scots, had seen quite enough and put Mary away for safe keeping, first at Carlisle but then moving her more deeply into the northern wastes. Still, Mary immediately began to plot her way back toward power in Scotland and England, even after her further removal to Bolton.

Yet Mary's downfall merely set the stage for a "great and prolonged political crisis"[12] centered on the succession but more fundamentally about the nature of the regime and its strategy. The crisis also put the cat among the pigeons in regard to Elizabeth's advisers. They were, and remained, in harmony of principle and strategic purpose, but now they, too, entered a testing time, and some scholars, perhaps influenced by the squabblings of Elizabeth's late years, have suggested that the advisers divided themselves into factions led by Cecil—supposedly a *politique* narrowly focused on English material interests—and Dudley—leader of a more aggressively Protestant clique. To be sure, Elizabeth's devotion to Dudley had vastly complicated the questions of the queen's marriage—in the early 1560s their romance might have led to nuptials—and thus of the succession and the hopes of regime stability as discussed in the previous chapter. But so were Cecil's designs inextricably linked to his relationship with the queen. He understood that a Leicester marriage would not only have jeopardized his influence on policy and strategy but might also spark an English civil war. Thus he captained the seemingly contradictory cause of a Habsburg marriage, not simply to keep Leicester in check but in hopes of reviving the longstanding English strategy to contain France by alliance with the Habsburg dukes of Burgundy. This line of thinking, however traditional, was to solve a past problem by exacerbating current ones. The rise of Hapsburg Spain had begun to undermine past English aims at balancing France, and this shift was reflected at court, some looking forward to a new alignment and others attempting to hang on to the past, as the queen most preferred. France was no longer the monolithic enemy and Spain's intervention in the Netherlands made their Burgundian presence begin to seem more threatening than comforting; this was a strategic revolution that England struggled to come to grips with. In the summer of 1568, civil war again erupted in France, and in the following winter, bad weather and Huguenot privateers in the Channel had forced Spanish ships carrying more than £80,000—a loan made by Genoese bankers sent to pay Philip's troops in the Netherlands—to seek refuge in Plymouth and Southampton. Guerau de Spes, the newly appointed but antagonistic Spanish ambassador in London, asked that the money be brought ashore for safe keeping. In the meantime, Cecil had discovered that, until the money was processed by bankers in Antwerp, it legally still belonged to the Genoese lenders, who might be enticed just to lend it to Elizabeth, particularly as the English had physical possession. The queen and Cecil could neither resist temptation nor gainsay the shift in strategic realities. They grabbed the loot, sparking an angry Spanish reaction that included trade sanctions that crippled London merchants; the Spanish Netherlands, and Antwerp in particular, was the entrepôt for English woolens, the country's staple export. Cecil's friends at court were delighted; from Devon, Vice Admiral Sir Arthur Champeroun wrote, "I am of the mind that anything taken from that wicked nation is both necessary and profitable to our commonweal."[13] For its part, the anti-Cecil faction grew into something of a Cecil-must-go movement. The movement included otherwise-impossible bedfellows, ranging from Leicester to de Spes, the French ambassador to obscure Florentine banker Roberto Ridolfi, who had ties to the Pope.

These multiple uncertainties made music for Mary, Queen of Scots and those who danced to her tune. Elizabeth had some sympathy for Mary's plight. Beyond their blood ties, Elizabeth could never countenance the deposition of a divinely anointed monarch. But Mary also had a broader base of support. This included traditionalists at court who, like Elizabeth, acknowledged the legitimacy of Mary's claims not only in Scotland but England; these were the sorts of nobles that had previously been swayed to support Mary Tudor, despite her Catholicism and the divisions that ensued. It further included the die-hard Catholics of the North. And, of course, Mary could court support from the Catholic ambassadors, especially de Spes—he was in many ways a more enthusiastic though certainly a less clever conspirator than she. But the key thread in the intertwining strands that led to the rebellion was the Duke of Norfolk, a man of princely rank, Catholic leanings, the acknowledged leader of the House of Lords, with the largest private fortune in England. He had long been considered as a possible match for Mary. Thus were matters of fundamental strategy enmeshed with soap-operatic personalities.

THE NORFOLK FACTOR

Thomas Howard, the fourth in the line of dukes of Norfolk, had risen by age thirty to the forefront of English politics. He was an attractive character, intelligent and cultured, also vaultingly ambitious. Shortly after celebrating Christmas of 1566, he returned from holiday to London to marry Elizabeth Dacre, whose husband of twelve years, Lord Thomas Dacre, had died in July. The duke already had taken young George Dacre, the heir to the extensive family estates in Cumberland, Westmoreland, and Bedfordshire, as his ward. The Dacres were a Catholic family, and the new duchess was an especially devout woman who, according to the Spanish ambassador de Spes, "hears Mass every day" and might soon convert the duke; Elizabeth Dacre also installed her equally devout mother in residence in the duke's household.[14] As noted above, the Dacres were also a powerful force along the border between England and Scotland.

In the month after the Norfolk-Dacre marriage, the Darnley murder set in motion the crisis in Scotland that led to the overthrow of Mary. But many other pieces of Elizabeth's chessboard were simultaneously in motion. To begin with, the queen had dispatched one of her most prominent and experienced counselors, Thomas Radclyffe, the Earl of Sussex, off to Germany to negotiate terms of hypothetical marriage with the Habsburg Archduke Charles IX. At the same time, the power of the Habsburg dynasty loomed as an increasingly proximate threat to English interests and the Protestant faith. In August, a month after Mary was imprisoned by the rebellious Scots, Philip II had dispatched the foremost soldier of Spain, the Duke of Alba, with ten thousand of his finest infantry and another twenty-five thousand German and other mercenaries, to suppress the Calvinist revolt in the Netherlands; Alba made no attempt to win Flemish hearts and minds but quickly established what the Netherlanders called the "Council of Blood," which arrested and executed the nobles suspected of causing the troubles. In December, Elizabeth finally informed the Spanish ambassador that she would be keeping the money seized from the ships carrying the pay for Philip's troops in the Netherlands; a week before, Philip, patience lost, had ordered Alba to seize English shipping.

Elizabeth Howard, the Duke of Norfolk's devout wife, did not survive to see all this tumult, dying in childbirth in September; her death plunged the duke into despair. But his duties left him little time for private mourning. What to do with the queen of Scots and how to deal with the new regime in Scotland were pressing questions. Mary's behavior had clearly been outrageous, and the new regency under James Stuart, the Earl of Moray (or Murray), Mary's illegitimate half-brother who ruled in the name of Mary's infant son James, was strongly pro-English. On the other hand, Elizabeth could not bring herself to openly embrace those who had deposed a lawful queen. In September, Norfolk led an English commission that was to meet with the two Scots parties at York to attempt to resolve the situation; Elizabeth would have liked to somehow restore Mary—and get her out of England—while keeping England's allies and the Protestant party in power. The commission was to examine, among other evidence, the so-called casket letters, love poems to Bothwell allegedly written in Mary's hand and implicating her in the Darnley murder. Acting in Mary's interest was her close adviser John Leslie, Bishop of Ross and the leader of the Scottish Counter-Reformation. The York meetings were brief and unproductive.

As a relief, in October the Duke of Norfolk went hawking with Sir William Maitland of Lethington, an astute ambassador to England and a savvy survivor of the lethal and conspiratorial politics of Scotland. Maitland had been first a compatriot of the Scottish regent, the Earl of Moray, but had become Mary's secretary and, despite keeping ties open to the new government, still looked to her interests. As Neville Williams, the duke's biographer, summarized the discussion over the sport: "Maitland shrewdly suggested that the only way of cutting the Gordian

Knot would be for Norfolk to marry Mary, who would be restored to her throne and in the fullness of time she and her issue would reign at Whitehall as well as at Holyrood House [the seat of government in Edinburgh]. Such a match would save Mary from dishonor and carry the Anglo-Scottish alliance a stage further."[15]

The Norfolk-Mary match had been bruited before, but now the hook was set in the duke's mouth with finality. Indeed, it had seemed to Moray that Norfolk had shown undue partiality to Mary's cause at the York conference, and this spin on events had also been circulated in London. When he returned south—a second conference had been set for Westminster in November—Elizabeth set a pretty trap in an interview with Norfolk. Would the duke not consider the marriage for the benefit of the realm and the safety of his queen? Norfolk swore that "no reason could move him to like of her that hath been a competitor to the Crown; and if Her Majesty would move him thereto he will rather be committed to the Tower, for he meant never to marry with such a person, where"—like Darnley—"he could not be sure of his pillow."[16] Whether the duke seemed to protest his resolve too much or not, the Westminster conference, at which the casket letters were publicly read and examined to the satisfaction of the privy council, ought to have made plain that Mary was a politically toxic substance. Yet Norfolk could not give up the idea. Maitland's logic—that marrying Mary would solve a world of problems at a stroke—also carried the lure of a crown for Norfolk. Yet achieving such a goal was a tricky task: it required Norfolk to abandon his friendship and collaboration with Cecil, seek to reconcile with Leicester, and enmesh himself with the Catholic zealots of the north. This was to forsake the most moderate and powerful of Elizabeth's advisers while bringing together the most forward Protestant courtier and the disgruntled and increasingly powerless border barons. It was a tricky tightrope for even the cleverest or most powerful politician and would prove too much for Norfolk.

Thus, in early 1569, a restless, rising anti-Cecil mood began to congeal among some at court. His policies might have put a desperately needed £85,000 in Elizabeth's purse, but they had resulted in a huge disruption in English trade and threatened war with Spain; Alba's army was employed in a brutal Dutch counterinsurgency for the moment but also represented a powerful striking force just across the Narrow Seas from Dover. The fluid anti-Cecil alliance included older but normally moderate diplomats such as the Earl of Sussex, also member of the extended Howard family but, like Norfolk, previously an antagonist to Leicester. Upon his return from the collapsed enterprise to secure a Hapsburg match, Sussex had been installed as president of the Council of the North. This element also numbered John Fitzallan, 19th Earl of Arundel, the nominal leader of what might be called the "loyal Catholic" party, and his son-in-law John Baron Lumley, but it also counted the more radical Catholics who wished, by first eliminating Cecil and then Elizabeth, to put Mary on the throne and restore Catholicism everywhere. Chief among these were Thomas Percy, 7th Earl of Northumberland, and Charles Neville, 6th Earl of Westmoreland, scions of ancient northern families who regarded Cecil not only as a heretic but also as a social and political parvenu, depriving them of their power and right to rule. But the earls were trimmers in comparison to the even more hotheaded lesser nobility of the north, including those in the Dacre family. In sum, other than opposition to Cecil, the alliance had almost nothing common with the Elizabeth's favorite, "Robin" Dudley.

Perhaps not surprisingly, Leicester's initial assault on Cecil was tentative at best. The traditional etiquette for attacking royal advisers without a direct confrontation was to advance charges of giving evil advice before the privy council when the monarch was not present; thus had Thomas Cromwell been removed to the Tower of London (and ultimately executed) under Henry VIII. But Cecil and Elizabeth discovered the plot and themselves called a preemptive privy council meeting. Later, when the queen was receiving Norfolk, Secretary Cecil, and others in her chamber, Leicester barged in, angering Elizabeth and provoking a tirade about the council meeting. Leicester was himself provoked to an attack on Cecil and his policies, which only brought on a stern rebuke from the queen. Norfolk got the message; he whispered to William Parr, the marquess of Northampton, "You see, my lord, how the Earl of Leicester is favored as long as he supports the Secretary, but now that for good reasons he takes an opposed position, she frowns upon him and wants to send *him* to the Tower."[17] Leicester also got the message that, while he might be Elizabeth's personal favorite, Cecil was the policy favorite. He began to lose enthusiasm for the Norfolk scheme, making it clear that if it came to it, he would tell the queen.

But Leicester's softening only drove the other conspirators and malcontents back on the Duke of Norfolk; they needed a champion. And if, for the duke, the marriage to Mary was the means for his own advancement, for Mary it was a path to freedom and a chance at power, and for the zealots the marriage was the means to eliminate Elizabeth, replace her with Mary, and restore Catholicism and the traditional political order. The duke's interest was ambition, but his bride-to-be and their backers were driven by political desperation and their faith and thus were more resolute. The nobles of the North began to plot more closely with the Spanish ambassador, de Spes, and through intermediaries like the banker Ridolfi and the Bishop of Ross; Norfolk was kept to the fringes. Thus the plot lacked any real leadership or consistent planning; it was many things to many people. Neither Northumberland nor Westmoreland, the northern earls, appears to have filled the void, and in the lower ranks there was even greater confusion. When the young Dacre, Norfolk's ward, died accidentally in March, the duke began trying to marry his sons to the surviving Dacre daughters and thus hang onto the Dacre estates. This further complicated matters for the supporters of the Norfolk-Mary match, and Leonard Dacre sued to return the property to the family. But the case fell to Cecil to decide. His ruling in favor of Norfolk, whatever its legality, certainly made the duke less a champion of the cause of northern rights and more beholden to Cecil. By the summer of 1569, Norfolk was pursuing his plan of marriage with little consideration or attention to what the northern leaders and the Spanish ambassador had in mind; Mary, through the Bishop of Ross, was in contact with them all but in a following rather than a leading position.

All through the summer, Norfolk hovered moodily around the court as Elizabeth made her annual progress. He was too timid to raise the subject of the Mary marriage directly with the queen, hoping Leicester or Cecil might do it for him and terrified that Elizabeth would find out on her own. When he got no help from Leicester or Cecil, he tried other members of the privy council, suggesting, as a general proposition, that if Mary were to marry some Englishman she might be set free. As July ended, the court arrived at Richmond Palace just up the Thames from London. Norfolk's secret had become widely known; he went fishing with Leicester, who revealed that some women at court had been gossiping about it. The queen gave him repeated opportunities to make a clean breast of matters. Shortly before leaving Richmond, Elizabeth summoned Norfolk, who had been briefly away in London. Did the duke have any news from town? None, he replied. "No! You come from London and can tell no news of a marriage?" On August 15, at Farnham, the queen invited Norfolk to dine with her alone. Despite heavy suggestions from the queen, the duke could not force himself to speak. "I was abashed at

Her Majesty's speech," he later said, "but I thought it not fit time nor place there to trouble her."[18]

Elizabeth began to smell danger; reports were filtering in of widespread discontent, provoked by a number of causes but often coming from northern England. The malcontents had been meeting regularly in Yorkshire and particularly in Durham to "allure the gentlemen" and prepare the revolt.[19] The government had mobilized northern militias through the summer, but the English system of militia service had yet to be reliably reformed and musters were haphazard affairs. Many troops were still equipped with longbows rather than pikes and harquebuses. From Scotland, Moray wrote to explain that the Scots had rejected the proposal for Mary's restoration and further declared it treason to uphold her authority; he would not support Norfolk's plans. The duke, again visiting London, approved a plan for Northumberland and Leonard Dacre to rescue Mary upon Norfolk's signal; Northumberland boldly asserted that the entire north was ready to rally to the cause. Elizabeth again called Norfolk to court, but he dawdled in coming.

At last the storm broke. Leicester had come down with "a tactical sickness" and implored Elizabeth to come and succor him on September 6, during which melodramatic meeting he spilled the beans on Norfolk. Predictably, the queen forgave her favorite but flew into a rage at Norfolk. The time for heavy hints and intimate dinners was past, and she ordered him to "deal no further with the Scottish cause." Norfolk tried to dismiss the matter, haughtily swearing that he had "a very slight regard" for Mary and that her position and fortunes were of no regard since his own "revenues in England were not much less than those of the Kingdom of Scotland . . . and when he was in his Tennis Court at Norwich he thought himself in a manner equal with some kings." Elizabeth did not enjoy the lecture and was sure she had a better grasp of the political realities than did the vain duke. The queen dismissed Norfolk with the observation that, in light of all the conspiring in the North and swirling around the queen of Scots, within four months of a Norfolk-Mary wedding she would be locked away in the Tower.[20] She could not allow such a powerful match without risking her throne and her life.

Norfolk hung around the court, both hoping for a royal change of heart and fearful lest a too-quick withdrawal appear as a signal for treason. Elizabeth suspected Norfolk's ambitions and prudence demanded that she plan accordingly. Mary was moved again for even safer keeping; the militia was fully mobilized—sixty thousand men turned out; and, in fear of Spanish or French intervention, ports were closed. The queen withdrew to Windsor and ordered Norfolk to attend her. She would keep her potential enemies close. Now it was Norfolk's turn to become tactically ill, with "an ague"; he could not arrive at Windsor until September 26. And when, on the afternoon of September 22, he had a letter from Leicester telling him he was headed for the Tower, Norfolk bolted, riding off the following night to his residence at Kenninghall Palace. From there he begged for mercy, writing the queen: "My enemies found such comfort at Your Highness's heavy displeasure that they began to make of me a common table talk" that made him "a suspected person" and that the Tower was "too great a terror for a true man."[21]

Norfolk's weakness and retreat was also a problem for the northern earls, particularly Westmoreland, to whom Norfolk wrote, begging that there be no uprising lest the duke pay for it with his life. But the plotting among the northern men had gone too far to be so easily turned off. Norfolk's message arrived while the earls, Dacre, and their companions were making final preparations; the lesser ringleaders—including the earls' two very Catholic wives—were so zealous that it was agreed that their rebellion would begin the following week, on October 7. But as word of Norfolk's plea for peace spread along with word of the uprising, confusion set in, and a number of the conspirators got cold feet. The Earl of Sussex, as president of the Council of the North and as a man of moderate and traditional politics, tried to mediate a solution, calling Northumberland and Westmoreland to a meeting at York; he hoped to "nourish that quiet until further in winter, that nights were longer and colder and the ways worse and the waters bigger to stop their passage, if any stir should be."[22] But Elizabeth, feeling she could not afford Sussex's patience or chance his potentially divided loyalties, took a tougher line and demanded they come to court; Norfolk had confessed that the earls had been in contact with the Spanish.

THE RISING OF THE EARLS

The summons to Norfolk provoked the earls to action. On November 8, they raised the standard of rebellion, proclaiming:

We, Thomas earl of Northumberland and Charles earl of Westmoreland, the Queen's true and faithful subjects: To all the same of the old catholic faith. Know ye that with many other well disposed as well of the nobility as others have promised our faith to the furtherance of this our good meaning, forasmuch as diverse, disordered and ill disposed persons about the Queen's majesty have by their crafty and subtle dealing to advance themselves overthrown in this realm the true and catholic religion toward God, and by the same abuseth the Queen, disorder the realm, and now lastly seeketh the destruction of these nobility, we therefore have gathered to resist by force and rather by the help of God and you good people to redress these things amiss with the restoring of all ancient customs and liberties to God's church and this noble realm. And lastly, if we should not do it ourselves we might be reformed by strangers to the great hazard of the state of this our country whereunto we are all bound. God save the Queen.[23]

They further refined and amplified this proclamation twice more, never mentioning the Queen of Scots or the Duke of Norfolk by name but insisting on the return of the old religion, the old political order, and the removal of "new" men like Cecil, all the while professing their loyalty to Elizabeth. As was the norm for resistance movements in Britain, it was the actions of "evil advisers," not the wrongdoing of the monarch per se, that legitimized active disobedience. And as badly as the rebellion was organized, planned, and logistically supported, and as short as its duration was to be, a remarkable seven thousand men rallied to its standard. In sum, the feudal obligation brought out the lesser ranks of England's north, though as K. J. Kesselring convincingly shows, the overwhelming majority of the earls' makeshift force came from the yeomanry. Clearly, the promise of a restored of Catholicism provided the raison d'etre of the rebel cause. Their principal banner recalled the Crusades by depicting the five wounds of Christ, and their principal targets were Protestant married ministers and churches. One Christopher Jackson made it his priority to terrorize the wife of Parson Edward Otbye; Jackson swore "a vengeance upon all fuckbeggar priests and the errant whores their wives."[24]

From Ripon in Yorkshire, where they celebrated Mass and burned Protestant books, the rebels moved generally south in the direction of Tutbury, where Mary was then held.[25] On November 25, Mary was moved again to Coventry, and the revolt began to run out of energy, its failures of planning and inability to sustain an army in the field beginning to tell. Still, the regime's inability either to clearly command the loyalty of the local militia or rapidly mobilize a force from the south in response allowed the rebels several tactical successes. On November 29, Westmoreland's nephew Christopher Neville led a force of three hundred toward Hartlepool, the port of Newcastle, not only an important prize in itself but potentially a source of reinforcements from abroad. As always, England's continental rivals were alert to opportunity and English rebels keen to enlist outside help. The Earl of Northumberland had received a message, purportedly written by Spanish ambassador de Spes, to make it a safe harbor for aid from the Duke of Alba's army in the Netherlands. Though Sussex had ordered the town fortified, local leaders had not done so, and Neville registered a near-immediate triumph, garrisoning the port with two hundred men.

The loss of Hartlepool alarmed the queen and Cecil—they were equally alert to the prospects of Spanish intervention—and spurred them to more urgent action. Her confidence in Sussex, who continued to counsel caution and that Hartlepool could easily be retaken in time, was wavering, and in addition to Hundson she dispatched trusted and long-serving privy council member Sir Ralph Sadler along with royal ships and five hundred musketeers. Meanwhile, Christopher Neville's raiders had rejoined the main rebel force gathering in early December before Barnard Castle, above Darlington on the River Tees and twenty-five miles southwest of Durham. The rebel earls were reluctant to move directly on York, and the Durham contingent was nervous about the threat from this direction; many of them had homes in the area and feared their property was vulnerable. Protecting the castle was a force of more than seven hundred loyalists under Sir George Bowes, a reliable soldier who had been tasked with escorting Mary, Queen of Scots, from Carlisle to Bolton the previous year. The siege of Barnard Castle was the largest engagement of the revolt and the rebels' high-water mark.

While Sussex had expressed confidence that the stronghold could withstand a siege, Bowes's men lacked heavy ordnance and were of doubtful loyalty and commitment. Though it had other dimensions, the rebellion was very much a Yorkshire civil war. Both sides recruited troops from the same places and peoples. And if Catholicism provided the insurgent rank and file with a powerful motivation, the same cannot

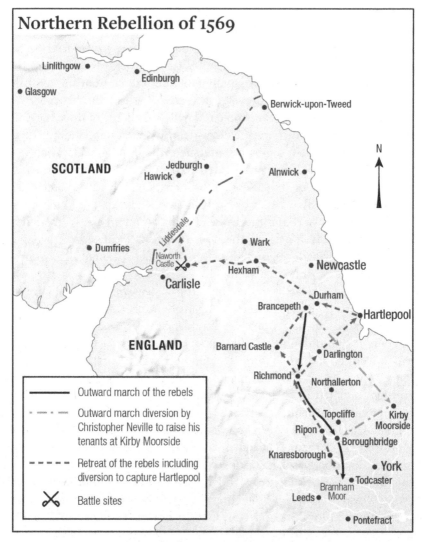

Figure 3.1. The Northern Rebellion of 1569.

be said for loyalists; although, in time, the Protestantization of the north would develop into a Puritan zeal, the process had not far advanced. William Cecil's son Thomas put the matter squarely for his father: "If these Yorkshire men be not backed with a stronger army of assured men from the south which may always command them, they will fight with but loose hearts."[26] Those southern reinforcements, though assembling, could not arrive in time to influence events at Barnard Castle. Men like Bowes and Sussex had reason to be cautious in confronting the rebellion, and it was not clear that Elizabeth was the stronger horse. They would have preferred more rapid, if necessarily smaller, reinforcements and believed that a well-armed and well-trained detachment would suffice, but given the larger political risks they faced, Elizabeth and Cecil preferred overwhelming advantages to put the end result beyond doubt.

Rebel cavalry arrived at Barnard Castle on December 2, the infantry shortly thereafter. The earls' army was at peak strength, probably more than five thousand, including as many as two thousand horsemen. Westmoreland took charge of the siege; Northumberland took five hundred cavalry to Durham, from whence Bishop Pilkington and Dean Whittingham had prudently fled. Though the rebels, too, lacked heavy artillery, they did manage by December 8 to open two breaches in the castle's outer wall. This led to defections from defenders to rebels; Bowes reported that 226 men—a third of his total strength—jumped the walls, despite the risk of serious injury in leaping thirty feet down. The defectors betrayed the castle's water supply and then opened the gates. At this point, the besiegers offered Bowes a chance to retreat with honor and in safety, taking himself, 330 horses and 100 infantry south to join Sussex at York.

Yet the victory at Barnard Castle did not supply the rebellion with any larger momentum. Though men continued to flock to their standard, the Northumberlands' pleas to Leonard Dacre fell flat. Seemingly at sixes and sevens about their next move, the rebels withdrew from Durham and made for Newcastle on December 13, the same day that the queen's reinforcements from the south, twelve thousand strong and with sufficient cavalry to assuage even the cautious Sussex, assembled at Wetherby, halfway between Leeds and York, and began to march northward. The following day, Elizabeth's ships arrived at Hartlepool, foreclosing the option of outside intervention, and the rebellion collapsed. On December 16, Northumberland and the rebel horsemen abandoned their infantry to their fate, fled to the Percy family stronghold at Alnwick, and two days later crossed into Scotland. Because Leonard Dacre had been slow to join the revolt, Elizabeth did not order him to be taken until mid-February. After the short fight at Naworth, Dacre too fled to Scotland.

Elizabeth viewed this as an insufficient result.[27] To begin with, the rebels had a safe haven from the borderers in southern Scotland, though Northumberland had been sold by his "host" and supposed protector,

Hector Armstrong of Harlaw, to the regent Moray. But in late January, Moray had been assassinated, so the prospects of bringing Northumberland to justice in England were not immediate. The earl was often seen strolling the streets of Edinburgh. Moreover, Westmoreland and his companions were soon talking of resuming the revolt in the spring. Back in his bastion at Berwick Castle, Hunsdon informed London that "the most part of the nobility of Scotland and especially on this [southern] side of Edinburgh think it a great reproach and ignominy to the whole country to deliver any banished man to the slaughter, accounting it a liberty and freedom evident to all nations to succor banished men."[28] Some border lords offered not just succor but military support in defense of Mary, whom they recognized as their rightful queen. From late January through February, Westmoreland and his new Scottish band led raids across the border in the traditional local manner, burning crops and taking prisoners. Despite Dacre's defeat, he took a substantial force across the border and Baron Henry Scrope, warden of the English West Marches and captain of the garrison at Berwick, reported that two thousand rebels roamed southern Scotland, openly maintained by Scottish nobles determined to restore Mary. Pushing the rebels out of northern England had only seemed to make them stronger, and with the murder of Moray, the English party in Scotland was at a low ebb of organization and support.

Elizabeth habitually preferred diplomacy to military action, but by March it was plain that the Scots would require more than gentle persuasion to give up the rebels. Further, the plight of "the King's Party" (the king in question being the infant James VI) was serious. Elizabeth had installed the pro-English regime and expelled the French a decade earlier, and if the Marians returned to power, there was every likelihood that they would restore the "auld alliance" between Scotland and France, as well as provide a platform for Spanish intrigues and potential invasion. Preventing that outcome was a prime directive of Elizabethan strategy, one that claimed for England what was essentially imperial power over Scotland; as Cecil had written, "It belongeth of very right to the Crown of England to give order to dissensions moved for the Crown of Scotland."[29] Perhaps a legally dubious claim, it was nevertheless a strategic necessity.

And despite this claim, the fledgling Elizabethan state lacked the ability to sustain a large army in Scotland; the only means of enforcing the queen's policy were large-scale and quite devastating punitive raids that might also give heart to the pro-English party. In April, Sussex and

Hunsdon from Berwick and Sir John Forster from the English Middle March launched a two-pronged assault toward Hawick, with each assault leaving a four-mile-wide swath of devastation in its wake. The target was Hume Castle, home of Lord Hume, a supporter of Leonard Dacre. Upon his return to Berwick, Hundson reported that "her Majesty had as honorable avenging of the receivers of her rebels and of all such as have been spoilers of her people and burners of her county as ever any of her predecessors had."[30] Given the standards of border warfare, this was a boast of brutality. But these initial raids did not yield the rebels, nor did subsequent raids in May or June. Finally, after a large raid by Sussex in August, the Scots nobles gave in, the King's Party gained the upper hand and the Earl of Lennox, Elizabeth's choice, was made regent. The Earl of Westmoreland fled to Flanders; Northumberland was finally, in 1572, sold to the English for £2000, returned to York, and beheaded.

But if the flame of the Northern Rebellion had flickered almost immediately and its Scottish aftermath had reaffirmed the idea of Protestant "amity" between the English and lowland Scots, it had also sparked a larger conflagration that would endure throughout Elizabeth's reign. As Kesselring aptly has observed, "A localized revolt that had not been able to generate nationwide assistance now threatened to become international in scope."[31] Perhaps more importantly, these strategic contests were defined in increasingly confessional and ideological terms.

A "GOOD OLD CAUSE" AND A NEW REGIME

A century later, after the civil wars that overthrew the Stuart monarchy, the poet John Milton and other propagandists for the British Commonwealth romanticized the "Good Old Cause." To be sure, this was an imprecise term, but its heart beat with a Protestant, imperial, and secretly republican pulse that would not only throb for centuries to come but can be detected in the development of the Elizabethan regime—and it is no accident that Queen "Gloriana" became mythically enmeshed in this ideological construct. As we have seen, the "monarchical republican" bent of men like William Cecil was, by 1560, already deeply planted and widely shared, and the fears of chaos and Catholic *revanche* repeatedly had propelled the matter of Elizabeth's successor to the forefront of conciliar, parliamentary, and public debate through the decade. Catalyzed by the events described above, this firmly framed the strategic discussion for the 1570s and 1580s. Thus, even as the Northern Rebellion reaffirmed what was traditional in English imperial thinking, it brought out two new strains particularly visible in the aftermath: Spain had begun to replace France as the greatest danger among the continental great powers, and the struggle for power and the character of war were, much against Elizabeth's wishes but with her consent, cast increasingly in ideological and confessional terms; the battle was being forced upon the reluctant queen. Further, these two strains were inseparable, for, as time would prove repeatedly, Philip II was more than an aspiring, dynastic Habsburg hegemon. He sought power ultimately to restore Catholicism across Europe and the fulfillment of divine will. Reasons of state vied in the contest with the glory of God, and though Elizabeth would continue to struggle to bridle the passion of her people and her more Puritan councilors, her horses had already begun to slip her lead; she had no choice but to ride whither they would go. It was imperative to bring the North under firm yoke.

Even in the public debate over the Norfolk-Mary match, there had been an effort to link Catholicism with treason. Just who wrote *A Discourse Touching the Pretended Matche betweene the D[uke] of Norfolk and the Queene of Scots* is not certain—it might have been Walsingham or Thomas Norton, just coming to prominence as an Elizabethan propagandist. The effort also certainly had the backing of Cecil, and the argument, reflecting a consensus view, is more important than the authorship. The pamphlet, published in mid-1569, attacked Norfolk, who unto his execution maintained his Protestantism, as a crypto-Catholic by association and Mary as "ambitious, a born Scot, a defamed person, who hath made a shipwreck of all honour and reputation, and lastly a branch of the house of Guise," the leading family of the Catholic faction in France and "a race that is both enemy to God and the common quiet of Europe." Under Mary's spell, Norfolk would betray both his faith and his country: "Did not Solomon, by matching with an idolatress Egyptian, become an idolater . . . to the plague of his kin and posterity?"[32]

In the wake of the rising of the earls, something needed to be done in northern England that would not just suppress "idolatry" but accelerate the project of Tudor centralization and the primacy of the Protestant religion. In June of 1568, the president of the Council of the North and archbishop of York, Thomas Young, had died. Young was also head of the Ecclesiastical Commission for the Province of York, the other principal instrument of government. These two bodies were traditionally "adapted to local conditions and staffed by northerners, or by men with long experience of the north, sensitive to the realities of the north."[33] Young had fit that profile, and his demise provided a timely opportunity for reforming both the church and government. This gave Elizabeth the opportunity to replace him as president with Sussex and then with Henry Hastings, the Earl of Huntingdon and a zealous Protestant more than happy to do the things at which Sussex quailed. An anonymous Catholic writer summed up Huntingdon thus: "In these parts this monster is god, king, bishop, president, catchpoll and whatsoever else to annoy the Catholics."[34]

Though the archbishopric went vacant for two years, Young's replacement was Edmund Grindal, an enthusiastic reformer with more than a little tolerance for Puritanism, even if he himself remained solidly within the Anglican communion. He would later serve a very brief tenure as archbishop of Canterbury, earning the queen's wrath and dismissal for his stout refusal to halt the practice of "prophesyings"—which were more like philosophical dialogues among the devout than charismatic Presbyterian "field conventicles"—among his clergy. "The significance of these two appointments," in Patrick Collinson's judgment, "was that a measure of 'thorough' was now to be introduced into the north. . . . The slow transformation of northern England was now accelerated" and "effective protestantization of the region began in earnest."[35] Durham's Bishop Pilkington now had an ally and bureaucratic protection, and Grindal recruited a cadre of similarly educated and motivated reformers. In classic counterinsurgency fashion, Grindal's campaign began in more densely populated cities and towns, anticipating that the old ways of the countryside would wither with time.

However, the most lasting efforts at reform came on the propaganda front, in the promotion of Protestant—almost Puritan—literature. The most influential was the printing of the Geneva Bible in both England and Scotland. The book, a translation from the original Hebrew and Greek into English led by Durham Dean William Whittingham, took its name from its original printing in the Geneva Republic of John Calvin. By the mid-seventeenth century, there were nearly two hundred editions of the Geneva Bible in circulation, "reach[ing] a larger audience than any other religious work published in the Elizabethan era."[36] Beyond making the scriptures widely available at home—including the homes of William Shakespeare, John Donne, and John Milton—its voluminous notes and commentary—also likely composed by Whittingham and another Marian exile, Anthony Gilby—were rife with Calvinist ideas and political commentary. The notes were also appended to the later King James Bible; even high Anglicanism carried the seed of Puritanism. In sum, these notes proved durably and widely influential, preserving views that were captured in neither court nor formal church records—quasi-republican ideas that would find echoes in the resistance to Elizabeth's Stuart successors. Not surprisingly, there were several Geneva Bibles aboard the *Mayflower* in 1620.

A second powerful instrument of influence was the 1570 printing of John Foxe's Protestant martyrology *Acts and Monuments* in an enlarged and richly illustrated edition with many anti-Catholic pictures. This was by law ordered to be placed in every English church alongside the Bible itself. The purpose, pointed out in a November 1570 letter to the archbishops of Canterbury and York and bishop of London, was plainly political: "The matter whereof being very profitable to bring hir majesties subjects to good opinion, understanding, and there liking of the present government of thes realme by trewe rehearsal and conference of tymes past. . . ."[37] This was a clear expression of the essential imperial ideas that the legitimacy and unity of a diverse polity were grounded in ideology, which in turn originated in faith, and that modernizing reforms were anchored in a proper understanding of past history. That both Cecil and Dudley signed the letter demonstrates that this idea overrode any "factional" differences and *politique* hesitations. Outside of London, York and Durham are likely to have been among the first to display this deluxe edition of Foxe's work.[38]

But the rebellion and the continued instability in Scotland provoked not just "thorough" and long-term reactions but more immediate and more violent measures; Elizabeth and Cecil were determined to make an example and to deter future revolt. Hundreds were executed in the north of England, and Elizabeth confiscated rebel lands and treasure, redistributing the goods among more faithful retainers. A flood of government-sponsored pamphlets was published, including several by Norton. His *Warning Against the Dangerous Practices of the Papists and Specially the Partners of the Late Rebellion* proposed that "every papist, that is to say everyone that believeth all the pope's doctrine to be true, is an enemy and a traitor." The wave of executions was entirely justified, since "no clemency, gentleness . . . or loving dealing can win a papist while he continueth a papist, to love her Majesty." Even, as the government had insisted originally, the earls had manipulated confessional issues for their own personal and political ends. They understood "papistry to be the very likely and apt color and mean to allure men to rebellion and treason against the queen."[39] Catholicism and disloyalty, if not one, were as near as made no difference. The right response was, therefore, armed force, powerfully and even brutally employed, and Protestant purity. As the popular ballad A Cold Pye for Papistes put it:

> Unto our Queen, Lord grant thy grace
> That she the sword from sheath may draw
> To vanquish such as hate thy law
> Then shall we from danger be free. . . .
> God grant our Queen may look about
> From hence to weed such Papists stout
> Then shall we be from danger free.[40]

Even for a divine-right monarch eventually much revered by her people, this sort of popular propaganda had consequences. It was, to be sure, a measure of the regime's weakness. And it began to foreclose options; there might be truces or alliances of convenience with Catholics, but no lasting peace with Papists. The immediate course of events strongly reinforced this message: in short order, Pope Pius V issued the bull Regnans in Excelsis, excommunicating Elizabeth and taken by many as authorizing her assassination; the banker Roberto Ridolfi began to plot with the Duke of Norfolk and the Bishop of Ross to do just that and put Mary on the throne; the Guise faction engineered the St. Bartholomew's Day Massacre of thousands of Huguenots in France. The struggle for power across Britain and Europe also was becoming a struggle, increasingly in English minds, between light and darkness. Henceforward, a strongly anti-Catholic Protestantism remained a critical tool for establishing and sustaining Elizabeth's legitimacy and the extending the government's control in England and, in time, its influence abroad. The privy council took on a more aggressively Protestant aspect: Cecil was raised to become Lord Burghley, Walsingham replaced him as secretary, and Leicester matured from youthful royal favorite to popular champion of the Protestant cause. French Huguenots and Dutch rebels increasingly turned to Elizabeth and England to protect the Protestant "liberties" of Europe against not only the Guise faction in France but the rapidly rising power and ambition of Philip of Spain. England was no longer simply a nation ruled by a Tudor dynasty; it was emerging as the leader of an international cause, a kind of Protestant crusade.

Scholars of sixteenth- and seventeenth-century English history and strategy frequently wonder at the continuing power of this anti-Catholic rhetoric, even as the number of English Catholics became almost vanishingly small. For many, these sentiments amount to a kind of political hysteria that distorted reasonable judgements. Moreover, the rhetorical power of "geopolitical Protestantism" persisted into the eighteenth century and was, if anything, far stronger on the Irish and American frontiers than in the London metropolis. It became an unshakeable "British" belief that their uniquely free domestic and international circumstances were constantly under threat from many quarters. The defense of British liberties demanded both martial vigilance and civic, ideological, and, often, confessional commitment.

This frame of mind drove Elizabethan strategy not only within England and Scotland but also, as we shall see, in Ireland, in northwest Europe, and in North America; the idea of a British regime as the guarantor of Protestant liberties displaced the last vestiges of Tudor dynastic rule—an irreversible change for which Elizabeth's Stuart successors were twice to pay the price. The political nation came to grips with the undeniable fact that the realm was more important than the ruler, indeed that the end of the Tudor line was all but inevitable—although Elizabeth teased out marriage schemes for quite some time to come—and the fate of the regime was inextricable from its success in erecting an imperial structure around it.

4

THE PORTUGAL EXPEDITION

If in the 1570s Elizabethans had begun to fear Spain more than France, they were in no hurry to confront Philip militarily. Indeed, the shift in great-power perceptions opened up new avenues for Elizabethan diplomacy and the revival of the matchmaking melodramas that the queen so seemed to enjoy and at which she excelled. Now, rather than entertaining a Habsburg match, Elizabeth considered marriage to the two French Valois brothers, Henry and Francis; if the traditional English strategic formula from the late eleventh century was to ally with Hapsburg Burgundians to balance against Valois France, now the equation was inverted to counter Philip's ambition. The second of Elizabeth's potential French matches was a more serious and extended "courtship." Henry Valois became King Henri III in 1574 and this disqualified him; neither Elizabeth nor her councilors would countenance another king as theirs, and the agonies of Mary Tudor and Philip of Spain were indelibly etched in their memories. Francis, first Duke of Alençon and then of Anjou, had been a handsome child, but smallpox had left him with a pitted face and twisted spine. That, perhaps, Elizabeth might have endured (and, in her mid-forties when the wooing began, her appeal as a mate was more political than personal) had Anjou been a more attractive strategic partner. As it was, he was an erratic politician, even by the standards of the age and, particularly worrisome from an English perspective, most of his adventuring came in Flanders and the Netherlands. And though England had negotiated two treaties with France, these were necessarily limited. Spain may have been the rising threat, but Elizabethan strategy continued to dictate that the Low Countries be kept free of all great-power domination.

But it was the long-running Dutch revolt—which would continue until 1648—that propelled Spain and Britain to the point of confrontation. The Duke of Alba's harsh campaign had, from 1567 to 1572, militarily suppressed the Netherlands; the rebellious Calvinist nobles and other malcontents under William of Orange had been reduced to operating as "sea beggars," stateless privateers plundering Spanish shipping from the Huguenot port of La Rochelle in France and the ports of southern England. When Elizabeth expelled them from their English sanctuaries in March 1572, it seemed the revolt might finally collapse. But the beggars then captured the ports of Brill and Flushing in Flanders, sparking a wider and general revolt, particularly in Holland. The Spanish response was a series of massacres; at Zutphen, the Duke of Alba reported to Philip, his soldiers "cut the throats of everyone they found and burghers, because [his son, the local Spanish commander] Don Fadrique had orders from me not to leave a soul alive and also to burn down part of the town."[1] Coming in conjunction with the St. Bartholomew's Day Massacre in France, not only aggressive Protestants such as Walsingham and Leicester but equally the judicious Burghley feared a Catholic coalition.[2] Through the 1570s, these strategic nightmares seemed increasingly real.

There was general agreement at court about the threat posed by Spain's rise and its menacing presence in northwestern Europe. If the Dutch were defeated, it would expose England to invasion. During the decade of the 1570s, the Spanish were unable, even following a series of policy reforms that renounced the excesses of Alba's regime, to eliminate Dutch resistance. This fact, in turn, sparked an English debate about the proper strategic response. This was a debate that would continue through subsequent centuries in England and continues even today in the United States: the debate between those, on one hand, who favor a "maritime" strategy, built upon diplomacy, defense of the "homeland," and, most of all, naval power, and those, on the other hand, supporting an engaged "continentalist" approach, in the belief that entangling alliances and direct involvement on the ground in Europe—even though on a small scale—were necessary to secure a favorable great-power balance. The debate over strategy also had, in the longer term, a lasting effect on English domestic politics, transforming a court divided by personality into one also differentiated by strategic orientation. Cliques became factions and, with time and under later kings, become something like early modern political parties.

The "continentalist" group, also described as "expansionist,"[3] was led by the Earl of Leicester, who through the 1570s made the leap from courtier and favorite to councilor and politician in his own right. Just behind the charismatic earl stood Sir Francis Walsingham, who had assumed Lord Burghley's job as secretary to the privy council (Burghley was now lord treasurer, and matters of finance were never far from the queen's mind). Walsingham provided an indefatigable Puritan energy, connections to the Puritan community, a first-rate organizational mind, and an effective intelligence network. But this faction also increasingly rode a tide of political opinion—within the privy council, at court, in Parliament, and in the larger political nation—that demanded aggressive action in the Dutch and French wars and the creation of a set of "pan-Protestant" strategic partnerships reaching even into northern Germany. They also believed that the Catholic powers, Philip and the Guise faction in France, were likewise ideologically driven and would never compromise their goal of re-Catholicizing Europe (and preventing Protestant penetration of the New World). They saw no real modus vivendi or durable power-sharing arrangement with such an enemy. There was, too, an eschatological overtone in their views of the competition with Spain. These were the fathers of what might be called British "geopolitical Protestantism," a complicated yet powerful mix of confessional and strategic elements and, especially, an enduring mode of rhetoric echoed in the apocalyptic tradition in American strategic thought.

Set against the Leicester-Walsingham faction was a more moderate group led by Burghley and a substantial minority of privy councilors. They offset the broad base of support for a more forward strategy by aligning themselves to Elizabeth's caution, conservatism, frugality, and flair for diplomatic drama; swimming against the tide of parliamentary, public, and popular opinion, they tried to swim with the royal tide. Burghley had by now worked so long and so closely with the queen that the lord treasurer instinctively knew her mind, how to frame decisions for her, what would appeal to her, and what would annoy her. He was also, as he aged and assumed the role of the queen's principal advisor, tempering his originally energetic Protestantism, though retaining his antipathy toward and fear of Catholicism. At the same time and in fundamental ways, the differences between the factions were not so great. Everyone agreed, for example, that the privateering quasi-war, especially in the Caribbean, was useful as statecraft and offered a good return for modest investment. That, above all, was what distinguished the mature Burgh-ley: limiting England's military and financial exposure and preserving strategic freedom of action. The queen, too, saw her realm as relatively weak, first concerned to avoid defeat rather than risking all for a decisive victory. She had little interest in leading a Protestant *internationale* that might pit the motley collection of Reformed European statelets, with the English lion leading a herd of much smaller cats, against the two Catholic great powers. Burghley saw Flanders and the Low Countries as England's "counterscarp," but he wished to defend it, if possible, with a combination local troops and British sea power. That is, he was willing to counterbalance a rising Spain but was skeptical of the prospects for inflicting a rapid, lasting, or decisive defeat upon Philip and worried about Elizabeth's ability to stomach or sustain a long war. Nevertheless, Burghley's strategic outlook had not fundamentally changed; he under-stood this war in both a global and ideological framework, as he later would reflect, at age 73, to parliament:

> Not as in former times when the [Hapsburg] Emperor Charles and the French [Valois] kings, the great Francis and the warlike Henry [VIII of England], made former wars for towns their greatest wars. . . . For in these wars none of them intended anything more than to be revenged of supposed injuries by burning or winning of some frontier town by besieging. And after revenges mutually had to the satisfaction of their appe-tites, wherein neither party had any special advantage, they fell to truce and in end with knots sometimes of intermar-raiges. . . . But now the case is altered. The King of Spain maketh these mighty wars by the means only of his Indies, not purposely to burn a town in France or England but to conquer all France, all England, and Ireland.[4]

The reference to Philip's "Indies"—meaning first and foremost Spain's colonies in America—marks another point of congruence across Elizabe-than factions: they saw that New-World wealth had tipped the scales of Old-World power. Britain and France had not exploited the discoveries of their early explorers as had Spain, and this made the threat from Madrid greater than that from Paris but also left Britain relatively weaker. The challenge from Spain was existential for the Elizabethan regime in England and Britain, immediate in northwest Europe, but in the long run could only be countered, contained, or defeated by striking at Spain's global possessions and its colonial financial complex.

THE ROAD TO THE *GRAN ARMADA*

A succession of three major developments from the mid-1570s to the mid-1580s incrementally but inexorably tipped the balance of Elizabethan thinking toward the war party. The first of these, ironically, was the implosion of the Spanish position in the Netherlands in 1576 that was the product of the death of Luis de Requesens, the Duke of Alba's replacement as governor and the author of a more moderate policy there. At the same time, Philip's fiscal-military house of cards went through one of its periodic collapses; in essence, the mountains of treasure imported from Peru were used to borrow, at usurious short-term rates, the funds that kept the Spanish military paid. When the money ran out, the angry Spanish forces in the Netherlands mutinied and sacked the trading town of Antwerp. This, in turn, united the Netherlands factions, from Flanders to Holland, behind William I, "the Silent," Prince of Orange, who proposed an agreement with the Spanish to remove their troops, suspend edicts against Protestantism, and leave it to the Netherlanders to reach a religious settlement among themselves. Such an agreement matched Elizabeth's desires in every particular, and when the Netherlands States General asked her to intercede with Philip, she readily agreed and went so far as to offer the Spanish her aid against French intrusion. The Spanish seemed to acquiesce initially, but when the following year Requesens's successor, Don John of Austria, seized the fortress of Namur and embarked upon a reconquest, the unity of the Netherlanders could not withstand the renewed pressure. With Don John's death arrived, in 1578, Alexander Farnese, the Duke of Parma, who matched Alba's determination with Requesens's political sophistication in a combination that would come close to destroying the Dutch revolt, splitting the United Netherlands into the Catholic and southern Union of Arras and the Union of Utrecht in the north, dominated by the Protestant provinces of Holland and Zealand. Thus did Parma destroy Elizabeth's hopes for a return to the moderate status quo—meaning tolerance for Protestantism, a Netherlands dominated neither by France nor Spain, and an English economy of force. It was increasingly clear that the Low Countries could not be saved without Elizabeth's intervention; Parma moved northward into Flanders and Brabant, methodically driving the Dutch.[5] A core British security interest was gravely at risk.

A second catastrophe for Elizabeth's strategy of balancing was Philip's conquest of Portugal. With the death of the young King Sebastian fighting the Moors at Alcazar in 1578, Portugal was thrown into a succession crisis and Philip had both the strongest hereditary claim and the military power to enforce it. By September 1580 the rehabilitated Duke of Alba had seized control of Portugal. Beyond the complete integration of the Iberian Peninsula and the lucrative overseas trade in the East Indies and East Africa, this also united the Americas under Spain. It further gave Philip a large navy of large craft capable of sailing in the open waters of the Atlantic and the mariners and the shipyards to sustain them. The additional ten galleons, "added to those of the Spanish Indian Guard [that protected the treasure fleets from the Caribbean], could give Philip an ocean-going war fleet almost equal in numbers to the royal navy of England."[6] It also gave Philip ports open to the Atlantic. In sum, the assimilation of Portugal into Philip's empire fundamentally altered the strategic situation in a variety of ways, helping to further secure the Mediterranean—which had been relatively quiet since the victory over the Ottoman fleet at Lepanto in 1571—adding the profits of the spice trade and the slave trade to the treasure of America, supplying the naval means to better sustain the transatlantic sailing routes and the routes of supply for Parma's armies. While Philip had yet to conclude that the road to victory in the Netherlands went through England, he and his advisors began to turn over the idea of the "Enterprise of England."[7]

The year 1584 marked a third step toward open war with Spain. Parma's advance through Flanders and Brabant was nearly complete, with only pockets around Antwerp, Brussels, and a few other towns keeping the Spanish from knocking on the doors of Holland and Zealand as they had in the mid-1570s; the Protestant-led Union of Utrecht was a military shambles. It came to the verge of political collapse with the assassination of William the Silent in July 1584. Absent outside intervention, the Dutch revolt was destined for the ash heap of history. Elizabeth's attempts to conclude a containment alliance with France ended—as did the queen's final marriage prospects—with the death of the Duke of Anjou. Further, the Guise-led Catholic League in France concluded, in December, a secret treaty taking Philip as their protector. This was revealed the following March, when the Catholic League issued a public declaration demanding that French King Henri III reform his government for the purpose of extirpating Protestant heresy. In May, Philip decreed the seizure of English ships in Spanish ports and in June, Henri caved to the League's demands. The English nightmare of a Catholic coalition had been realized. Elizabeth had to decide whether to defend the continental counterscarp—and defend it with the Dutch alone—or to retreat behind the wooden walls of her navy and rely on her militia at home. For Leicester, Walsingham, and their followers, the choice was clear: Philip was committed to an ideological and confessional conflict that allowed no sharing of power with Protestant heretics. "They saw in his persecution of Netherlands Calvinists, in the intrigues of his ambassadors, in his connivance at Papal attempts in Ireland, clear proof of his 'insatiable malice' against all things Protestant."[8] Once the Dutch were done, the northern European counterscarp would become a jumping-off point for Parma's troops in an invasion of England itself. England had to be defended in the Netherlands. The conservative faction was not convinced. "If the Queen would meddle no more in the matters of the Netherlands, but most strongly fortify her kingdom . . . gather money, furnish her navy with all provisions, strengthen the Borders towards Scotland with garrisons, and maintain the ancient military discipline of England,"[9] hoped Burghley, all might still be well. Further, the factious and unreliable Dutch were rebels against their lawful sovereign.

But this cascade of catastrophes made it clear that this sort of "offshore balancing" approach favored by Elizabeth and articulated by Burghley could not produce the strategic outcomes that the English political nation held dear. All that really remained to decide was the nature and the extent of the military response. There had been thoughts of sending Drake out on another government-sponsored, substantial raid, or "descent," to "annoy the King of Spain," but the prospect of an official commitment in the Netherlands made naval operations in home waters a priority, lest the Spanish strike back while the queen's ships were away. The negotiations with the Dutch began at the end of June, when their envoys had an initial royal audience. The first item on the agenda was a repeat of the offer of sovereignty of the Low Countries; Elizabeth again rejected it immediately. The Dutch tried a second time—and, with William of Orange dead, they lacked a figurehead for military and political unity—but Burghley made it plain that the best they could expect was an offer of protection. Then, per Elizabeth's habit, came "sharp bargaining" over the number of English troops, financial support, and the garrisoning of the "cautionary towns" of Brill and Flushing as collateral for the loans.

On August 12, an initial agreement was reached, subject to ratification by the queen and the Dutch Estates General, for England to provide four thousand foot, four hundred horse, and seven hundred further troops in garrison. But when word reached the negotiators that the Duke of Parma had taken Antwerp, even Elizabeth was inspired with a greater sense of urgency and upped her offer to five thousand infantry and one thousand cavalry, as well as the garrison forces, and agreed that the Earl of Leicester—the erstwhile royal favorite whose absence Elizabeth had heretofore been unable to bear—would be offered as overall commander.

That this commitment crossed a new threshold in Elizabethan strategy-making is attested by the fact that the queen, "notwithstanding our prerogative" in the direction of strategy, felt compelled to issue a formal *Declaration of the Causes Moving the Queene of England to Give Aide to the Defence of the People Afflicted and Oppressed in the Lowe Countries.* The pamphlet made a stark contrast to those circulated in the aftermath of the Northern Rebellion and had a wider audience. It was addressed "not only to our own natural loving subjects, but also to all others our neighbors, specially to such Princes and States as are our Confederates, or have for their subjects cause of commerce with our countries and people." It can even be understood as a strategic communication with Philip, for Elizabeth was at pains to blame his counselors rather than the Spanish king. But though Elizabeth owed "homage and service only unto the Almighty God" and was "not bound to yield account or render the reasons of [her] actions to any others," she nonetheless chose to make known her intentions and "upon what just and reasonable grounds" she was going to war; she would also need financial support from parliament and was, at any rate, too good a politician not to make her case in public. The pamphlet captured well Elizabeth's notion of a limited war, downplaying the confessional and ideological dimension, mentioning only once the "mutual amity observed" between Englishmen and Netherlanders in "Eccelesiastical as [well] as Secular" matters; issues of trade and the balance of power comprised the main argument. It was the Spanish who had disturbed the long-standing peace of northwest Europe by "being exalted to absolute government, by ambition, and for private lucre"; they "have violently broken the ancient laws and liberties of all the countries." Elizabeth also noted the many "late examples of the violent hostile enterprise" of Spain, including collusion with the pope in Ireland, with the "intent to pursue a conquest," in which Elizabeth could "manifestly see in what danger our self, our country and people might shortly be" if such an invasion were to happen. She rehearsed similar past arguments about Scotland, taking care to mention the mischief made by the French house of Guise "and their Niece the Queen of Scots." All she sought in supporting the Dutch was a return to the traditional status quo, "a restitution of ancient liberties and government by some Christian peace, and thereby a surety for ourselves and our realm to be free from invading neighbors, and [for] our people to enjoy in those countries their lawful commerce and intercourse of friendship and merchandise."[10] Thus the declaration is notable for what it did not say, or more precisely, what it left to others to say in other pamphlets, in pulpits, or in public. The ideological and confessional character of the conflict did not, in Elizabeth's mind, need to be emphasized; she had agreed for the moment to ride the tiger of the Protestant interest, but wished to keep it on a tight leash and to dismount at the earliest practicable opportunity. She also feared the Spanish and Catholic tiger of the Counter-Reformation and thus appealed to Philip in dynastic terms. Even while crossing the threshold of a "continental commitment" to a Calvinist crypto-republic, the queen framed the campaign—and a revolution in strategy—in conservative terms.

Yet this caution likewise had consequences; Elizabeth's limited commitment was reflected in a confused strategy. Leicester's expedition to the Low Countries in 1586 and into 1587 was beset with myriad problems, and while its failures can be overemphasized, it certainly served to sour Elizabeth on such a large-scale, land-force commitment in the Netherlands or on the continent in general. Indeed, the queen continued to negotiate with the Duke of Parma even while Leicester led her troops into battle. By the time of the Spanish armada in 1588—and there were worries it would come in 1587—Elizabeth was ready to shift strategic direction. Militarily the expedition and the campaign of 1586 was a shambles from the start. England lacked almost every requirement for sustained land-force power projection: the leadership, the finances, the manpower, the organization, and the command structures. And, of course, it was a measure of Dutch weakness that they had come begging to Elizabeth in the first place.

To begin with, the coalition had contradictory aims. The Dutch were on the verge of declaring their independence—disappointed by Elizabeth, they would declare their republic to be sovereign in 1588—while Elizabeth still clung to the notion of restoring the status quo. The coalition also lacked military unity of command in ways that would endemically plague the British-Dutch "strategic partnership" for the next century and more, culminating most notably in the frustrations of the Duke of Marlborough. Leicester was nominally in charge, but Elizabeth's refusal of sovereignty handicapped him from the start, and when he assumed, on the Dutch offer, the title of "absolute governor general," Elizabeth flew into a fury and humiliated Leicester into resigning. Burghley was also working to undermine both the mission, which was a much riskier strategy than he wished, and Leicester's personal authority at home; the debate leading up to the decision for war had exacerbated the factional rivalries in the court. The earl—whose experience and talents were political more than military—simultaneously clashed with Sir John Norris, the deeply experienced—though equally grasping—captain of the English mercenary force that had been operating in the Low Countries for a number of years. As we shall see in a later chapter, Norris was a thoroughgoing professional, disdainful of the noble dilettante. Moreover, when Leicester's followers flocked to volunteer in the expedition, he forced Norris's longtime subordinates to the sidelines.

The English officer corps was almost as factionalized as the court, and the differences between "professional" and "gentlemen" exacerbated the quarrels. Paul Hammer succinctly summaries the army's organizational and logistical problems: "After an absence from war on the Continent for so many decades, the administrative structures of Leicester's army, including the basic arrangements for pay, discipline and supply, had to be virtually reinvented piecemeal. The result was not merely confusion, but also massive corruption."[11] The corruption infuriated the cheeseparing queen as much as Leicester's bid for vice-regal powers. Elizabeth had translated her troop commitments into a ridiculousy precise estimate of £126,180 and 10s per annum[12]—a serious effort that would consume about half her normal revenue but, as so often in war, a calculation measured with false precision. The costs, inevitably, went up and auditing the expenditures was not only not in Leicester's interest but beyond anyone's competence. Finally, Elizabeth's instruction "rather to make a defensive [than] an offensive war and not in any sort to hazard a battaille without great advantage" put Leicester in an impossible tactical box. The Duke of Parma, methodical as he was, was not about to wait on Leicester to ready himself. He opened the 1586 campaigning season by attacking the town of Grave, which he took after initial and bloody repulses. He then moved along the River Meuse and then the Rhine, forcing Leicester to dance to his tune. Leicester responded by a daring assault on Axel in

July and then toward Zutphen, just north of the Rhine. These operations were haphazardly commanded but at least created a stalemate. Zutphen also became an iconic moment in the English understanding of the war, for it cost the life of Sir Philip Sidney, poet, Leicester's nephew, son-in-law to Walsingham, and model of martial Protestant virtue. "His grand funeral at St. Paul's cathedral in London on 16 February 1587 would serve as a propaganda vehicle to whip up flagging support for the war."[13] Elizabeth did not wish to lead a crusade, but many of her subjects saw the struggle in such terms.

The queen's commitment to the war in the Netherlands was indeed flagging in early 1587. The year began with the Spanish reclaiming the expensively bought fort at Zutphen and the nearby post at Deventer—where the local English commanders and their starving and underpaid troops deserted to the enemy. After a seven-week siege that summer, and heroic efforts by the English garrison, Parma took the fort of Sluis when Leicester could not mount any relief. The Dutch, knowing that Elizabeth was in not-very-secret talks with Parma, were preparing to fight on their own and for independence. And Elizabeth increasingly was concerned that, for Philip, preparations for an amphibious invasion known at the Spanish court as the "enterprise of England" were foremost in his mind; to the queen, the "forward" strategy had begun to look like overstretch. It looked as though the Spanish fox already was in the English henhouse; in August 1586, Walsingham had exposed a Spanish-backed plot by Anthony Babington and other die-hard English Catholics to assassinate the queen. This conspiracy also, in February 1587, brought an end for Mary Queen of Scots, who had approved the plot. Elizabeth was in desperate financial straits, as well; two years of fighting in the Netherlands had consumed the entirety of her "chested treasure" of £300,000, the savings she had been carefully accumulating for a decade. The talks with Parma were going nowhere; they merely served to divert English attention from the assembly of the *Gran Armada*. Indeed, the talks continued—as did the queen's hopes—until the moment the Spanish fleet appeared off the coast of Cornwall. Thus, in 1587, Elizabethan strategy shifted back toward a defensive posture, and military preparations for militia defense against invasion and a battle at sea received the highest priority.

The story of England's encounter with Philip's *Gran Armada* has been often and, occasionally, well told. The sailing and sighting of the "Invincible Armada," the initial skirmishes, the employment of "fireships" and the battle off Gravelines in Flanders, the fortuitous blowing of the

Theatre of Maritime Operations, 1588–1589

Figure 4.1. Theater of Maritime Operations, 1588–1589.

"Protestant wind" that scattered the Duke of Medina Sidonia's disorganized fleet, and its later wrecks off the coasts of Ireland are all central components in the making of Elizabethan myth. Less well remembered is the effectiveness of the Dutch in bottling up Parma's army and its barges. But perhaps the most strategically revealing moments of the encounter came in the aftermath, in the Portugal expedition that followed.

THE ENGLISH ARMADA

On August 9, 1588, the day after the clash off Gravelines, Lord Burghley had written to Walsingham that he was "not of the opinion that the Spanish fleet will suddenly return from the north or the east, being weakened as they are, and knowing that our navy is returned to our coast where they may repair their lacks and be strong as before."[14] It took an additional two weeks to confirm that the Spanish fleet had sailed northwards past the Orkneys and thus past the point of no return where they must loop entirely around Scotland and Ireland to sail for home. With the immediate danger of invasion also past, at the end of August 1588 Elizabeth summoned her closest councilors to ponder her next move. For all the rejoicing over the defeat of the Spanish, no one expected that it was a decisive moment; Philip would come again. Now was the time to mount a counteroffensive to exploit what surely would be a fleeting moment of Spanish weakness. The first impulse was to try to intercept the American treasure fleet, but the English fleet was in no condition for that, according to the reports of Charles Howard, the Earl of Nottingham and lord admiral, and Francis Drake. Nonetheless, some countering blow had to be readied, the initiative seized, and the naval victory exploited. Sir John Norris was also brought in to consult on land-force matters.

What would become the Portugal expedition of 1589—"the English Armada" to Spanish historians[15]—is, like the Northern Rebellion two decades previously, a little-studied but greatly revealing story of British strategy-making. It was also a textbook example of the ineradicable "maritime" or "blue-water" element that emphasized naval power and colonial commerce and sought to avoid entanglement in continental European affairs in British strategic culture and the improvised, "public-private" method of generating military forces that betrayed the weakness of the Elizabethan state. By mid-September 1588, it was agreed that the survivors of the wreck of the *Gran Armada* were likely to return to Spain and Portugal for refitting and that a raid of the sort that Drake specialized in would forestall the building of a new Spanish fleet. Burghley made note of a September 20 meeting to decide objectives: "(1) to attempt to burn the ships in Lisbon and Seville; (2) to take Lisbon; (3) to take [the Azores, the way station for the treasure fleet]."[16] Thus from the first, the Portugal mission was expansively and contradictorily defined. Even allowing that "Seville" might really mean the port of Cadiz, mounting two raids either simultaneously or sequentially was a large ambition. If done at the same time it would demand dividing the English force. If done one after the other, any hopes of surprise—all but essential in successful "cutting-out" attacks—in the second case would be gone, and, practically speaking in the age of sail, the window of opportunity was likely to be small. Second, raiding and "taking" operations were inherently at odds. Raids could be mounted with relatively fast-moving, smaller forces; "taking"—let alone taking and holding—called for heavier, larger forces, particularly ground forces that would require substantial transport and other forms of logistical sustainment. "Taking" two places—and the Azores are almost one thousand miles from Lisbon and fifteen hundred miles from Plymouth—would more than double the amount of effort required. But Burghley's note marked only the beginning of an expanding set of objectives. In the hands of the Leicester faction, the "taking" of Lisbon quickly became a scheme to restore the Portuguese pretender; Drake had been an unceasing advocate for the idea since the Spanish invasion of 1580.

If Elizabeth's fleet was in no condition to support this increasingly ambitious project, neither was her purse. Neither, for that matter, were English or Dutch land forces, since Parma's invasion force would no doubt return to its methodical campaign to suppress the remaining pockets of resistance. Almost from habit—and with no real alternative—the weak Elizabethan state looked to a joint-stock partnership with private adventurers to produce the fleet and forces it needed. By mid-September, an initial estimate called for the queen to contribute

> six of her second sort of ships, victualed for such number of sailors as they shall require, and provided of all sorts of munition for their sea freight. That Her Majesty will, either by authority or by contract with the city of London and other towns, cause to be supplied twenty good ships of 150 tons or upward, victualed and provided as her own. . . . That

> Her Majesty lend the two late-taken Spanish ships, with their artillery and tackling. . . . That Her Majesty's commission be granted for the levying of 6,000 able soldiers . . . only furnished with sword and dagger for the easier charge of the country. That it will please Her Majesty to disperse towards the voyage in ready money twenty thousand pounds.

Other line items in the request specified the requirements for artillery and "calivers"—infantry firearms—other logistics and support requirement, and an indemnity to the private "enterprisers" if the queen called off the mission. The Dutch were expected to participate to the tune of up to three thousand "shot"—that is, infantry with firearms—as well as shipping for transport and other supplies.[17] Elizabeth's backing would ensure that private investments would make up another £40,000. In a very broad commission issued on October 11, Elizabeth gave Drake and Norris essentially everything they asked for.

But "this method of financing the expedition necessarily meant some weakening of the Queen's control over its aims and operations" and that her "strategic purposes might well take second place" to the political and financial interests of Drake, Norris, and the other backers.[18] Beyond the immediate gains that might be had from privateering, Drake's circle and London merchants were salivating at the riches they expected to realize from the trade concessions they would receive from a restored Don Antonio, illegitimate claimant of the Portuguese throne but standard-bearer of the anti-Spanish faction in the wake of King Sebastian's death in 1578. Portuguese domains included resource-rich colonies in Brazil, West Africa, India, and the East Indies. Elizabeth's desire to disrupt the rebuilding of Spanish fleet was the least important mission to everyone else. This structural weakness was exacerbated by the intelligence, which arrived just after the commission was signed, that the remnants of the Spanish fleet had been driven by the prevailing winds not to Lisbon or Cadiz but eastward into the Bay of Biscay, with forty or more ships at Santander and another substantial group even farther away at San Sebastián. The winds that had blown the armada on its way home might likewise pin the English expedition in the Bay of Biscay, not only exposing it to rowed Spanish galleys but at least delaying if not preventing its sailing to Lisbon to restore Don Antonio or to the Azores to intercept the treasure fleet. Winds, weather, and tides further confounded English plans.

As the mission expanded, so did the planned force and the cost. Almost immediately it became clear that Elizabeth would have to put up her £20,000 in full before private investors would chip in. Drake was energetic in assembling the force for a planned February 1 sailing date but was spending at an alarming and unexpected rate. Norris was dispatched along with fifteen hundred troops to the Netherlands to inform the States General of their expected contributions, including providing for the extra troops Norris had brought with him—but which the Dutch had not requested—while Norris withdrew his veterans for the expedition. The Dutch did not care for this idea and said they could not afford either the money, the men, or the ships Elizabeth demanded. Lord Peregrine Bertie Willoughby, who had replaced Leicester as English commander in the Netherlands, did not care for Norris or his idea to strip the Flanders front of experienced units. Willoughby complained to the privy council on October 28 that the companies sent over with Norris "are come hither altogether unfurnished and unprovided of arms. . . . I am so straitly scanted and of mine own spent myself so near the bones that I am not able to do anything."[19] The following day Norris whined to Walsingham "how ill affected my Lord Willoughby is" and "the small regard he hath showed to have heretofore to Her Majesty's letters."[20] The fight between the two English generals helped to diminish the waning and never-great Dutch interest in the expedition. Willoughby failed to pass along Elizabeth's proposal to maintain the English garrisons in Bergen op Zoom and Ostend, while Norris, as a contemporary Netherlands historian recorded, appeared to the allies as "manly and brave but much too arrogant."[21] In the end, the States General did agree to support the expedition, but at a lesser level than planned and at the cost of much time and misunderstanding—they also, in March, involuntarily contributed as troop transports some sixty smaller "flyboats," which the English appropriated.

As the February sailing date came and went, Elizabeth became increasingly concerned not only about the mounting costs but the divergent ends of the mission itself, particularly the effort to restore Don Antonio. On February 23, she felt obliged to try to discipline Drake and Norris, issuing instructions—closely edited by Burghley so as to erase any doubts or possible misunderstandings—reminding them, "Forasmuch as the chief and principal end of the setting forth of our army under your charge tendeth chiefly to two purposes, the one to distress the King of Spain's ships, the other to get possession of some Island of the Azores thereby to intercept the convoys of treasure that doth yearly pass that way to and from the West and East Indies, we would have you direct the whole course of your proceeding in such sort as may best serve to accomplish and perform the said two ends and purposes."[22]

In regard to any attempt to restore Don Antonio, the queen did not rule it out, but she was increasingly skeptical of the pretender's claim that the people of Portugal would risk a rising against Spanish rule absent large-scale outside support, requiring many more troops than Elizabeth or her Dutch allies could generate. Therefore, she instructed her commanders, "We would have you carefully and substantially inform yourselves before you proceed to attempt anything to that purpose. . . . And in case upon enquiry you should find that that neither the love borne unto [Don Antonio] is so great as he pretendeth and that the forces of the King of Spain are such as nothing can be attempted without very great hazard, our pleasure is that you shall then forbear to attempt anything towards Lisbon for any enterprise to be there attempted other than destroying the ships there."[23]

In sum, Elizabeth was issuing discretionary orders—given the need for private investment and participation and Drake and Norris' own contributions and organizational efforts, she had no choice—but making her strategic priorities plain. Yet she remained worried that, once finally away and on their own, the adventurers would disregard her desires. Thus she appointed Anthony Ashley, a clerk of the privy council, to travel with and oversee the expedition and to "keep a journal of all public actions and proceedings in way of counsel or in fact."[24] It was a threat that Elizabeth would be watching and hold the expedition's leaders accountable.

Additional logistical problems and contrary winds kept the expedition in port from mid-March until it finally sailed on April 18. This "counter-armada" totaled 180 ships and, officially, more than seventeen thousand troops; the number of soldiers is likely to have been inflated by as many as four thousand, according to later audit. Costs had risen to more than £96,000, of which Elizabeth's share was almost £50,000.[25] Moreover, much against the queen's wishes, her new favorite, the young Earl of Essex, had stolen away from London and, after a frantic thirty-six-hour ride to Plymouth, stowed aboard the royal *Swiftsure* to be a part of this golden opportunity for fame and fortune. As R. B. Wernham dryly observed, "Such a man, bearing all the prestige of a peer of the realm, could not but have a considerable influence upon the conduct of the expedition."[26] Essex was already deep in debt and determined that "if I speed well I will adventure to be rich."[27] He later boasted, "Although I had no charge, yet I made my brother general of the horse, my faithful friend Sir Roger Williams colonel-general of the infantry, seven or eight of my fast friends colonels, and 20 at least of my domestics captains, so as I might have party enough when I would."[28]

In such spirit were many Elizabethan military operations conducted. At least the expedition did not sail directly for Portugal rather than Santander. Drake and Norris had, however, passed along intelligence several weeks before departing that "there are arrived to the number of *200 sail of ships* of divers nations at *the Groyne* [that is, Coruña] *and other* ports of Galicia and Portugal with store of munitions, masts, cables and other provisions for the enemy." The italics are in the original, ensuring that the queen and her advisors would not miss the point that Drake and Norris already were inclined to divert from the agreed plan. Therefore the commanders' intentions were that "if the wind will not suffer us to bear with Biscay and those parts"—that is, to sail either in or out of the bay where previous intelligence had located the refitting Spanish fleet—"to attempt the destroying of the shipping in the foresaid coasts of Galicia and Portugal."[29] This Coruña intelligence was almost too good to be true. Taking so many prizes so early in the expedition would satisfy investors, do enough damage to Spanish shipping to satisfy Elizabeth, and allow the expedition to avoid the winds and currents of the Bay of Biscay. Indeed, if the prizes were rich enough, they would also obviate the need to go to the Azores and thus, happily, leave plenty of time left over for the Portugal excursion. And too good to be true it was: only a handful of ships were found in port. But having committed to Coruña, Drake and Norris had to make at least a show of effort; one of the ships was the thousand-ton *San Juan*, one of the capital ships of the 1588 invasion fleet.

The circular bay of Coruña, about a mile wide, lay just east of Cap Finisterre at the northwest corner of the Iberian Peninsula. The port was protected by the castle of San Antonio on a promontory at the eastern end. Outside the castle was an upper town above a lower town clustered around the actual harbor. On April 23, Drake and Norris landed about seven thousand men a mile east of the town, established a beachhead, brought some artillery ashore, and prepared for further operations. The two Spanish galleys in the harbor rowed away. Well before dawn on April 26, Norris attacked the lower town, flanking the town wall and taking its defenders from the rear. With their harbor gone, the men of the *San Juan* set her aflame, and the remaining ships were abandoned. The Spanish garrison made a sortie against the English beachhead but were easily repulsed. So far, so good; the victors then sacked the town, finding an "infinite deal of wine," which they immediately drank. They also discovered some fine clothing that had been part of the armada baggage, but which carried infectious diseases that would prove even more lethal to the English than did the wine. The easy victory may also have gone to Norris's head, for he now decided to attack the more heavily fortified upper town. His initial bombardment failed, as did a subsequent attempt to mine a tower overlooking the town wall. The botched effort destroyed one of his two precious demiculverin. These medium-weight cannon, relatively mobile but not heavy enough to quickly batter a breach in well-maintained walls, were the biggest artillery pieces allowed to the expedition; Norris later protested that "the want of the artillery that we demanded from Her Majesty" accounted for many of the expedition's failures.[30] The English commander also left the seaward approach uncovered, which allowed the Spanish galleys to resupply the garrison. A small breach was blown on May 3, but because "the English soldier"—the militia and raw recruits, particularly—"is not well acquainted with matters of breach" the attack went in too quickly, was repulsed, and then was crushed when the targeted tower fell over. Three days later, Norris was spooked by the report of an approaching Spanish force initially estimated at ten thousand. He marched his men away several miles eastward to Puente de Burgos, where he found the Spanish encamped on the far side of a two-hundred-yard stone bridge. Leading his men in an attack over the bridge, he routed the Spanish, inflicting heavy losses and sustaining few, though the aggressive Norris himself had his head sliced by a Spanish sword when he fell over "with very earnestness in overthrusting" with his pike.[31]

On May 8, Norris began reembarking his troops in Drake's ships. The leaders of the expedition learned exactly the lessons they wished to learn from the experience at Coruña: "that an army of 10,000 men, good soldiers, may pass through the whole realm without great danger." Norris not only thought that Elizabeth would be pleased by "the success of the war of Portugal"—this is how he thought of it, not as the "war of Spain"—which would "give Her Majesty encouragement to be at some charge for the maintenance thereof."[32] Drake and Norris thus asked the queen for real siege guns and another thirty companies of infantry. Assuring themselves that the stores they had destroyed already would delay the mounting of an invasion campaign in 1589 (and ignoring intelligence from prisoners that the ships refitting in the Bay of Biscay were expected at Coruña in May to stage a new attack on England or Ireland), they made for Lisbon. When she learned of this, Elizabeth was not at all pleased. She complained that Drake and Norris "went to places more for profit than for services," denied their reinforcement request and, in a long letter, tried to administer a "douche of cold water," as Wernham put it. Elizabeth insisted "that your first and principal action should be to take and distress the King of Spain's navy and ships where they lay" and that they had better "accomplish it before your return as ye think to answer for your doing otherwise than yet you have given us cause to be satisfied with you."[33]

The expedition was also wanting for ground forces. Something like a third of the reported, but inflated, strength of 18,485 had never made it out of English waters. Another three thousand went home or to La Rochelle in France after the Coruña interlude, and sickness had begun to ravage the remaining ten thousand. Perhaps worst of all, the three weeks spent at Coruña had eliminated any element of surprise in Lisbon, and the Spanish governor general, the Cardinal Archduke Albert, lost no time in clamping down on those known or suspected of favoring Don Antonio's cause or of holding anti-Spanish sentiments. On the plus side, the wandering Earl of Essex arrived with queen's ship *Swiftsure*, adding to the firepower of Drake's fleet. Despite that, a May 15 council of war rejected the idea of a direct dash up the River Tagus past the forts that protected Lisbon and a coup de main on the port itself. They stuck with their original plan for what would be a relatively uncontested landing at Peniche, forty-five miles north of the city. The next day, Essex landed a vanguard of two thousand, the earl leaping into shoulder-deep water whereupon he supposedly "killed a Spaniard hand-to-hand." Alas, rocks and a heavy sea slowed the rest of the landing and caused a boat to go down with all hands, and it took several hours for Norris to get the main body ashore, allowing the local Spanish garrison to counterattack. These militia were driven off and the town and castle taken.[34]

Taking forty-eight hours to rest and consolidate their force, now down to six thousand with only forty-four cavalry, Norris and Essex began the march to Lisbon on May 18, while Drake sailed away, promising to meet them on the Tagus. A large Spanish force covered their advance, and it took fully six days for the English to slog along the road to Lisbon.

Disease weakened the men, as did the mounting heat and the lack of pack animals and carriages. Late on May 23, they reached the outskirts of Lisbon, and Norris led a reconnaissance party toward the town, which appeared nearly empty. A few beggars welcomed Don Antonio home, but there was no indication of a widespread popular uprising; indeed, from the moment of the landing it was apparent that most of the Portuguese were either intimidated by the occupying Spanish or hostile to Don Antonio. The next morning, the Spanish launched a surprise raid which, though beaten back into the Lisbon walls, killed two English captains and about forty troops. But the Spanish could afford to sit and wait.

> There was little need for them to interfere. The city was well and continuously supplied from across the river. Most of the Portuguese officials, indeed most of the Portuguese inhabitants, had either fled across the river or gone into hiding. Those few who had dared to attempt anything for Don Antonio had been caught and most of them hanged or beheaded. The garrison already outnumbered their besiegers among whom sickness was taking an increasing toll and who had now spent almost all the powder and match they had been bale to cary with them. Norris had no artillery with him and the walls of Lisbon were [high and strong].[35]

The English expedition, in contrast, could not afford to wait, and without the promised uprising they had not strength enough to assault the Spanish fortifications. Norris confronted this reality in a May 25 council with his colonels, of whom only Ralph Lane—whom we shall meet again—retained any optimism, and he would only recommend waiting another three days for Don Antonio's supporters to show themselves. Three days was too long for Norris. The next day he withdrew to Cascais, where Drake had turned up with the fleet and sixty Hanseatic and French ships loaded with corn, naval stores, and copper that Drake had intercepted at the mouth of the Tagus. This booty not only was the first entry in the credit column for the expedition, but it allowed Norris and Drake to hang on in Cascais—the Spanish were still in no mood to come out of Lisbon's walls—in the event that reinforcements turned up. On June 6, two small barks arrived with word from Elizabeth that no reinforcements were to be had and orders to send the Earl of Essex home immediately. With perhaps as few as four thousand effectives in the ranks, all prospects in Portugal were gone; there was nothing left but to try to salvage the Azores leg of the expedition.

That, too, collapsed almost immediately. Though the surviving troops had been reembarked, the lack of wind kept the large but increasingly ragtag English fleet pinned near the coast. This made for ideal conditions for the rowed Spanish galleys, twenty of which made a raid on Drake's stragglers on June 9, costing the English several ships and further confusing the fleet's organization. When at last the winds picked up, they blew strong from the south, preventing any progress toward the Azores. The fleet became hopelessly scattered. The English ships were drawn into the port of Vigo, which they looted and then burned. In a final attempt to perform some of their original mission, Drake and Norris split their forces, and, as the accomplished soldier Anthony Wingfield wrote in his account of the campaign, "to man and victual twenty of the best ships for the Islands of the Azores with General Drake, to see if he could meet with the Indian fleet; General Norris to return home with the rest."[36] Still the contrary winds blew, building in intensity. Drake did not await the consolidation but put to sea with the bulk of the fleet on June 20; Norris, with thirty-three ships further up the river, was unable to catch the tide but sailed for home the following day. Both these squadrons were further battered by storms. Drake eventually gave up on the Azores altogether, but Norris, who had lost perhaps seven further ships, got to Plymouth first, on July 2. Norris alerted Walsingham in understated terms: "We are afraid that Her Majesty will mislike the event of our journey."[37] Essex, who had returned a week before, immediately sued the queen for a pardon.

It took a while for the full extent of the expedition's failures to be reckoned and assessed. It was not, perhaps, as the Spanish historian Luis Gorrochategui Santos claims, "the greatest naval disaster in English history," but it was complete waste of precious Elizabethan resources at a crucial moment.[38] The first order of business was to try to refit the queen's ships for service and return such troops as survived to the Low Countries. But the captured Hanseatic hulks had to be returned, which was not only a diplomatic setback but meant that Elizabeth had to write off her £50,000 investment, with neither financial nor strategic profit to show. Whatever opportunity there was to deal a crippling blow to the Spanish navy had been lost, and though it would take some time for Philip to mount another invasion threat, the ships refit in the Bay of Biscay ports were soon escorting treasure fleets across the Atlantic.

It was also apparent that Spain's grip on the Iberian Peninsula and the Mediterranean was much firmer than thought; however much the Portuguese or Moroccans chafed at Spanish power, there was no way for England to exploit the situation. And with the assassination of Henri III in France, making the Protestant Henri IV of Navarre next in line for the throne, crises on the continent soon demanded the attention of English strategy-makers.

Drake and Norris got off lightly in the official inquiry before the privy council, and many participants and supporters continued to view the Portugal expedition as a lost opportunity. Yet both Norris and Drake fell out of favor; Norris, for all his experience, did not receive another major command until 1591 and Drake until 1595. But more profoundly, the maritime power-projection strategy that they had championed was discredited, at least for the moment. Important tactical lessons had been learned about amphibious operations that could and would be exploited elsewhere. At least, compared to the Spanish, English admirals and generals had achieved a level of cooperation that was impressive. And there would forever be a place in the English strategic imagination for amphibious raids, or "descents," as they would come to be called, and Drake would again be regarded as a national hero. As English sailors, soldiers, and colonists in the Americas would discover, the problem of projecting substantial and sustainable military power across oceanic distances at a "contested" target remained a very tough task; absent benign conditions on the far shore, maritime power had distinct limits. Whatever the defensive value of England's "wooden walls," Elizabeth's navy remained a brittle battering ram. Moreover, thrusts at the periphery of the Spanish sphere did not seem to be worth such effort; compared to the balance in the Low Countries or the succession crisis in France, Portugal was a sideshow. And, as the Spanish war dragged on, vulnerabilities in Britain would again seem to be higher priorities.

5

THE TYRONE REBELLION

Sir Henry Bagenal, marshal of all English military forces in Ireland and a member of Queen Elizabeth's privy council, awoke to face critical decisions on the morning of May 27, 1595. He was camped with a force totaling about fifteen hundred men, a mix of "shot" (infantry armed with matchlock-ignited muskets, arquebuses, and calivers) and pikemen, and supplemented by two hundred fifty cavalry outside the fort at Monaghan, an isolated garrison nestled amongst the hills, woods, and bogs of Ulster. The marshal successfully had completed his mission, which was to relieve and resupply this tenuous outpost besieged by Irish insurgents led by the leaders of the Maguire and MacMahon clans. But Bagenal's worry was how best to get back to Newry, whence he had marched two days previously. Newry was the most forward supply depot of the English army in northern Ireland, and on May 26 Bagenal's column had been steadily harassed by the forces led by the Earl of Tyrone. Tyrone, or to his fellow Irish, Hugh O'Neill—he had risen to become "*the* O'Neill," or chieftan of the clan dynasty—had become the most powerful leader across the province, uniting disparate and oft-feuding chieftains in resistance to the encroaching English. More immediately for Bagenal, O'Neill—who also had eloped with his daughter, Mabel—had modernized and reformed Irish military practice, introducing a higher percentage of firearms, giving his forces much greater lethality than the Scots "gallowglass" mercenaries whose primary weapons were the axe and the bow and who had for decades been the Irish warlords' principal strike force. O'Neill had likewise improved the supply and introduced better discipline both among individual soldiers and in command. Bagenal anticipated a difficult day.

The first day of the march westward from Newry to the Monaghan outpost had been uneventful and easy, but it covered just eight miles. Bagenal wanted to complete the revictualing of the garrison with as little muss and fuss as possible and so chose an indirect and more northerly route to avoid the most likely ambush sites. Unfortunately, as Bagenal's men made camp for the evening, several hundred of Tyrone's cavalry appeared on a hill about a quarter of a mile distant. The English horse quickly drove off the Irish, but the element of stealth was gone; Tyrone, previously informed by spies in Newry of Bagenal's preparations and departure, had located and no doubt well scouted the relief column. Thus, as one of Bagenal's lieutenants, Tutcher Perkins, reported:

> Next morning after eight miles march the Earl of Tyrone brought all his forces to a strait which we were to pass, and turned out seven or eight companies of foot to skirmish with us, placing their battles [that is, their main body] some quarter of a mile off upon a hill. These 700 or 800, being continually second from their battle, held us play some three hours and annoyed us much by reason of the narrowness of the passage, a bog being on their side and a wood on the other to our great disadvantage. After we had passed the strait the enemy's powder was well nigh spent. . . . Afterwards they no more skirmished with us for that time, but still we might perceive their forces increase. . . . We found that Maguire and MacMahon besieged Monaghan, but they rose as soon as we came. We encamped on a hill close to the Abbey. Our loss was 12 slain and 30 hurt; the enemy's 100 slain and many hurt.[1]

This running three-hour skirmish at the hamlet of Crossdall on May 26 was indeed good reason for Bagenal to worry about the 27th. To begin with, he was deep in enemy territory. His location and dispositions were known. His supplies were limited, and in particular he was low on powder, the most precious of all logistics needs. Bagenal could not stay at Monaghan, nor could he maneuver more deeply into Ulster; he had to get back to Newry, where at least he could be sheltered and resupplied by sea. The marshal commanded a large and powerful force that, although fleshed out with recent recruits, included veterans of Irish service and newly arrived reinforcements who had been fighting in France. However, the network of narrow roads was extremely limited and would serve to string out his command and make it very difficult to concentrate; he could not count on the English advantages in open-field battle and discipline in the compartmented terrain. Moreover, the extended skirmishing of May 26 had a demoralizing effect on his troops. They had expended a proportion of their precious ammunition, suffered significant casualties—Perkins's figures probably undercount those of the English and overestimate Tyrone's—and had faced a numerous foe who had demonstrated no little tactical competence. As Perkins observes, Tyrone had rotated his "shot" to keep up a menacing fire for three hours, quickly replacing units whose ammunition was gone with fresh units. This was particularly disturbing to the English, who were accustomed to think themselves tactically superior to the Irish. At Newry, one of the company commanders redeployed from Brittany had expressed concern about the shortages of ammunition. "Captain," replied William Russell, lord deputy—essentially, the viceroy—of Ireland, "you are not now in France or the Low Countries, for you shall not be put here to fight as there."[2] A week later, Russell would report to the privy council that "the traitors' arms and weapons and their skill and practice therein far exceed their wonted usage."[3] Finally, it was almost certain that Tyrone had shown only a fraction of his overall strength. And so Bagenal reckoned that, on May 27, he had to find another way back to Newry other than retracing his route through Crossdall, where now Tyrone was gathering his force and improving what had already proven an excellent position for ambush. At about ten o'clock in the morning, Bagenal's troops stepped off, moving eastward from their camp but on a more southerly path toward Clontibret Church, a little more than six miles from Monaghan and somewhat more than four miles from Crossdall; Bagenal was betting that he could get his column past this crossroads before Tyrone could reposition his larger force to block him.

Tyrone won the race. The ground at Clontibret was as favorable for ambush as Crossdall had been; the route on which the English marched was flanked by a bog to the north and hills to the south. English Captain Francis Stafford described the Irish dispositions:

> The Earl [of Tyrone], discovering the Marshal's intentions, commanded his brother Cormac, Henry Og, who married the Earl's daughter, [and] MacMahon with all their own troops and some 300 shot of the Earl (and a battle of pikes to our judgment of 600 or 700) to possess a hill which stood

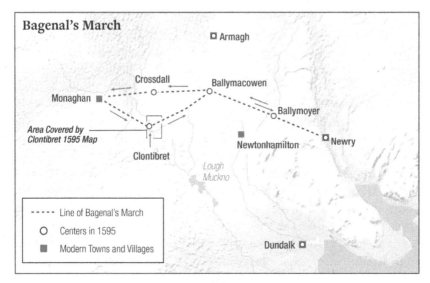

Figure 5.1. Bagenal's March.

somewhat upon our right hand in the way we marched. The distance between the Church and a strait which of force we must pass I conjecture of not half a mile. Upon the left hand of the way was a red bog where was placed a number of shot. The Earl himself, accompanied I protest as I could judge with 300 horse and a number of shot and Scots was behind us.[4]

Bagenal rode at the front of his column and quickly realized that his one hope was to attack into the ambush and push through it as rapidly as possible, avoiding at all costs another drawn-out engagement that would exhaust his ammunition, thereby expose his pikemen and his trains, and risk the disintegration of his entire force. But again Tryone acted first, and, against all past practice, began to close with the English, as Stafford detailed: "We had no sooner past the Church Clantubrett but we were charged in the vanguard with Cormac, in the rearguard with the Earl and his troops (which were pike in batalia) in sundry place. Their shot and the Scots playing upon our wings, we were fain to abide the whole forces . . . and never marched above a quarter of a mile in all that [five hours'] time."[5]

Unable to batter his way through and soon out of ammunition, Bagenal's column was prepared for destruction. Tyrone led his forces closer, to within thirty paces of the now-exposed squares of English pikemen;

the Irish shot kept up suppressive fires while the O'Neill prepared his own pikemen and cavalry to deliver the knockout punch. But as Tyrone arranged his troops, one of the Irish petty nobles in English service, James Sedgreve, recognized the earl and sprang forward in a suicidal charge, followed by a small band of English troops. Sedgreve and Tyrone "splintered their lances at that first impact," wrote Lorcan Ó Mearáin in what is otherwise a sober account of the battle, "then gripping each other they fell to the ground locked in 'that fatal embrace' which each knew must end in the death of one of them."[6] Sedgreve's bravery—though fatal to him—unhorsed Tyrone and thus stupefied Irish command and control. In the chaos, the stalled English column at last began to move forward

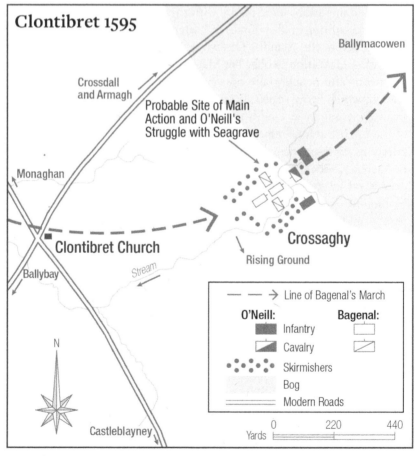

Figure 5.2. Clontibret 1595.

past the bottleneck at Clontibret and make their way eastward toward relative safety at Newry. English losses were substantial—the estimate was 31 killed and 109 wounded, though the numbers may have been greater since the units involved remained unable to conduct further operations for some time after—but not nearly as bad as they might have been.

The psychological impact of Clontibret far outweighed the tactical effect. The epitome of English professional competence, Sir John Norris, whose troops had been those shipped from Brittany to Ireland and who was shortly to take the field himself, reported to Robert Cecil, who had already begun to work with and assume the role of his father William Cecil, Lord Burghley as Queen Elizabeth's principal strategic advisor. Norris, long close to the Cecils, pulled no punches: "The state of the northern rebels [is] far different from that it was wont to be, their arms better and munitions more plenty with them." Tyrone's strength had paralyzed the existing English forces in Ulster and was changing the political balance across the island: "The whole country [is] much altered from their wonted position to obey her Majesty's laws; for amongst the nobility, the towns and people there are few that will come into a [Protestant] church, which betrays their interior disposition."[7] Sir Ralph Lane, whom we will encounter at length in the following chapter, was likewise part of the English reinforcements to Ireland, and put the matter even more grimly in correspondence with Burghley, telling "your Lordship that in no memory either of the living or of record in chronicle this Kingdom ever stood in greater danger of being utterly lost if either the Spaniard by himself or by the Scot should invade us in any part of the realm."[8] By the mid-1590s, the long-festering problem of Ireland had forced its way—or rather, was forced by the growing power of Tyrone—to the front of Elizabethan strategic consciousness. What had been a secondary and even tertiary strategic concern in London for the first forty years of the queen's reign would soon become the largest theater of operations for English military forces, eventually dwarfing all others, fighting not just the troops of Tyrone but of Spain. Ireland also would serve as an increasingly important element in English strategy-making, an issue of domestic security and regime legitimacy, but equally a first and precedent-setting step in the process of building a transoceanic empire that would place "Britain"—if that reality was still far in the distance, the idea already had taken deep root in the English geopolitical imagination—first among European great powers. The answer, to many in London, was not simply conquest but colonization, civilization, and Protestantism, uplifting the benighted Gaels as the imperial Romans had done for the British and establishing a formula to be followed on farther frontiers in North America, a spirit one day to be echoed on the Great Seal of the Commonwealth of Massachusetts: "Come over and help us." Thus Ireland was also a school, and a hard one, for soldiers and state-builders. As ever, balancing the first-order need for security with the desire for social, economic, confessional, and political progress was a tricky business.

For four decades, Elizabeth had schemed and fought her way back toward the front rank of European powers, but her efforts were constrained by limited resources and an essentially defensive posture, patrolling the walls of the "counterscarp" along the western littoral of the continent, turning back the tide of the Counter-Reformation, supporting the Protestant party in Scotland, ever on guard against invasion from abroad, rebellion at home, and the prospect of assassination. Her final, and ultimately greatest, contribution to English strategy was to open the doors to westward expansion and colonization. To the east, north, and south, Elizabeth and her councilors sought to hold the line in concert with their allies; to the west, they sought new legions of subjects, power, and the strategic depth they would need to compete in the age of empires.

PAST POLICY

In yielding to her Irish impulse, Elizabeth tapped into a long-standing English desire. The rebellion led by the Earl of Tyrone, which the Irish came to call the "Nine Years' War," arguably had been in the making since the 1530s, when Thomas Cromwell sought not only to bring Protestantism to England but to extend his program of reform to the outlands of Henry VIII's domains, to consolidate and centralize English power, and to Anglicize political, social, and legal structures. This put the focus on the English settlement centered around Dublin known as "the Pale," and its effect was to divide the English community in Ireland; while some embraced the plan, it was also a challenge to the customary powers of the "Old English" magnates, including some families that had arrived with the original Norman conquest of Ireland. The greatest of these—the Butlers of Ormond and the two FitzGeralds of Kildare and Desmond—were recognized as English earls and held what were essentially quasi-independent palatinates. More aggressive were the "New English" agents sent by Cromwell to speed the implementation of his program.

Viewed from London, the reforms were a reassertion of monarchical rights based on the original conquest; modern, more efficient principles of government; and, of course, a less corrupt and purer church. In Ireland, and particularly to Thomas FitzGerald, son of the Earl of Kildare, Tudor centralizing efforts were a mortal threat to the position and power of the Old English nobility. FitzGerald—known as "Silken Thomas" for the silken tassels he wore circling his helmet—rallied a "Geraldine League" in open revolt, creating a small army and invading the Pale from Munster in the south. The earl also made his revolt a larger Catholic cause, branding Henry as a heretic; beyond the matters of faith, this made the Irish Catholic cause an international one and, more importantly, gave the revolt an appeal across the traditional Irish politics of clan and region. These were two notes Tyrone would play with virtuosity. Silken Thomas's rebellion was crushed and the FitzGerald estates seized, but with Cromwell's fall from power in London, the winds of change in Ireland faded before they reached Gaelic society. Henry did create, by act of the Irish Parliament in Dublin, the "kingdom" of Ireland to supplant the medieval "lordship" of Ireland, which had originated in the twelfth-century conquest and a subsequent papal bull legitimizing it. The act also expressed the intent to bring all of Ireland under English rule. "This was a task of the greatest magnitude," wrote Wallace MacCaffrey. His conclusion has withstood the test of time:

> It was to prove to be the most far-reaching undertaking of the Tudor monarchy other than the making of the Reformation. . . . What was required was nothing less than the transformation of a whole society. The Gaelic world lacked virtually every element that an Englishman saw as necessary to right order. . . . For the Englishman there was a relatively simple recipe for ending what he regarded as social chaos. His own home society provided the model on which the Gaelic world must be reconstructed. . . . Above all, public and private authority must be clearly separated. The [Gaelic] clan chiefs must become mere landowners while clansmen were to be subject to one lord only, the King. All alike must be subordinated to the rule of the common law, administered by royal justices and relying for its enforcement on the obedience of the population to the representatives of royal authority.[9]

Such a political goal—one could fairly call it "regime change"—also had a transforming effect on English strategy-making. Elizabethan strategists did conceive the struggles against Spain in ideological terms and hoped that one day reformed religion might replace Catholicism on the European continent; both Protestants and Catholics longed to reunify "Christendom." But that they left to the realm of aspiration, not planning. War in northern England and Scotland, in the Netherlands, in France, in Portugal might be cast in confessional terms and result in periodic atrocities, but it was considered to be war among civilized and recognizably Christian parties. Wars against Catholic powers were also cast as strategically defensive struggles even when, as in Portugal, they were operationally offensive; the first order of business was to defend traditional British interests and establish an international refuge for Protestants. Elizabeth might pine to reestablish a continental sally port at Calais, grasp greedily at "cautionary towns" in the Lowlands, or aspire to maritime and trading greatness, but the appetite for European empire was weak, as was the military capacity. Ireland—and later America—would prove different in almost every respect. The English thought they first had to civilize the Gaelic Irish before they could be brought to understand the truth of true Christianity. If, to English eyes, Irish society was chaotic, the land of Ireland was also "waste," seemingly all but undeveloped except in the Pale, where English ways ruled. Thus what was required was a strategy of imperial expansion, of military offensives; conquest must precede civilization, but it was not sufficient to establish a durable regime. Ireland was also a theater in the great-power struggle with Spain. The great English fear was that Philip would do to Elizabeth what she had done to him in the Netherlands: give support to a festering rebellion on a distant frontier, funding proxies that would exhaust resources.

This "Irish Model" is also of critical importance for this study because it established a framework for colonization of English America. Irish colonial service also frequently became a schooling ground for English military officers sent to the New World. The habits of strategic and colonial thought that guided British imperial expansion for the next two centuries were roughed out and refined in Ireland. And measured purely on the scale and cost of military operations, the Elizabethan undertaking in Ireland came, eventually, to dwarf the level of effort either on the continent or at sea; in exasperation, the queen eventually overcame her natural parsimony in favor of a spare-no-expense approach and, perhaps even more remarkably, learned to retain confidence in an on-scene commander despite setbacks and infighting at court. Elizabeth's Irish wars were entirely unromantic affairs and thus take a back seat to the tales of the repulse of the *Gran Armada* and swashbuckling sea dogs in popular memory. But, and especially when regarded through the lens of what was to come in America, the influence of the Irish Model, and its application during the Tyrone Rebellion in particular, must be examined more thoroughly. There were also a number of cross-cultural barriers that complicated strategy-making: in Ireland, as in native American societies, the collective clan or tribe held ownership or stewardship of land; leadership positions were based upon military and political prowess or authority, bound, contingently, by clan or tribal custom; succession was neither strictly hereditary nor military, but a combination of the two that also rested on a clan consensus about who would make the most powerful chieftain. The choice generally was made during the life of the current leader, sometimes with his blessing and sometimes against it. The English looked to settled law, custom, and politics to provide a social stability that Irish and tribes of North America did not want or fully grasp; the result was a nightmare for English strategists, as James P. Myers explains: "As 'pacified' chieftains died off and were replaced by their *tanists* [traditionally-chosen leaders] or as England, for a number of reasons, failed to defend the new authority bestowed upon the chieftains against the power of the clan," there inevitably was a jockeying for power that required a new set of arrangements, whether arrived at by fighting, negotiating, or, usually, some combination of the two.[10] In short, the native Irish and American political systems drove the English to distraction and made the settling of their imperial frontiers a risky and uncertain project.

The original Norman Conquest had added but the thinnest veneer of feudal order to the native Gaelic order, and with the passing of centuries the newcomers tended to adapt to local ways rather than transform them. Even in the sixteenth century, the English Pale encompassed a very small slice of the island, from just south of Dublin through Drogheda up to Dundalk at the Ulster border; all three of these were port towns and a short sail across the Irish Sea from England. Inland settlements followed the river lowlands westward, particularly the Liffey and the Boyne. Englishmen did not like to go into the rugged hills; the Wicklow Mountains just south of Dublin and those which formed the Moyry Pass heading northwest out of Dundalk and toward Ulster posed a threat to English lines of communication and settlement and made the frontiers of Leinster contested grounds. In this regard, these were very much like the routes to the interior of North America—the Connecticut, Hudson, Mohawk, Suqhuehanna, and Potomac River corridors—would be in the following centuries. Exposed to the sea, Munster and the south had a substantial English presence, but Connaught and, above all, Ulster remained resolutely and remotely Gaelic. Englishmen would long depend on supplies from the sea; while this enabled military operations and colonization, it could also be a weakness.

It did not help that Gaelic Ireland was lightly populated, with few towns and poor roads. The level of development diminished exponentially with distance from the coast. In another analogy to North American patterns, the Irish economy depended on cattle "booleying" or, in anthropological terms, "transhumanence," the seasonal movement of both herds and people, shifting from lowland to upland fields in summer months. Herding was also the basis of a complex social and political structure built around "septs," a quasi-kinship structure that shifted according to both heredity and power, particularly military power. Cattle-raiding was a form of sport, culture, and power, a brew preserved in the Ulster Cycle of Irish epics, whose Homeric expression is *Táin Bó Cúailnge*—the "Cooley Cattle Raid." The prizes in such raids not only included the livestock (which also paid off mercenaries, including the "gallowglass" mercenaries who came over from western Scotland and the islands) but political submission and tribute. Political and military skill were the keys to power in Gaelic society and constantly put to the test. For the English, "convictions of racial superiority critically shaped attitudes about how best these remote regions could be 'civilized'—how these unruly subjects could be reformed, their over-mighty lords tamed, thuggery and feuding replaced with law and order, and labor channeled into production rather than destruction. Crown strategies ranged from annihilation to assimilation."[11]

Crown strategies had heretofore also enjoyed limited success; hence the wide range of approaches attempted. Henry VIII, for example, had shifted in his later years from conquest to conciliation, offering Irish chieftains a choice of "surrender and regrant," whereby he would substitute English titles—more legally secure and stable than the system of tanistry that was Gaelic practice—for Irish ones. But this so contravened Gaelic law and custom that Henry's short-term solution created greater long-term difficulty. By the middle Elizabethan era, the need to solve the Irish puzzle was becoming more strategically urgent, not only because of unrest among the Irish. The Reformation and Counter-Reformation further added a confessional edge to the Renaissance English *mission civiliatrice*. As she had moved to try to latch the northern, Scottish postern gate, Elizabeth would try to bolt the western gate in Ireland; a revolt by Ulster chief Shane O'Neill in the 1560s had not only been difficult to suppress and resulted in raids into the Pale but also threatened to spark French support for the Gaelic lord. The English response, developed largely by Sir Henry Sidney, the lord lieutenant for Ireland, was first dubbed the "Ulster Project" and then, in the 1570s, the "Enterprise of Ulster." The O'Neill revolt ended with Shane's death, and the return of relative peace and stability in Tyrone—the O'Neill homeland—under his successor, Turlough Luineach, put the enterprise again on the back burner. As always, Elizabeth wished to cuts costs, had other strategic priorities, and, again almost as always, looked to pursue public ends with private means.

THE ROAD TO REBELLION

What would come to be called the Tyrone Rebellion had begun as a sporadic affair, with only few substantial engagements and much raiding, negotiation, diplomacy, and deceit; Clontibret marks an early point of punctuation but hardly the beginning of hostilities. The Maguires and O'Donnells had been openly at war with Elizabeth for several years and even the Earl of Tyrone, promoted by the English as a proxy, had destroyed an English garrison at a fort on the Blackwater River months before Clontibret. But this war became more than a series of skirmishes. It would become an existential affair for the Gaelic Irish lords, a desperate last-ditch attempt to preserve power, position, and a political culture. It also became the centerpiece of late Elizabethan strategy, a move to secure their British backdoor to their European adversaries and to conquer, colonize, civilize, and develop a British Ireland. The Ulstermen were fighting a defensive struggle, though they preferred to take the operational offensive when they could. The English were waging an offensive and expansionist campaign as part of a British imperial design, in character much closer to the Northern Rebellion than assisting the Dutch or the French along the continental counterscarp or maritime raids on Spain or her colonies. Both sides in Ireland employed regular and irregular methods. The Spanish, when they finally got involved, were taking a low-risk and potentially high-reward opportunity to create an Irish quagmire for English resources. They despaired of deposing Elizabeth, but they could "annoy" her as she did them.

The conflict originated in the renewed English attempts to Anglicize and colonize Ireland, though, as with all Elizabethan policies, this was a start-and-stop affair constrained by the government's weaknesses and, during the late 1580s and early 1590s, the demands of war with Spain and, in regard of land forces, fighting on the continent. Sir John Perrot became the lord deputy in Ireland in 1584; he was part of Leicester-Walsingham faction at court and the instrument of intended reforms. His principal task was to shepherd the colonization of Muster. His efforts were "programmatic in method"—he followed the colonize-and-civilize line—and "maximalist in objective," and he took office promising "to bring [the Irish] to the same felicity and quietness which her majesty's subjects in England to live in."[12] This was a palpable threat indeed to his Irish listeners, not just the Gaelic lords but the established English in Ireland. When events diverted resources and court attention elsewhere, factions of the queen's privy council in Ireland, the English executive and administrative body in Dublin commonly known as the "Irish council," exploited the weaknesses of Perrot's position by lodging complaints in London that further eroded the lord deputy's support. The real wonder is how he lasted in office until January 1588; in the year of the *Gran Armada*, Elizabeth could not afford a quarrelsome lord lieutenant.

Thus Perrot's replacement, Sir William FitzWilliam, was his strategic and temperamental opposite. He was an experienced diplomat who had previously served in Ireland, and his patron was the pragmatic Lord Burghley rather than the more ideological Leicester and Walsingham. London's intent was now to keep Irish matters firmly subordinated to larger strategic concerns and the sea wars with Spain. Alas, FitzWilliam's own pragmatism shaded quickly into corruption that provided what was likely the immediate spark to the Tyrone Rebellion. Generally, FitzWilliam's weakness gave license to ambitious and independent New English subordinates, including Bagenal, English marshal in Ireland and commissioner of Ulster; Perrot had feuded with the Bagenal family. Then in 1589 and 1590, a succession crisis in the MacMahon clan provided Sir William with an opportunity for a land grab in Monaghan, enriching both the government and himself. The new claimant on the MacMahon title, Hugh Roe, came to Dublin to validate his position, but by a murky legal process was himself tried for treason and executed and his lands seized and regranted. To the Gaelic lords of Ireland and Ulster in particular, this was a devastating attack on their social, economic, and political power and a preview of what was in store for them if they did not submit to English authority in every detail. And it was especially a direct assault on the power of Tyrone, for the MacMahons were an essential element in the O'Neill power structure. The O'Neills would have to protect the MacMahons, or their own power might be called into question.[13]

Taken together, the tenures of Perrot and FitzWilliam represented, to Irish eyes, an especially provocative combination of aggressive intent and military and political weakness. Their terms of office also coincided with and helped contribute to a consolidation of Gaelic power in Ulster; Elizabeth's desire for a period of calm had the exact opposite effect. The maneuverings of the Irish factions, as can be imagined, is extremely complex, the personalities and politics intertwined in multiple ways. The net result, however, was a disaster for English interests, in that it produced an alliance between the O'Neills and the O'Donnells, the dominant factions of eastern and western Ulster, traditional rivals but united in their perception of an encroaching English threat. Hugh Roe O'Donnell was a leader every bit as charismatic as Tyrone. They also made a complementary pair: O'Neill, the senior, was wily, worldly, and a diplomatic strategist; O'Donnell was young, energetic, and a natural military leader.[14] Adding to the potential for conflict was a revival of "Catholic-nationalist" sentiment in Ireland, stoked by a cadre of passionate priests who were also angling to involve the pope and the Spanish in their cause. And, in the reckoning of Hiram Morgan, Irish politics was crippled by a structural, constitutional crisis that placed English and Gaelic orders into an irresolvable conflict. One could no longer be both the English Earl of Tyrone and "the O'Neill" of Ulster; one had to be one or the other. Hugh O'Neill preferred to regard himself as sovereign and not to depend upon English sufferance; to Elizabeth—for whom, and from the first day of her reign, legitimacy and sovereignty were life itself—Tyrone's revolt would appear insufferable. O'Neill was ready to deal with the English, but as equals; Elizabeth demanded submission.

The crisis escalated even as FitzWilliam was replaced by Sir William Russell, whose patron was the Earl of Essex, by then firmly established as the queen's favorite. He was also the emerging leader of the aggressive

Protestant faction at court—by 1594, both Leicester and Walsingham were several years dead—coming to challenge the aging Burghley and his son and political heir Robert as the dominant voice in matters of strategy. The choice of Russell reflected another shift in thinking in London, this time back in favor of a military solution. But his deputyship was nothing short of disastrous. A veteran of the Dutch wars who had distinguished himself at Zutphen and who was briefly governor of the "cautionary town" of Flushing, Russell came to office with inadequate experience, no new troops, and a weak personality; he usually deferred to the fissiparous and indecisive Irish council. With Tyrone operating in the background, the fighting in Ulster was done by proxies. First the Macguires and then O'Donnell broke into open revolt. A government column sent to relieve a siege of Enniskillen Castle was soundly defeated and Tyrone, in an attempt to translate that into a favorable political settlement, travelled to Dublin to confront Russell and the council. But the effort was disrupted by Bagenal, who arrived, under the pretext of a formal "submission," to present a list of accusations of Tyrone's treason- ous behavior. Russell and the council, more impressed with their own weaknesses than Bagenal's charges, equivocated, and Tyrone, reciting Irish complaints and his supposed inability to suppress the legitimate grievances of the Ulstermen, rode off with an impressive propaganda victory. Elizabeth was furious that the leading rebel had been let go: "This slight manner of proceeding both eclipsed the greatness of our estate [in Ireland] and served to glorify [Tyrone], to comfort all his followers and to the amazement of those [in Ireland] who have opposed themselves against him."[15] Indeed, the English display of weakness served to increase the size of the rebel confederacy, which mushroomed through late 1594 and early 1595 to cover not just western but eastern Ulster as well and into northern Connaught. Correspondingly, Irish expectations escalated; they demanded a return to the status quo wherein the English would recognize their sovereignty and, in particular, return the Monaghan lands to the MacMahons.

By April 1595, Elizabeth had had enough. She directed Burghley to proclaim Tyrone a murderer, a traitor, a "known practiser with Spain and other Her Majesty's enemies," and, worst of all, a usurper who would be a sovereign "prince of Ulster." Publication of the charges in Ireland was delayed until June to coincide with the deployment of troops under Sir John Norris, but Tyrone's appearance in person at Clontibret eliminated whatever suspense and pretense remained. The outcome also opened a packet of larger questions. Could any English commander produce a decisive victory in Ireland? Could the aging Elizabeth stay the course until such a result was achieved? Would the Spanish do more than support and occasionally supply the Irish? There was also the question of English political and financial support. Elizabethan England was, in the 1590s, growing weary of war. Whereas, originally, her subjects had been more aggressive than the queen, a decade of maximum effort against Spain had made parliament, in particular, chafe under the burdens of taxation. Moreover, as experience testified, a war in Ireland would not be cheap, easy, or short. England's government had long suffered from divided political and military chain of command in Ireland. There was bad blood between Russell and Norris. Both were difficult personalities and, beyond that, typified the divide between those in the English establishment who were military "enthusiasts" and had connections at court—Russell—and the cadre of cautious long-service military professionals—Norris—who had fought and survived in Flanders and elsewhere for decades. They were also representatives of what were now full-blown factions at court, one of Essex and another of the Cecils. The struggle for power also had begun to anticipate Elizabeth's death and the likely accession of James Stuart, the son of Mary Queen of Scots and coming to maturity as James VI north of the border, as the next English king.

Tyrone also posed a new kind of military threat in Ireland. Due to the modern methods and firepower that Tyrone had introduced to complement the traditional strengths of Irish forces, the prospects for a decisive battlefield encounter were slim, at least without an arduous campaign of occupation and irregular skirmishing that caged the Irish and left them with no other choice. Such a war would require investments in men, money, time, and, most of all, royal patience. And what the Spanish might do was hard to assess. Philip II was nearing seventy and, in his quests to extirpate Protestantism, become the dominant power in Europe, and drive the Ottomans out of the Mediterranean, had kept Spain constantly at war, spending the treasures shipped from his American empire many times over and causing multiple bankruptcies. Ireland might be an opportunity to do unto Elizabeth what she had done to him in supporting the Dutch, but it also might be an opportunity to cut a deal that acknowledged respective spheres of influence and permitted the exhausted great powers to recover.

To be sure, the Tyrone confederacy faced immense challenges as well, both political and military. Though O'Neill had, over the years, established himself as the primary power in Ulster, the very nature of Gaelic politics meant that he had to cajole, persuade, and occasionally intimidate more than simply command. O'Donnell was himself a regional overlord managing yet another coalition. As the rebellion spread from Ulster down to Connaught, it became more powerful but less cohesive; a war to preserve the Gaelic order was also a war to preserve the Gaelic disorder. Exploiting their naval mastery, the English might strike at any part of Ireland as opportunity offered. Unity of command literally was impossible for O'Neill and O'Donnell—in keeping with tradition, they took hostages from among the sons of their supposed allies to ensure continued obedience—and unity of effort unlikely over time. Defections, either for purely personal or local reasons or in response to English bribes and pardons, were a continuous worry. Synchronizing military efforts was likewise a challenge, even between the two principal chieftains. And if the English had operational and tactical challenges in subduing a dispersed and seminomadic population and sustaining an occupation in very rough country, O'Neill and O'Donnell had an equal or greater job to do in supplying such armies with the arms and ammunition—particularly powder—that made them more threatening than mere Irish raiders. For such supplies they depended upon the Spanish and thus on an extended sea line of communication.

ENGLISH FAILURES, IRISH SUCCESSES

The big events of 1595, Elizabeth's proclamation and Tyrone's victory at Clontibret, did not produce an immediate eruption of large-scale fighting in Ireland. To begin with, Spain was still the primary enemy for London, and the main effort for the summer campaign season was yet another maritime expedition planned by Sir Francis Drake and William Hawkins, an attempt to realize Drake's dream of seizing and holding Panama and using it as a base of operations. Such a central position in the Caribbean would disrupt the Spanish flow of silver; the isthmus was the key node in transferring the bullion mined in Peru from the Pacific to the Atlantic. Elizabeth also invested heavily in the enterprise, providing the six largest ships in the fleet of twenty-seven and covering two-thirds of the cost. But the expedition—wait for it—was plagued by uncertainty, beginning with the divided command and rivalry between Drake and Hawkins, both of whom were prone to argument. The Spanish were aware of the massive English preparations and readied their fleet in response, a move interpreted in London as indication of another looming invasion. The Drake-Hawkins mission was close to being canceled when the news arrived that a Spanish treasure ship was stranded in Puerto Rico, and that became the new target. Unfortunately, when the English approached the harbor at San Juan, it was at full readiness; Hawkins, who had been sick throughout the Atlantic crossing, promptly died the next day. Nevertheless, Drake pressed what proved to be a very costly and unsuccessful attack. When it failed, he made a stab at Panama, but it too failed; Drake died of dysentery on the trip home.[16]

When the survivors limped their way back to Plymouth, the news of the catastrophe was almost enough to scuttle an even larger maritime expedition outfitting in the late spring of 1596. Reflecting the moment of enthusiasm for maritime strategy, the Lord Admiral Howard, cautious enough in command of the fleet sent out to repel the *Gran Armada* of 1588, had been converted by Drake into an ardent advocate for an offensive, blue-water strategy: "not to fear any invasion but to seek God's enemies and Her Majesty's where they may be found."[17] The admiral was also politic enough to offer joint command to the Earl of Essex, who had made his reputation in the Portugal expedition of 1589. What remained unclear, however, was whether the effort should be aimed at Calais, in support of Henri IV against the Catholic forces in France, or directly at Spain, at Cadiz. By the time Elizabeth had resolved upon a relief of Calais, it had fallen to the Spanish. This in turn sparked renewed indecision, as did reports of yet more naval preparations in Spain. Like the Portugal expedition, the sack of Cadiz was initially reported and spun as a smashing victory, with four Spanish galleons captured and holds filled with plunder, and certainly the dashing earl returned in increased glory as the manifestation of Elizabethan martial virtue. However, the true strategic result was less spectacular—the majority of Philip's navy was elsewhere—and, as in 1589, disillusionment set in. Indeed, the Spanish did mount another armada, only to see it smashed again by the "Protestant wind," this time along the coast of Galicia well before it might have engaged an English fleet. The maritime raiding strategy was given further trial in 1597, but again found wanting.[18] Another cost, this one indirect, was that the series of failures helped to convince the French that they should make a separate peace with Spain. By the Treaty of Vervins of May 1598, England was shorn of its great-power partner and counterweight to Spain on the continent. The mismatch between

Elizabethan geopolitical ambition and its military and financial grasp repeatedly discombobulated strategy-making.

These maritime misadventures imposed substantial opportunity costs on affairs in Ireland; diplomacy and negotiation were all the English could manage and a truce was arranged. This was fine by Tyrone, whose position and confederacy slowly grew. Yet, in the wake of her proclamation and Clontibret, Elizabeth was locked into a hardline negotiating stance that neither her council in Ireland nor her commanders could advance. Tyrone's demands were equally extreme, and not only did the on-the-ground realities in Ulster and elsewhere in Ireland tilt in his favor, but he was in the process of negotiating an alliance with Spain. Philip II sought revenge for Cadiz and dispatched three military missions to Ireland to make preliminary plans for a Spanish invasion.[19] The principal negotiations were conducted quietly by Ensign Alonso Cobos, O'Neill, and O'Donnell. They estimated that a successful intervention would require six thousand Spanish troops and arms for ten thousand Irish. The Irish rebels also offered to make Philip their ruler and to name a viceroy. The war was no longer simply a defense of Gaelic society and political order, a defensive war to preserve traditional ways. It was now an Irish "national" war and threatened to become a part of the Counter-Reformation confessional struggle. Though Irish identities were then powerfully local and a part of the larger European political and confessional struggle, common culture helped to bridge provincial, familial, and clan divides. This "nationalism with Irish characteristics" did give the island a sense of native sovereignty.[20] If combined with Philip's muscular Catholicism, this raised the stakes to a level Elizabeth could no longer ignore.

Following Russell as Elizabeth's viceroy came Thomas Lord Burgh, who arrived in Ireland in May 1597 and was dead by October. The old warhorse Sir John Norris, too, died in September, the effects of old wounds exacerbated by Irish service and exposure. Indeed, the health of Englishmen in Ireland almost inevitably suffered. Though Burgh had but a short tenure and thus made little progress in dealing with Tyrone, he did bring a certain clarity to English military strategy. Perhaps his training as a diplomat made him better at what was becoming a confusing but combustible mix of Irish insurgency overlaid with the prospect of great-power confrontation with Spain. To Robert Cecil, Burgh wrote, "Branches will sprout as long as the root is untouched. Bring the axe thither, and they do wither; lop them, others spring; cut [the root], all decays." In other words, anything less than a direct strike at Tyrone and O'Donnell, and particularly at Tyrone in his Ulster base, would produce only an evanescent effect. Burgh promised to choke and to chew on Tyrone until he was brought down. "I will encamp by him, force him, follow him, omit no opportunity be day or night to prove his quarters. . . . I will, God willing, stick to him and if need be lie on the ground and drink water ten weeks."[21] Burgh's health was too delicate to fulfill such a promise, but he had identified both the nature of the Irish problem—Tyrone's military ability to field and sustain a substantial force that had more conventional capabilities than traditional Irish raiding parties, and the resulting political power among the Irish that such forces gave him—and the solution—persistence in bringing Tyrone to bay. Absent the Tyrone nucleus, the rebellion would dissipate. Of course, putting Tyrone down now also demanded keeping Philip out.

Burgh also helped to enshrine a broader three-part strategy for bridling Ulster. In addition to a direct assault from Dundalk into eastern Ulster, Tyrone's homeland, a supporting effort would drive northward from Connaught toward western Ulster into the Tyrconnell base of O'Donnell, and a third, amphibious assault would sail up Lough Foyle toward Derry and then suppress the surrounding country, home to lesser Irish warlords but also rich pastureland that acted as a kind of support zone for all of Ulster. In some ways, Burgh did no more than codify conventional English operational wisdom, and the challenges of carrying out this concept remained daunting, but the tasks were now explicit and defined. In 1597, in the face of the threat of the Spanish "Second Armada," the seaborne element of the plan was beyond attempt. Moreover, Sir Conyers Clifford had barely been able to stem the tide of rebellion in Connaught proper, and thus his march toward Ballyshannon culminated quickly and he was lucky to get his small column out without being destroyed by O'Donnell, who quickly mustered an overwhelming force in defense. Burgh himself did well. In early July, he set out from Newry toward Armagh, defeating Tyrone's effort to defend at the line of the Blackwater River and building a fortified bridgehead on the south bank that not only covered the approach but made the north bank untenable to the Irish. However, with just three thousand infantry and five hundred horse, Burgh's campaign likewise culminated and could go no farther without resupply and reinforcement; the assault across the river had been a bloody affair that had cost Burgh's brother-in-law, Sir Francis Vaughan, his life. It was not until October 10 that the Blackwater fort was safe, having been held against Tyrone's counterattacks, and resupplied. Burgh's reward was a vicious "Irish ague" that carried him off within three days. Sir Henry Bagenal eulogized Burgh to the queen in terms that expressed the deep disappointment of those most devoted to—and self-interested in—extending English rule in Ireland: "It hath pleased God to take to his mercy my most honourable Lord your Deputy: a gentleman who, for his forwardness and valour in your service, was as zealous in his prosecution thereof as any whatsoever his predecessors in my time and did with as great honour to Your Majesty, during his short continuance, acquit himself in all his actions."[22]

Gracious words, but words that skirted the fact that, in his short continuance, Burgh had only exceeded a very low previous standard. Despite a clear definition of military objectives, in fact the 1597 campaign did nothing of lasting value to bring Tyrone to heel, and London had no option but further appeasement and delay when truce negotiations with the earl opened in December in Dundalk. The talking continued into the spring of 1598, but the military situation continued tilting toward Tyrone, who was building an ever-larger force, and away from the English. The Blackwater fort quickly fell into disrepair, and with Burgh gone, there was no unified leadership; the loyal Old Irish Duke of Ormond conducted the negotiations with Tyrone while de facto military command fell to Bagenal, the marshal.

By the time the truce expired in midsummer, Tyrone felt strong enough not only to lay siege to the Blackwater fort but to send second and third columns to invest the castle at Cavan, directly west of Dundalk, and deep into Leinster, threatening the Pale itself. Elizabeth responded to this danger as best she could, but something less than fifteen hundred reinforcements had arrived in Dublin by the beginning of August. The Duke of Ormond led a successful campaign to secure Leinster, near his own homeland, and left it to Bagenal to relieve and resupply the meager garrison of three hundred at the Blackwater fort. In truth, this advanced post had become as much a burden on the English as it was an irritant to Tyrone. As the veteran soldier Henry Brounker told the younger Cecil, "the place was too little and the garrison too weak" to supply itself when invested by Tyrone, who had no intention of storming the place when he could starve it, and by August the garrison had eaten its horses.[23] Tyrone also could afford to lie in wait for Bagenal's relief column, whose movements he monitored and whose plans could be no surprise.

The predictable ambush was a smashing result for Tyrone. Bagenal had left Newry on August 12 with almost four thousand foot—mostly

Irish but with a seasoning of veterans with continental experience—and a little more than three hundred cavalry, a very small complement of horse to scout hostile country. He rested at Armagh the next day then moved toward the river, knowing he faced the prospect of a major encounter. Bagenal divided his force in three groups of two regiments each, intending that, when the certain ambush came, each group had sufficient power to defend itself and that substantial reinforcements would be in close support; he feared having a larger force caught in compartmented terrain and cut up in detail as had happened at Clontibret. But gaps between groups inevitably opened, and Tyrone intelligently had posted what also was a numerically superior force, with Tyrone himself directing the attack on Bagenal's left flank and O'Donnell the right. The initial encounters were by fire, and it was one-way traffic: Tyrone's front was protected by a bog and O'Donnell's by a wooded plantation.

Shortly after crossing the "Yellow Ford" over a brook, Bagenal's leading regiment, under Colonel Richard Percy, found its way blocked by an extended trench four feet deep and five feet wide. Percy's entire regiment was under fire as it struggled to get itself and its artillery across the brook and past the trench. The guns stuck in the soft ground and eventually a wheel came off the heaviest and the oxen pulling it were shot down. As it struggled forward, the regiment became increasingly disorganized, losing many of its musketeers when they exhausted their powder. The Irish charged with both infantry and cavalry and destroyed Percy's regiment even within sight of the fort. Bagenal himself was with his regiment, second in line behind Percy. Instead of concentrating his entire force, he rushed to reinforce Percy's remnants, aggressively leading forward a small section of cavalry. The marshal was shot in the head and killed immediately, and his regiment too was broken up and slaughtered.

With Bagenal dead, command of the column devolved to Sir Thomas Wingfield, who commanded a regiment in the main body. Retreat was the only option. Wingfield told his leading commander, Colonel Henry Crosby, to cover the ford and the withdrawal, but Crosby sent elements forward to try to rescue the survivors of Bagenal's attack, himself becoming embroiled and foiling Wingfield's efforts. Crosby's men, too, then had to be rescued. To make matters worse, a soldier replenishing his supply from one of the powder carts in the main body dropped a match into an open barrel, setting off a tremendous explosion that not only killed more of Wingfield's troops but added to the confusion and terror. And finally, the third element, only dimly aware of events to its front, blundered

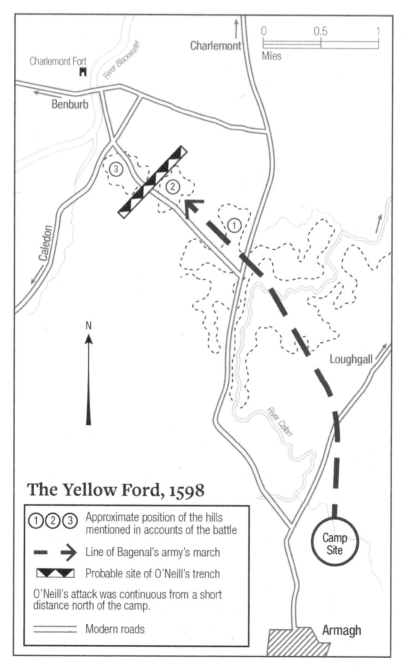

Figure 5.3. The Yellow Ford, 1598.

forward. English command and control had broken down entirely. But for the actions of the rearmost regiment of Colonel Richard Billings, Bagenal's entire force might have been destroyed. As it was, barely fifteen hundred crawled back to Armagh, and the English left thirty officers dead upon the field, beginning with Bagenal but including important northern Irish loyalists. The fort on the Blackwater fell. The only force blocking Tyrone from a march on to Dublin had been wrecked. The Battle of Yellow Ford was the worst disaster ever suffered by the English in Ireland.[24] The English situation across Ireland was dire. Cyril Falls summarizes well: "Tyrone was already master of all Ulster but Newry and Carrickfergus. . . . O'Donnell established himself in complete control of Connaught. . . . In Munster the case was far worse. The province was already seething when Owen MacRory and Richard Tyrrell, Tyrone's best professional commander, burst into it by way of Limerick. . . . The whole elaborate structure of the Munster plantation had collapsed at a stroke. Among those who escaped was Edmund Spenser, but according to tradition one of his boys was burnt to death in the flames of his castle at Kilcoman."[25]

Tyrone, true to type, assumed that his stunning military successes put him in a much-improved position to negotiate with the English. The Dublin Irish council certainly was intimidated and feeling dangerously exposed. Their response to the news of the Yellow Ford was a picture of pusillanimity: "We are to put you in mind how far you may incense Her Majesty's indignation towards you, if you shall do any further distress" to the prisoners taken; conversely, they suggested "how far you may move Her Majesty to renew a favourable conceit of you by using favour to these men." And, with "your ancient adversary the Marshal [Bagenal] being now taken away, we hope you will cease further revenge."[26] No one in Ireland seemed able to see the war as Elizabeth did. By crossing into open rebellion, asserting his sovereignty, and, most important of all, challenging the queen's sovereignty—a personally sensitive issue and fundamental to both her domestic and international security—Tyrone had changed the character of the Irish conflict. The traditional Irish way of war, as habitual to the Irish council as to the Gaelic lords, had been subsumed in a more existential conflict; no compromise would do. As Elizabeth, queen of vitriol as well as of England, wrote to Dublin: "We may not pass over this foul error to our dishonor, when you of our Council framed such a letter to the traitor, after the defeat, as never was read the like, either in form or substance, for baseness, being such as we persuade ourselves, that you will be ashamed of your own absurdities and grieved that any fear or rashness should ever make you authors of an action so much to your Sovereign's dishonour and to the increasing of the traitor's insolency."[27]

As a practical matter, however, Elizabeth had no immediate riposte to Tyrone except to pour in troops as fast as she could. A series of levies was sent from England to Ireland through the winter, as was a contingent of veterans from the Low Countries. Vast contracts for uniforms, arms, and supplies were let and shipping identified for a potential Lough Foyle expedition. These all reflected a major shift in the focus of English strategy, particularly considering that France and Spain had made peace, leaving the Dutch to stand alone on the continent. And the death of Philip II—who, to the end, kept a close rein on Spanish strategy and diplomacy, suggested that Spain might be hamstrung for some years by the succession to his son, who might prove less aggressive both in strategy and in religion.

THE ESSEX AFFAIR

But more than materiel, the English in Ireland lacked leadership, both military and political. Burgh's tenure had been brief, but he had yet to be replaced. Ormond, loyal but suspect as an Old Irish grandee, was clearly not the answer. Neither had been Bagenal, as his past political sins and rash military actions at the Yellow Ford made plain. The Irish council was a weak reed, especially in the current circumstances, and while the English might rent lesser Irish lords for a season or two, they had yet to forge alliances that could weather the mounting defeats. Finally, English strategy in Ireland remained subordinated to the situation at court, on the continent, and at sea; any rumors of a new Spanish fleet created paralyzing fears. Elizabeth's solution, one that reflected her growing personal as well as strategic commitment to Ireland and defied her past pattern of hedged bets, was to call upon the manly personification of English military prowess and Protestant virtue, Robert Devereux, the Earl of Essex, Earl Marshal of England, the tormenter of Spain in Portugal and at Cadiz, Elizabeth's favorite. As Robert Cecil revealed to Sir Conyers Clifford on December 10, 1598, "I think Her Majesty is now resolved of her General to be the Earl Marshal, and he shall have a good army of 12,000 or 14,000 foot and 1,000 horse."[28] No one could now accuse Elizabeth of half measures; she was sending the best she had and supplying him as she had no previous commander—not on the continent, not in any maritime expedition, and never in Ireland. Elizabeth was all in. And unlike his godfather the Earl of Leicester in the Lowlands a decade previously, Essex would be lord lieutenant in Ireland, the undisputed civil and military authority. Essex "left London on 27 March 1599, riding through a double lane of citizens four miles long, who called down the blessings of heaven upon him."[29]

The procession was, perhaps, the high-water mark of Essex's expedition to Ireland. Indeed, the combination of his failures and his paranoia about how they were received in London would soon enough drive him into attempting a kind of coup—also a badly botched adventure—that would cost him his head. Despite the fact that Essex had been the front man at court for an aggressive approach to Ireland and Tyrone, and had assured the queen that a rapid and decisive campaign would suppress Tyrone, he had not wanted to take the command or the responsibility for the war himself. Even before leaving England he began to realize the political, operational, and logistics problems he would confront in Dublin: the limp Irish council, the debilitated state of a much-shrunken army, corruption and incompetence in supply services, the lethal climate. He whined to the privy council that they "might rather pity me than expect extraordinary services from me," that he suffered from a "rheumatic body," and that the queen—so far from setting him up for success, had him "sent out maimed beforehand" by refusing his request to make the marshal of the army at home, Essex's stepfather Sir Christopher Blount, a member of the Irish council. In fact, Elizabeth was quite right to fret that Essex would regard his Irish service as a way to rally and enrich a faction of loyalists, for, despite explicit orders to the contrary, he appointed the young Henry Wriothesley, Earl of Southampton, future patron of Shakespeare, as his senior cavalry commander.[30] Wriothesley was also recently released from prison along with his bride, Elizabeth Vernon, waiting lady to the queen. In sum, Essex and his intimates were behaving little differently than the earl had when he stole away to Portugal in 1589.

Upon arriving in Dublin, Essex promptly forsook, to the relief of the Irish council, his promise to execute the root-and-branch strategy against Tyrone in Ulster; he would "forbear for a while the invasion of Ulster and in the meantime prosecute the rebels of Leinster to see if those inner

**Battles of the
Tyrone Rebellion**

♜	English Forts
✕	Battle Sites

Figure 5.4. Battles of the Tyrone Rebellion.

parts of the Kingdom might be freed."[31] The Lough Foyle excursion would also have to await reinforcements and shipping. Initially, Essex requested only a delay until summer, when sufficient grass and other forage would be available, and the Leinster operation would be small, limited, and culminate in a rendezvous with Sir Thomas Norris, John Norris's son and president of Munster, who would report on the situation in the west. To be fair, the English position in Ireland was at an ebb. On the other hand, it was Tyrone's successes that had driven it there. As long as Tyrone's army was intact and able to take the field, there was no chance of pacifying outlying provinces for long, let alone penetrating central Ulster.

Essex left Dublin on his Leinster expedition on May 9, 1599, planning to be back in Dublin and to launch the Ulster assault by mid-June. Initially, the Leinster operation went quietly. There were no major encounters with rebel forces, but neither did many locals come forward to proclaim their loyalty, as had been hoped; of Ireland's four provinces, English strength in Leinster was the greatest. Yet upon conferring with Sir Thomas Norris at Kilkenny, Essex decided to leave Leinster—not to return to Dublin but to journey further westward into Munster. En route, he laid waste to Cahir Castle and arrived at Limerick on June 4. Again huddling with Norris and now Sir Conyers Clifford, governor of Connaught, Essex went further west in search of a rebel force under James Fitzthomas, fighting some minor skirmishes, wearying his troops, and extending his line of communication but failing to provoke anything decisive. By the middle of June, Essex and his army were in western Munster, with rebel-infested areas in his rear and thus forced to take the long road home. The return march, along the eastern coast of Ireland, was meant to avoid the inland areas that were rebel strongholds and to allow for support from the English navy if need be, but it was a constant invitation to the ambushes at which the Irish excelled. Approaching Arklow, midway between Wexford and Wicklow, in June, the Duke of Ormond's vanguard, hastening toward the safety of the town, became separated from the army's trains, which were lightly guarded. "The rebels saw their opportunity and moved into the attack. For a short while it looked as if there might be a Yellow Ford in the making. Essex and Southampton, however, with a handful of horse, held them off until the rearguard came up. Thereupon the rebels scattered into the shelter of bog and scrubland and the English made their way safely into Arklow. Next day they moved on to Wicklow and a few days later Essex was back in Dublin."[32]

Essex' Leinster-Munster experience cemented his belief that the challenges he faced were all but insurmountable. Having now encountered them at close quarters, the earl wrote to Elizabeth that the Irish were determined "to shake off the yoke of obedience" and "root out all remembrance of the English nation in this kingdom." Tyrone not only had more troops, but they also had "better bodies and perfecter use of arms." These insurgents were very hard to bring to battle, being content "to skirmish and fight loose," but, lacking artillery, were "neither able to force any walled town, castle or house of strength nor keep any that they got." Essex now understood that a successful campaign in Ireland would be long and costly, that the English could not live off the land—indeed, it would be necessary to destroy all crops and cattle to deprive the Irish of sustenance—but would have to be supplied across the sea, and the English navy would have to prevent Tyrone's forces from being supplied by the Spanish. Yet Essex himself had lost heart for Ireland and become paranoid about what might be happening in London and what poison his rival Robert Cecil would be pouring in the queen's ear: "Why do I talk of victory or success? Is it not spoken in the army that Your Majesty's favor is diverted from me? Is it not lamented of Your Majesty's faithfullest subjects both there and here that a [Baron William] Cobham or a [Sir Walter] Ralegh—I will forbear others [such as Robert Cecil] for their places' sake—should have such credit and favours with Your Majesty when they wish the ill success of Your Majesty's most important action?"[33]

The earl made matters worse by writing in a similar vein to the privy council. The prospect of a rapid and decisive campaign, which seemed so vivid in London at the beginning of the year, had vanished somewhere in Leinster. Back in Dublin, Essex had no difficulty in getting the Irish council's agreement that neither a direct assault on Ulster nor a landing in Lough Foyle were possible; of a total establishment of about sixteen thousand, no more than six thousand troops were available for mobile operations. By mid-July, Essex had all but given up.

Worse soon followed. On August 5, Connaught governor Sir Conyers Clifford and his force of almost two thousand were ambushed as they marched through the Curlew Hills. The tactical engagement was becoming depressingly familiar to the English: Clifford's column was exhausted and spread out. A detachment of O'Donnell's retainers, the O'Rourkes, only about a third of Clifford's strength, fell on the vanguard. It soon ran short of powder and fell back in disorder on the main body, spreading confusion and panic. An English cavalry charge allowed for an escape, but not before Clifford, his second-in-command Sir Alexander Radcliffe, and 239 other troops were killed and a further 208 wounded. The psychological defeat was even heavier than the physical loss. Robert Cecil accounted it one of the worst of all Irish disasters, coming as it did when London again was gripped with armada fear and reports of Essex's difficulties were only beginning to trickle in. But it was entirely crushing to Essex. To the privy council, he painfully explained that "instead of thinking this a summer's work or an easy task"—as Essex had boasted before he left England—"Her Majesty and your lordships may believe this is such a war as, if Her Majesty will prosper in it, she must keep a strong army with liberal maintenance" for years to come.[34] Pulling together "the lords and colonels of the army," Essex held a council of war that, not surprisingly, concluded that they could not "advise or assent to the undertaking of any journey far north," be it directly into Tyrone's homeland in east Ulster, from Connaught in the west, or the Lough Foyle amphibious assault in the north; every element of the English plan was abandoned.[35] What Essex did begin to plan was a coup: "He proposed to Southampton and Sir Christopher Blount going over to Wales with 2,000 or 3,000 troops and making good his landing there until he could gather sufficient forces to proceed further, not doubting that his army would soon so increase that he would be able to march on London and make his conditions as he desired."[36]

In a final but fateful gesture, Essex gathered the remnants of his shrinking army to make at least a demonstration on Tyrone's front, or, as he wrote to the queen, to sacrifice himself in some gallant way that might redeem his standing at court. The earl had become desperate, if not quite deranged. Awash in self-pity, he told Elizabeth that "the rebels' pride and successes must give me means to ransom myself, my soul I mean, out of this hateful prison of my body. And if it happens so, your Majesty . . . shall not have cause to mislike the fashion of my death though the course of my life could not please you."[37] But as Essex approached Tyrone's position, it was apparent that the Irishman's force was too strong—he may have enjoyed as much as a four-to-one advantage, including in cavalry—and his positioning, in wooded ground and across a river, all but impregnable. Instead of sacrificing himself, Essex sent Captain Thomas Smith into Tyrone's camp.

The Irish earl, ever ready to preserve his force when a political maneuver might reap a commensurate or greater reward, leapt at the opportunity. He must also, well versed as he was in English domestic politics and faction, have known his man. Tyrone sent a message back saying that if Essex "would be guided by him, he would make him the greatest man in England." This Essex melodramatically misinterpreted as the chance for single combat he had imagined and challenged Tyrone "to meet me in the field so far advanced beyond the head of his *kerne* as myself shall be separated from the front of my troops, where we will parley in that fashion which best becometh soldiers." The next day, when it was apparent that Tyrone had a quite different sort of parley in mind, sending word that he wished to submit to the queen's mercy and discuss terms, Essex took the bait. At a ford in the river Lavan, Essex found Tryone, mounted alone in midstream with the water rising to his horse's belly. Essex, too, pushed his steed into the water, as the river was too wide to parley across.[38]

The two met quite alone, and there is no record of the conversation. But the consequence was all Tyrone could have desired: six weeks' truce, renewable until May 1601; Tyrone to keep all the territory he then held and no new English garrisons established; a commission of both sides established to set borders. Essex, too, in his broken condition, regarded this as a triumph and immediately sent Captain Lawson as a messenger to Elizabeth. Lawson reached court on September 16. The queen packed him back to Ireland the next day, carrying a pair of stinging rebukes to Essex. The first letter, written two days prior to Lawson's arrival, was a biting analysis of Essex's conduct of the campaign. The queen reminded him that Tyrone and Ulster were the objectives and wanted to know why Essex had wasted the season going anywhere else. What was Essex thinking? "How often have you told us that others, that proceeded you, had no judgment to end the war; who often resolved us [that] until Lough Foyle and Ballyshannon were planted, there could be no hope of doing service upon the capital rebels? We must therefore let you know, as it cannot be ignorance, so it cannot be want of means for you had your asking, you had choice of times, you had power and authority more ample than ever any had or shall have."[39] The second letter, written in response to Lawson's report, was harsher still. Elizabeth complained that Essex had kept her in the dark when conferring with "the traitor" and had made a very bad bargain on top of that. "You have prospered so ill for us by your warfare" that the queen disavowed the treaty. To trust Tyrone was "to trust a devil upon his religion. . . . Unless he yield to have garrisons planted in his own country to master him; to deliver O'Neill's sons . . . and to come over to us personally here, we shall doubt you do but patch up a hollow peace."[40] Elizabeth had sent Essex to Ireland to crush an insurgency and force a rebel to submit, and he had negotiated a treaty of equals with a traitor that left the latter independent, politically strengthened, and his troops intact. Hearing his queen's rebuke, Essex himself became a rebel, taking ship for England September 24 along with his closest followers. They botched the coup as badly as they had botched the campaign in Ireland. By September 29 the privy council had condemned him and by October 1 he was under house arrest, though he did not mount the scaffold for another year and a half. R. B. Wernham's timeless judgment on Essex was that "*omnium consensu capax imperii nisi imperasset*": had he not held high command, everyone would have thought him capable of it.[41]

MOUNTJOY TAKES COMMAND

Having seen off Essex, Tyrone went down to Munster for the last months of 1599 to try to undo the little effect that Essex's march had produced; it was, in effect, a victory parade. The O'Neill's position had never been better: the alliance with O'Donnell had made Ulster strong, not just against the English but in recruiting other Gaelic chiefs to his cause. O'Donnell, in particular, had been remarkably successful on his raids into Connaught; the death of Sir Conyers Clifford was more a reflection of the weakness of the English there than a cause of it. The allegiances that Essex had won in the summer of 1599 were grudgingly given and an increasing number of lesser, local leaders across the island were hedging their bets. Those in the south were unwilling to be ruled from Ulster, but Tyrone had also been building support from Spain and from the pope, further making the war for Ireland a part of the larger Spanish bid for European mastery and Counter-Reformation. To transform his ineradicable Ulster insurgency into a larger movement that might achieve a lasting liberty, Tyrone sought outside great-power assistance and to impart ideological cohesion; Irish Catholic practice, like Irish politics and society, was a very local and often helter-skelter affair. The Spanish were increasingly providing supplies, such as powder and some artillery, which gave Tyrone and O'Donnell greater conventional strength and was beginning to make them a threat to English strongholds. And by casting the Irish struggle as not only a defense of Gaelic feudal society but also an offensive to restore Catholicism, Tyrone tried to advance a cause that could help unite otherwise fiercely local and factious Irish leaders.

Tyrone's prime diplomatic directive was to cultivate the Spanish. The notion of doing to Elizabeth in Ireland what she had to him in the Netherlands had an innate appeal to Philip II and interested Philip III even more when he came to power upon his father's death in 1598. The new monarch's initial instincts were defensive—rumors of a brewing English descent like Essex's raid on Cadiz were rife—but in the summer of 1599, he did send a token of a possible future Spanish commitment in the form of a large cargo of arquebuses, pikes, power, lead, and match to the Irish. Perhaps an even more important cargo was Sergeant Major Don Fernando de Barrionuevo, a special envoy sent to sound out Tyrone and O'Donnell's intentions and assess their capabilities while also scouting potential landing points for a Spanish amphibious force. Landing at Killybegs on the north coast of Donegal—"one of the best ports of Ireland . . . able to take a large armada" and easily fortified[42]—Don Fernando met with Tyrone, O'Donnell, and their lieutenants. The Irish reaffirmed their fealty to the Spanish crown, and the Spanish officer lamented the delay in sending troops as well as arms, urging the Irish confederates to remain united until a supporting operation could be mounted.

Tyrone's relationship to the Catholic Church was likewise deepening. In some ways, Counter-Reformation Catholicism mirrored geopolitical Protestantism in finding much of its meaning in public expression and political and martial struggle, and in Ireland this expressed itself in the kind proto-nationalism described above. Tyrone was very conscious of the larger trends shaping his times. But, as Thomas O'Connor convincingly argues, it appears that the earl was something more than a *politique* or a "floating spirit, caught in a political and cultural whorl greater than himself." He was a man who had "experienced some sort of religious conversion in the mid-1590s which left its mark."[43] In sum, for Tyrone as much as any of Elizabeth's most puritanical commanders, the distinction between faith and power was blurred. Certainly Tyrone sought advice and counsel from and employed ardent Catholics as easily as he built a coalition of Gaelic Ulster lords. Father Edmund MacDonnell, the dean of Armagh in exile, was his "ambassador" in Spain, but the indefatigable advocate for intervention in Ireland was Fr. Mateo de Oviedo, the papal nuncio in Spain. A further effort was mounted by Dr. Peter Lombard of Waterford, a graduate of the Jesuit school at Louvain in France which had been established to recruit and train missionaries to England. Louvain produced some of the most wily, committed, and active opponents of Elizabeth. Lombard's job was twofold: convince the pope that Tyrone would prove a better champion of Catholic freedoms in Ireland than the Old English Catholics, and seek papal support, in the form of excommunication and indulgence, for Tyrone's military efforts. Thus by the turning of the year 1600, Tyrone's revolt had grown into an even more complex insurgency. An effort to preserve "Ulster exceptionalism" was giving way to an attempt to provoke a general rising, and the war was becoming a more integral element in the European great-power and confessional struggle.

Spain's calculus also was changing. Although Elizabeth had hoped for a respite from conflict, Philip III was as zealous for Counter-Reformation as his father and his approach to strategy more aggressive; he directed the Duke of Lerma to prosecute a war of "blood and iron" to suppress the continuing Dutch revolt. Lerma's efforts would play a major role in bringing on the Thirty Years' War, the climactic chapter in Europe's wars of religion. Further, Philip III was a kind of bureaucratic reformer. His father had been an extreme micromanager, working excruciating hours to read official correspondence, annotate it, and, when he was ready, respond to it. Indeed, Philip II's lethargic but obsessive command style, in combination with Spain's ingrained habit of multiple councils, had contributed significantly to England's repulse of the *Gran Armada* of 1588. One of the effects of speeding up decision-making was to delegate authority, particularly to Lerma. The duke became Philip III's *valido*, which made him a royal "favorite" much as Essex, but he also played the role of strategic adviser, akin to Cecil. The result was increased interest in Ireland, a project Philip II had long considered but never undertaken.[44]

In the summer of 1599, Philip's military envoy to Ireland, Don Martin de la Cerdà, had returned to Spain with a positive appraisal of the Irish situation, one likely dictated by Tyrone, and on July 1 a junta of councilors presented a memorial, a kind of memorandum for decision, to the king. As John J. Silke observes, it was a succinct statement of the overall strategic rationale for Spanish intervention. As for the English, Ireland was a smaller piece in a larger, global game of power. As things then stood, "the [Spanish] plate fleets were forced to ply out of season in order to avoid the attention of the [English]. This placed a strain upon the [Spanish] royal navy and exposed the ships to risk from storm. Now an expedition to Ireland would set free the coasts of the Spanish empire from attack. . . . . Spain was now in a position, the argument continued, to conduct an offensive war against England; a diversion was the safest, as it was the cheapest and most effective, entry into England."[45]

The memorial offered three other compelling arguments, also likely Tyrone-inspired. To begin with, it was now or never: "If Spain did not answer the Irish pleas, the Irish would be forced to accept terms and thus would be added to Spain's enemies." And aiding the Irish would divert English forces from the Netherlands, "forc[ing] the return of Holland and Zealand to their proper obedience." Lastly, this would be a big reward for a very modest investment. "An army sent to Ireland need consist of only six or seven thousand men: 20,000 Irishmen, most of them armed . . . would be ready to join the Spaniards; no resistance would be offered" and "the sea off the Irish coast was free from rocky shoals." Cerdà's arguments made sense and the council made them forcefully, but Lerma was initially cautious, pleading poverty and that fleet and an invasion force could not be readied in time. After several months' delay, Philip III put his foot down: "This enterprise must so further God's service, and the earnestness and zeal shown by the council for it must so animate those entrusted with its execution as to overcome all difficulties foreseen. I myself will see that the money is provided, even at the expense of what is necessary for my personal state. . . . The expedition must go this year [1600]; to that end, the council will put all in order with the utmost speed."[46]

By luring the new Spanish king to intervene at last, Tyrone had more than doubled down on his rebellion. The prospect of a negotiated settlement with Elizabeth, already faded, was all but gone. A return to the status quo was no longer possible. No longer was the war fought for solely Irish reasons.

Yet what really altered the course of the Tyrone Rebellion was the replacement of Essex with Charles Blount, Lord Mountjoy. At last, Elizabeth had found her general. Though a member of the Essex faction at court, Mountjoy distanced himself—just enough—from the earl's excesses that would soon cost Essex his life. More critically, Mountjoy's energy, adaptability, attention to detail, and persistence made him an almost ideal commander for Ireland. This, too, was the chance he had looked for all his life. Though a distinguished soldier, Mountjoy had served at nearly every echelon of command without ever finding the opportunity for distinction and glory that he, like every Elizabethan courtier-officer, craved. Mountjoy was a close student of the arts of war and a protégé of the crusty professional Sir John Norris, and indeed, Essex had ridiculed him as too bookish—for Mountjoy was as well a discerning theologian—in 1599, when both were candidates for command in Ireland. In sum, Mountjoy could be patient where past viceroys had been in a rush, and Elizabeth, not fearing a rival, could be patient with Mountjoy in ways she never could with his predecessors. It was to prove a winning combination.[47]

Mountjoy arrived in Ireland in late February 1600 to find Tyrone at the zenith of power and influence and on the loose in Munster. Essex's final appreciation of the situation had been accurate: the English still controlled the fortified towns but not much else, and the Irish nobility, both Gaelic and Anglo-Irish, had lost confidence in and even some respect for English arms. Tyrone had more manpower, and his hardy kerne were better adapted to life in the field than the English. Their migratory ways and cattle herds gave the Irish a mobility the English could not match. A serious Spanish intervention could give the Irish the ability to take the towns, which were, in many cases, already trading with and giving succor to the rebels. Nonetheless, the English retained critical advantages. Their command of the sea was unlikely to be challenged—though armadas had been a source of panic, they had yet to prove a source of success for the Spanish—which gave them operational advantages and a strategic depth that would be all but impossible for Tyrone to match. So, too, the English cavalry, heavily armed, riding powerful English horses much larger than Irish breeds, and equipped with the stirrups that made the horses a far more stable fighting platform, was an enduring tactical advantage. Whichever side could make time their ally would prevail.

There were other subtle advantages that Mountjoy could count. Perhaps the largest would prove to be a very able secondary commander in the person of Sir George Carew, who had been named president of Munster. Carew was a competent soldier and clever politician, in both the Irish and English sense. He developed a knack for exploiting the differences among local Irish lords and between the locals and Tyrone, and Carew was also intimate with the Cecil faction at court and a frequent correspondent with Robert Cecil. Over time, Mountjoy would learn to trust Carew, not an easy thing to do or something that an Essex could have done, and to allow Carew to exercise independent authority and military initiative. He also was well served by (and patient with) the querulous Sir Henry Dowcra, who would conduct the long-planned amphibious assault up Lough Foyle; by Sir Arthur Chichester, who would lead a second thrust into Ulster from Carrickfergus in the northeast near modern Belfast; and by the Earl of Ormond, the stout, consistently loyal and charismatic Anglo-Irish lord. Indeed, Mountjoy's "command style" became a judicious mix of attention to detail and delegation. He had an insatiable but not paralyzing appetite for intelligence. Further, he was zealous in tending to his troops' morale and made it his business to make constant circulation among them. In sum, he would prove an extremely careful commander, cautious until the moment when he saw opportunity and then willing to run a large risk for a large reward.

Nonetheless, it was not until September that Mountjoy felt comfortable making a foray toward Ulster and that campaign proved a fizzle. Tyrone had fortified the mile-long Moyry Pass with three lines of trenches between two hills, covered by thorn bushes in front—nature's barbed wire—and by musketeers on the flanks, and the approaches were soddened by fall rains. On October 2, Mountjoy launched an assault that eventually drove the Irish from the first of the three lines, but at great cost. Though Tyrone withdrew to Armagh and Mountjoy razed the defenses, the English lacked the strength to push farther north. Mountjoy had to content himself with buttressing the outpost at Newry, well beyond the pass but only halfway to Armagh, which had been the original goal of the campaign.

Nor did other elements of the Ulster plan achieve more than mixed success. Hopes for a thrust toward Ballyshannon, on the south coast of Donegal Bay, were scrapped in June for want of troops. Sir Henry Dowcra had come ashore at the tip of Lough Foyle in mid-May and by May 22 had moved inland to Derry, which would become his main base of operations and headquarters. He was briefly opposed by O'Donnell's forces, but when Hugh Roe withdrew to the west, Dowcra tried to push further inland. O'Donnell returned at the end of June and, in a spectacular raid, carried off two hundred English cavalry horses, an action in which Dowcra suffered a javelin wound. More seriously, Dowcra's men began to go sick by the scores. He had, at last, planted a foot in the very north of Ulster and secured a useful port, but he was too weak to do much more. The real fruit of the effort was political; lesser Irish chieftains began to defect. First came Art O'Neill, son of the clan chief displaced by Tyrone. Then, in October, came Neill Garve (Anglicized from the Irish "Garbh," or "the Rough") O'Donnell, brother-in-law to Hugh Roe. This was a much more substantial coup than O'Donnell's horse-thievery, though the haughty and acquisitive Neill Garve would eventually prove too ambitious for the English. "I cannot compare him to anything more like than a quince," wrote Dowcra. "Let him be sugared and dressed with much cost and he will be good for somewhat, but undoubtedly, to speak truth of the man, I am of the opinion that the Queen must of necessity bestow more upon him than his body is worth before she shall reap any good of his service; although the man is valiant . . . he is subject, to extreme covetousness whether he be rich or poor, and unseasoned by any manner of discipline, knowledge, or fear of God."[48] But in Ireland, where to English minds the enemy of an enemy was a friend, Neill Garve was good enough. The English gave Neill Garve license to raid throughout O'Donnell country, and in one action at Lifford he killed Hugh Roe's younger brother Manus.

The year's biggest successes in Ireland came to Sir George Carew. Once planted in Munster, he quickly grasped that Tyrone's position there was a hollow one, a reflection of past English weakness rather than rebel strength. There were three real powers in Munster. One was Florence MacCarthy, a wily diplomat himself who proved content to watch and wait; at the end of October, MacCarthy professed loyalty to Elizabeth and was given a safe-conduct. The second was Dermot O'Connor, an able soldier but, in Carew's judgment, a Connaught mercenary who could be bought. Carew's scheme fell through, but O'Connor was disgraced and withdrew to Connaught. Last and most worrisome was James Fitzthomas, known as "the Sugane Earl" (*sugane* being the Gaelic word for "straw rope") because he had attempted to assume the old Geraldine title of Earl of Desmond, a name that still carried great weight. Carew had hoped to use O'Connor to capture Fitzthomas. When that misfired, he had the true Earl of Desmond, kept in the Tower of London during his youth, brought back to Ireland in hopes of making him a puppet. At first, all went according to plan, but the young Desmond made the fatal mistake of openly worshipping as the Protestant he was raised to be, thus losing any credibility among the strongly Catholic Geraldine faithful in southern Munster. Nonetheless, Carew chipped away at the Sugane Earl's position, throwing all his available field force against another Geraldine leader, Edmond Fitzgibbon, forcing his submission after a quick siege of his castle at Kilmallock, centrally positioned between Limerick on the Shannon and Cork, on the sea.

A final distinguishing feature of Mountjoy's strategy was that winter saw no break in his military efforts. In the Christmas season of 1600, he concentrated on clearing the Wicklow area, the mountainous region south of Dublin, home to the O'Byrne clan and a source of constant raids into the Pale. By doing so, he surprised the O'Byrnes, a neat trick in itself, and nearly captured their chief, Phelim McFeagh, scaring him to the point that he would make submission in the spring. The campaign thus secured a limited but important objective that would pay dividends in the coming year. Mountjoy's efforts also impressed his subordinates. "I never saw any L[ord] Deputy take the like pains in my life," wrote Captain Nicholas Dawtry, a hardy professional soldier, to Robert Cecil, "for he gives his body no rest, and although he were a very sickly gentleman in England yet he keepeth health here the best of any man, besides that he is endued with notable virtues befitting a general in such things to discern between man and man. . . . He hath secrecy in so excellent a measure that his intent cannot be discovered before it is done; also he hath affability to please all men of service and severity to make the wicked live in fear of him."[49]

But perhaps the biggest success of Mountjoy's initial campaigning was on the home front. Though there was genuine progress in Ulster and across Ireland, the achievements could look much smaller from the vantage point of London. The niggling touched a nerve of petulance in Mountjoy. More seriously, he was in deep danger of becoming embroiled with the Essex plot; his long-running and deeply passionate affair with Essex's sister Penelope, Lady Rich—herself knee-deep in the brewing Essex coup—made him suspect. And indeed, Essex had reached out to Mountjoy for support that, if given, would have been treasonous. Thus, Mountjoy wrote to Robert Cecil in late November to preempt, reassure and to warn: "I am sure I can never be unfaithful to Her [Majesty], but for all other things wherein I have hitherto extraordinarily precise, I will no longer undertake for myself, for I do not see it marked or at least regarded, and the general infection of this kingdom is such as I am afraid of myself if you keep me here [in Ireland] any longer. And yet while I am honest (as that shows me to be so yet) I give you this warning of it."[50]

In return, Elizabeth wrote a remarkably—given her past frustrations with Irish deputies and the percolating Essex plot that would soon come to a head—encouraging and almost self-deprecating response. Mountjoy had previously complained that his position was little better than that of a scullion. Elizabeth replied with a gentle jest: "Mistress Kitchenmaid . . . with your frying pan and your other kitchen stuff [you] have brought to their last home more rebels and passed greater breakneck places than those that had promised more and did less. Comfort yourself therefore that in this that neither your careful endeavor nor dangerous travails nor heedful regards to our service . . . could ever have been bestowed upon a Prince that more esteems them." The queen's conclusion expressed a willingness to be patient and a confidence in a commander that can only have confirmed Mountjoy in his methodical approach to the war: "No man can rule so great a charge without some errors, yet you may assure yourself I have never heard of any had fewer." Elizabeth signed herself "Your Sovereign that dearly regards you."[51]

THE SPANISH TAKE KINSALE

Securing his London front was essential for Mountjoy in view of the trial to come: a Spanish armada—the sixth, counting the expeditions of 1579 and 1580—would at last put ashore a substantial force to create a second front in Britain itself. Philip II had formally agreed to assist Tyrone in 1596, and his governor in the Netherlands, Cardinal Archduke Albert, had prepared a "Discourse on Diversion," arguing that the road to England must run through Ireland, at least as long as Flanders was contested ground.[52] The conclusion of a peace with France at Vervins in 1598—a treaty that left Elizabeth the odd one out in West European politics—and with Savoy in January 1601 created a window of opportunity for Spain to play the Ireland card while restoring its larger military strength and financial health. Several preparatory missions had been dispatched to the Irish rebels, but Philip II's death left the Spanish enterprise of Ireland in his son's hands. Mountjoy's successes of 1600 had begun to tip the balance in Ireland away from Tyrone, and by early 1601, it was now or never for the Spanish in Ireland.

Spanish operational planning was as indecisive as Spanish strategy-making. A rough outline was drafted in 1600, and the assessment was that to put six thousand infantry ashore and secure a port would require about fifteen thousand tons of shipping with twenty-five hundred sailors and fifteen hundred further troops to guard the ships, even if they rapidly unloaded and returned to Spain.[53] But a practical puzzle was where to land, and the solution also depended on the size of the force. Tyrone's son Hugh O'Neill, then in Spain, argued the family position: if the landing force was as large as planned—six thousand or more—it should land in Munster, in the south of Ireland, which offered more prizes and was easier to operate in and live off of. Moreover, the landing would reignite the rebellion in Munster, rousing the MacCarthys and the Desmond loyalists. However, the landing force needed to be at least that large to sustain itself and the military initiative until the Ulstermen could march south to rendezvous. A smaller force should sail farther north to Donegal Bay, link up with Tyrone and O'Donnell, and help them break the noose that Mountjoy was tightening around Ulster.

Throughout the spring and early summer, the invasion force was assembled at Lisbon; troop strength was set at six thousand, even though it would be impossible to ship them all at once. In what was to prove an unfortunate arrangement, Don Diego de Brochero y Añaya was appointed naval commander and Don Juan del Águila captain general of land forces; each was supreme in his element but neither exercised overall power, and though the two had fought together in France and were experienced professionals, each was a strong-willed personality. Even before the armada sailed for Ireland, an argument arose over where to land. Águila, for whom England was the primary enemy, favored a landing somewhere in the St. George's Channel, to use southeast Ireland as the jumping-off point for an invasion of England. He also thought a landing in Munster, in southwest Ireland, was the worst option, that the local Irish chiefs would hedge their bets and a Spanish force would have to dig in and support itself until relieved by Tyrone and O'Donnell. Brochero thought the St. George's Channel too dangerous—it was shallow, roiled by unpredictable currents, and most exposed to the English navy—and favored a landing in Donegal Bay. The two were at such loggerheads that the decision was referred to Philip and his council, which refused to intervene except to say that the final choice was to be Águila's. Further complicating the command arrangements and the argument over where to disembark was the arrival in Lisbon, in early August, of the papal nuncio Mateo Oviedo and Don Martin de la Cerdà. These two, strongly attached to the Irish rebellion, presumed to speak for Tyrone and O'Donnell and insisted that the southern Irish would rally to the cause and thus Munster—and particularly the port of Cork—was the best option. Again the decision was sent back to the king. Afraid of the loss of papal support, Philip and his council now gave Oviedo and Cerdà the deciding voice. Águila gained one concession, however: because Cork was well fortified, he strongly objected to attacking there, and Oviedo approved the smaller port of Kinsale, just to the south and west of Cork, as an alternative.[54]

The armada for Ireland put to sea at first light on September 3, 1601. Thirty-three ships, including thirteen hired for the mission, carried just over 4,400 infantry but only six pieces of artillery and supplies of powder, match, and lead that were short of likely requirements. Brochero, Águila, and Oviedo rode in the flagship San Andres; Cerdà was at the last left behind, having contracted malaria during the long wait in Portugal. The Spanish viceroy, Don Cristóbal de Castel-Rodrigo, was relieved to see them go. He wrote to Philip's secretary to complain about "what an amount of work it had been . . . to send off that armada under two different heads, two men besides so opposite in their humors. One wanted to go north, the other to the south, while both . . . rested as much as they could. And yet there was no end to the demands they made. . . . Never, never advise the king to divide a command so equally between two leaders, neither of whom had any respect for the other."[55]

The fleet enjoyed a fair wind and week later approached Ireland. This provoked a final showdown about where to land in a meeting called by Brochero on the flagship. In addition to the military principals—minus the senior regimental commander, who also had fallen out with Águila—master pilots and sailors familiar with the Irish coast were summoned to attend. Any hope of further communication with Tyrone and O'Donnell had evaporated, and the weather was becoming tempestuous and the winds turning against the Spanish. Despite the fact that he was falling ill, Oviedo's opinion carried the day, and Brochero, fearing the effects of a storm on the fleet, ordered his captains to rendezvous at Kinsale and, if that were impossible, still farther down the coast at Castelhaven.

On the evening of September 27, the Spanish came into sight of the Irish coast and took on pilots to make a landing the following morning. That night, however, the storm finally struck, driving two galleons—the Spanish naval leaders had insisted on using these large but cumbersome ships—and six smaller craft away from the main body and dispersing the landing force. The missing ships carried a number of senior military commanders, most other munitions and match, and eight companies of infantry, 674 men in all. Águila struggled ashore at Kinsale on October 2 and within a week had assembled a force of just less than 3,400. Things immediately seemed to go worse when he learned that the leaders of the MacCarthy and Desmond factions were in English custody. Águila's fears of Munster perfidy then took on a self-fulfilling character when he rejected the offer of two thousand men from another chieftain, Daniel O'Sullivan Beare, who promised—in return for arms for half his men—to block the likely English routes of march and hold off a siege of Kinsale until Tyrone and O'Donnell could march southward.

Ruling the local Irish out of his reckoning and commanding such a small, poorly armed, and poorly provisioned force, without *maestres de campo* (tactical, regimental commanders), Don Juan dismissed the notion of taking the field and decided to fortify himself as best he could until he was reinforced by the armies of Ulster and Spain.[56]

The Spanish landing had added a new and powerful piece to the Irish chessboard, but even had Águila's operation been flawless, it would not in itself have been decisive. The question now was who would react first and best to the changed circumstances: Tyrone, O'Neill and Philip III, or Mountjoy and Elizabeth.

The English had long understood that the Spanish might intervene in Ireland and in early 1601 had accurate intelligence reports of the expedition fitting out in Lisbon. Robert Cecil, as prudent and organized as his father had been, made a note in late April that he must find shipping for another four thousand troops to Ireland. Mountjoy and Carew, with whom he was developing a good partnership, reasoned their way through the likely Spanish courses of action, including likely landing spots. While a landing in Ulster would give the most direct aid to Tyrone, adding another three hundred miles of sea travel, exposure to interception by the English navy, and the limits of northern ports suggested that a landing in the south was more likely; Carew considered Cork the best bet. Moreover, as the English themselves had come to learn, onward operations once ashore in rugged Ulster would be a challenge to the Spanish. Donegal Bay might seem an attractive port, but it was ringed by hilly country; the terrain that helped to keep the English at bay would tend to bottle up the Spanish.

At the same time, Mountjoy, having campaigned through the winter and determined to keep constant pressure on Tyrone, had no thought of simply waiting on the Spanish. The forces in preparation in Lisbon might be sent to the Netherlands instead of Ireland, and Mountjoy thought he might be able to snuff out the rebellion in Ulster before the end of the year: Dowcra's efforts at Lough Foyle and Derry were beginning to bear fruit, and Sir Arthur Chichester had made the most of limited resources at the Carrickfergus garrison, driving Tyrone's nephew, Brain MacArt O'Neill, well to the west and away from the coast. These three lines of attack into Ulster—including Mountjoy's own drive from the south—were all aimed directly at Tyrone's heartland, and though Tyrone's host was larger, it was unwieldy, and the earl would be hard-pressed to respond to attacks coming from every point of the compass.

On June 8, Mountjoy, with a force of about three thousand, again approached the Moyry Pass. The defenses were not manned, but Mountjoy had to halt to await supplies. Over the next week, he formulated an ambitious plan, telling Dowcra that, while Mountjoy held Tyrone's attention, Dowcra should if practicable first strike southwest to sieze Ballyshannon rather than having Carew attack northward from Connaught. Dowcra's thrust also would have cut off O'Neill, thus dividing the Ulster armies, and posed a threat to any Spanish landing in the west. Once at Ballyshannon, Dowcra was then to turn east to rendezvous with Mountjoy. Despite the likelihood of a Spanish landing in Munster, Mountjoy told Carew to first concentrate on Connaught. Dowcra complained that he lacked the strength to take and hold Ballyshannon and further that he lacked the match needed for his muskets and therefore could only hold what he had already taken. With deflated ambition, Mountjoy nonetheless kept pushing northward, forcing Tyrone to give battle at Benburb, which lies about halfway between Armagh and Tyrone's seat at Dungannon but is also north of the Blackwater River. The engagement was a tactical draw but the net effect a big win for Mountjoy; he held the garrisons established through the previous campaign and the winter and planted a further one at the Moyry Pass. Operational patience, persistence, and superior logistics capacity allowed Mountjoy to translate English advantages as none of his predecessors could.[57]

On August 12, Robert Cecil in London received reports of the Spanish invasion fleet at sea. The gale that struck the Spanish likewise delayed the transmission of this intelligence to Ireland, but when alerted Mountjoy moved immediately southward, to Kilkenny, from where he could quickly respond wherever the Spanish might come ashore. At Kilkenny Castle he met with much of his senior command on September 22, including Sir George Carew; the Earl of Ormond; and Sir Richard Wingfield, the marshal of English forces in Ireland. The next day, word arrived that Kinsale was the Spanish target. With the crisis approaching, Mountjoy was at his very best. He wrote to Elizabeth with an appreciation of a great challenge but a clear mind. The moment of decision was at hand, and the enemy in his sights:

If we beat [the Spanish], let it not trouble you though you hear all Ireland doth revolt, for (by the grace of God) you shall have them all return presently with halters about their necks: if we do not, all providence bestowed on any other place is vain. . . . I apprehend a world of difficulties with as much comfort as ever poor man did, because I have now a fair [opportunity] to show how prodigal I will be of my life in every adventure that I shall find to be for the service of my dear Mistress, unto whom I am confident God hath given me life to do acceptable service, which when I have done I will sing *Nunc dimitis* [sung at evening prayer, anticipating one's death].

To Cecil, after a full accounting of the powers of the Spanish and Irish, Mountjoy expressed a similar confidence more colloquially: "And now, Sir, that you know (as I hope) the worst, I cannot dissemble how confident I am to beat these Spanish Dons as well as ever I did our Irish Macs and Os."[58]

MOUNTJOY AND O'NEILL RESPOND

During most of her reign, Elizabeth had grown used to, if still exasperated at, field commanders promising rapid victory while delivering disaster then blaming others—unscrupulous colleagues and contractors, rivals at court, anything and everything. She had also grown used to deconstructing such excuses and had come to second-guess and scrutinize every detail of every report. She had learned the need to keep her generals, admirals, and gentlemen adventurers on a short leash. Yet upon receiving Mountjoy's report to Cecil, she ordered it read aloud in council, "as being written in a style wherein she discerned both the strong powers of your own mind in promising yourself all happy success (against such an enemy) and the lively affection you bear to her person."[59] Very late in life, the queen had found a general, and, for once, she felt she could loosen the choke chain. She was not alone in her confidence. A bill was rapidly brought to parliament, which had heretofore begun to chafe at the endless expense of Elizabeth's wars, for supplemental funding and passed through the House of Commons by December 5. With the real prospect

Figure 5.5. The Road to Kinsale.

of dealing a decisive blow to Tyrone and a major defeat to Spain, the English political nation was of one mind.

Mountjoy also moved rapidly to assemble a force to lay siege to Kinsale, dispatching Wingfield and other lieutenants to the Pale and Ulster to rally troops and ship artillery. He himself went first to Cork and by September 29 was reconnoitering the Spanish position at Kinsale. There was little Mountjoy could do until he collected his forces, but he wanted to attack before Tyrone and O'Donnell arrived, keep the Spanish penned in, and deter any potential uprising in Munster. Even with a fraction of his troops on the scene, Mountjoy made camp just half a mile from Kinsale. Whatever its value as a harbor, the town sat in a bowl and was not an easily defended position; the ridgelines that anchored Mountjoy's lines, however, were naturally so. The town also sat a mile or so up the Bandon River, northwest from the harbor bay. To the southeast, but on opposite sides of the river and not easily supplied or supported from the town, lay two fortified promontories, Castle Park on the west bank and Ringcurran Castle on the east bank. Mountjoy's camp lay to the north of town, where two further hills overlooked Águila in Kinsale. With but thirty-five hundred troops, the Spanish commander lacked the strength—and after his trials, perhaps the energy—to mount a forward defense. Late in October, English shipping arrived with artillery and entrenching tools, and Mountjoy occupied Spittle Hill due north of Kinsale and began digging parallel trenches. By the end of the month, he had assembled a force of six thousand foot and six hundred horse.[60]

The Irish did not and probably could not match the urgency and efficiency of Mountjoy's movements; O'Neill and O'Donnell were able to move about Ulster with ease and subsist their troops there, but moving a large body the full length of the island was unprecedented. While the rapid contraction of the English force posture across Ireland—Mountjoy summoned forces from Ulster, Connaught, and Leinster—made it safe for Tyrone and O'Donnell to go to Kinsale, the very nature of their insurgency helped to betray their cause. Irish command was consensual and contingent, as, to a large degree, were the terms of military service; Tyrone had created and led an exceptionally dangerous irregular force, but not a centrally controlled professional one. His line of march would be long and, even if successful, would leave his lines of communication to Ulster exposed; Mountjoy enjoyed both interior land lines and control of the sea. Moreover, for both O'Donnell and Tyrone, the first order of business was to try to stabilize the situation in Ulster; Mountjoy's incursions into Tyrone country and the multiple English toeholds in Tyrconnell were existential threats. But O'Neill and O'Donnell could hardly leave the Spanish by themselves in Kinsale; this was the larger war they had wanted.

It was O'Donnell who moved first. Águila had sent word upon landing that "we are awaiting your most illustrious highnesses" at Kinsale, and O'Donnell broke off his siege of Donegal Abbey directly.[61] Like Mountjoy, O'Donnell believed that the moment of decision was at hand, and the point of decision was Kinsale: "He thought it of little importance that the English should remain or dwell in the castles which they had seized in his territory, for he was sure they would abandon them at once if the Irish and the Spaniards were victorious in the contest with the Lord Justice at Kinsale."[62] At the same time, O'Donnell was losing ground across Tyrconnell, both to the English and his cousin Neill Garbh; the speed of his response was both virtue and necessity. He summoned his retainers and the troops and those of the O'Rourkes, a total of perhaps fifteen hundred infantry and four hundred horse, to Ballymote in County Sligo in the first week of November and prepared to march southward. His track took him through the eastern part of Connaught. Crossing the Shannon, O'Donnell was joined by Captain Richard Tyrrell, adding another five hundred foot soldiers and two hundred light cavalry, but his attempts to seduce the lords of western Leinster went unrequited. He paused briefly at Athlone in hopes of a rendezvous with O'Neill, but Tyrone was still assembling his forces and O'Donnell soon crossed into County Tipperary in north Munster.

By contrast, O'Neill had doubts about whether he should lead his army in person to Kinsale. He was said to have a superstition based on a prophecy that he would lose his life in Munster, and although he was under pressure from the English in Ulster, his situation was better than O'Donnell's. To begin with, he needed to decide who would rule in his absence and who would succeed him if indeed he were to die at Kinsale. In this he took a risk, too, naming his teenage son Hugh as tanist, roughly the Gaelic equivalent of being named heir apparent, leaving aside his brother Cormac, who had previously been Tyrone's deputy. Skirting the English posts in eastern Ulster, O'Neill assembled his army at Lough Ramor in County Cavan. It took him the better part of a month to do so. Many of his men were reluctant to go so far from home and, of course, the campaign would far surpass O'Neill's logistical capacity. Sir Geoffrey Fenton, the secretary of state for Ireland, had a hard time believing that O'Neill would undertake such a risky march; as Mountjoy moved toward Kinsale, he also feared O'Neill might turn east to make a large raid into the Pale.[63] By the second week of November, O'Neill met his troops—2,500 foot and 550 horse, though the English thought the force almost half again as large—at Lough Ramor and in short order plunged southward toward Munster.

In addition to containing and besieging the Spanish in Kinsale, Mountjoy wished to forestall the rendezvous of his enemies, and the gap between O'Donnell's march and O'Neill's departure seemed to offer a chance not only to prevent the juncture of the Irish and Spanish but to defeat the Ulstermen in detail. Thus, as O'Donnell began to move south, Mountjoy dispatched Sir George Carew with two thousand infantry and four hundred horse from Cork to intercept Red Hugh, and on his way to Ardmayle Castle near Cashel in eastern Tipperary, he had picked up additional forces from the Pale. But Carew moved cautiously; he believed—thanks to poor intelligence and Ulster propaganda—that O'Donnell had three times his strength. And Carew's troops included Irish militia as well as Irish nationals among his regulars. Carew assumed O'Donnell would wait for O'Neill before pushing farther south, and, with the Sieve Phelim mountains between his army and O'Donnell's and the few tracks soaked with late November rains, Carew was content to block and wait.

Thus Carew was caught entirely by surprise when O'Donnell took advantage of a snap freeze to slip his force through the hills south and west of Cashel and into Limerick, marching twenty-seven miles in a single day. With shame, but also with admirable accuracy, he reported to Mountjoy, "This long march is incredible but, upon my reputation, I do assure your Lordship it is true. When I went from your Lordship, the mountain which they passed was not passable by reason of great rain; and so did all the noblemen of these parts tell me. . . . But the traitors . . . seeing an opportunity offered by this great frost, marched over that unpassable mountain, and by their infinite long march got the start of us."[64] Carew made a perfunctory pursuit as far as the abbey of Owney in Limerick, but, afraid that O'Donnell would beat him to Kinsale, sprinted back to Mountjoy's camp within four days, where he sought to restore his honor by asking his chief if he might lead the assault once the Spanish fortifications were breached.

He needn't have worried. Instead of speeding to the relief of the Spaniards in Kinsale, O'Donnell continued westward, rallying support in Munster and eliminating isolated English outposts. Moreover, these maneuvers opened the line of march of O'Neill as he moved his force southward. For his part, Mountjoy had begun the methodical process of strangling Águila, breaching the town walls, beating back a brief but violent Spanish counterattack, and capturing the two forts guarding Kinsale harbor. In this last effort Mountjoy was assisted by the fleet of six warships under Sir Richard Leveson, dispatched from the port of Rochester on the Medway. Leveson's arrival proved even more timely when, a week later, an additional Spanish force landed slightly to the west of Kinsale, at Castlehaven. Commanded by Admiral Don Pedro de Zubiaur, this included six ships and six hundred fifty men from the original invasion force, but which had been blown off course, reorganized at Coruña, and quickly returned to Ireland but was prevented by adverse winds from entering Kinsale. Upon receiving the news of Zubiaur's landing, Leveson divided his fleet, leaving a few at Kinsale but taking his five-hundred-ton flagship *Warspite* and escorts to strike at Castlehaven. In a short but sharp engagement, Leveson forced four of Zubiaur's fleet aground. Although Zubiaur had gotten most of his embarked troops ashore along with a few cannon and Leveson's fleet was somewhat battered, the English retained control of the sea.[65]

Zubiaur's force, though small, was nonetheless a magnet for the lords of West Cork to rally to the rebel cause. The O'Driscoll clan handed over several castles in the area and Daniel O'Sullivan Beare added several thousand followers, although many of them remained unarmed. However, Zubiaur believed his principal mission was to secure the Castlehaven harbor for the long term rather than putting immediate pressure on Mountjoy, who, though threatening Águila in Kinsale, now might be trapped by the Irish coming from the north and west. In the end, Zubiaur would only contribute 120 Spanish with the West Cork Irish—a total of something less than a thousand—to the army of O'Donnell and O'Neill in the week before Christmas. "I am giving arms to those who lack them," he reported to Philip III, "and powder and biscuit—all that they can carry." He also knew that wasn't enough and warned the Spanish king that any decisive victory in Ireland was only possible "if your majesty speedily sends an abundance of arms, ammunition, and provisions. Let not your majesty let slip this great opportunity."[66]

But Mountjoy, too, had lost the opportunity to finish off the Spanish quickly or prevent the junction of the Irish earls and their Munster supporters. The English had received about six thousand reinforcements, but the winter weather, lack of food and forage, and appalling sanitary situation in their camps above Kinsale—now with fortifications facing northward to keep the Irish out as well as circling the town to the south to keep the Spanish in—essentially eliminated the effect of the fresh troops. Fynes Morryson, Mountjoy's secretary, who later wrote the standard account of the Irish campaigns, put the number of English effectives at just over sixty-five hundred, commenting, "I do thinke that a more miserable siedge hathe not been seene or so great a mortalitie without a plage."[67]

The Spanish were likewise suffering, and some deserted to English lines. Carew summarized the situation: "The Spaniards on there parts endure infinnit myserye growne weake and feint with there spare diet, being no other than water or ruske; dogs, catts and garons is a feast when they can get it."[68] Águila was becoming increasingly peeved at the Irish earls for their seeming unwillingness to attack Mountjoy; the Spanish commander was equally aware of the English difficulties and argued that a synchronized assault would be successful. But the Spanish were generally dismissive of the Irish ability to fight in a continental, conventional way. A previous Spanish observer had concluded that the Irish "need veteran soldiers to teach them how to form squadrons, as they are not used to this war tactic nor to the rest of those things which are so common in the military world." Diego Brochero, naval commander at Kinsale, complained, "They make war as the outlaws and bandits of Catalonia and Calabria do."[69]

THE BATTLE

In substance, O'Neill agreed entirely with the admiral's analysis. His great victories had indeed been large-scale ambushes, made more effective by a judicious adaptation of modern firepower and better organization. Moreover, his overall strategic success originated in his understanding of Irish society and politics. He did not ask his men or his allies to do things they were incapable of doing. Thus, As Hiram Morgan writes, Águila's plan, a sort of hammer-and-anvil approach circulated by Ensign Alférez Bustamente, for the Irish to take up battle formation on a hill just outside the English lines while the Spanish sortied from Kinsale, must have appeared quite mad to Tyrone.[70] While Águila was not asking the Irish to do more than demonstrate in support of his attack, the idea of massing in the open against the English contravened the Irish way of war, and, as O'Neill well knew, a formal "demonstration" required a level of command sophistication and troop discipline that his men did not have. At the same time, none of the contestants could afford to wait indefinitely; their armies were all wasting away. Though the message from Bustamente was something of an ultimatum, it still sparked debate among the Irish. The common account has it that a fiery and combative O'Donnell—who had already lost primacy in Tyrconnell—convinced a hesitant O'Neill and O'Sullivan Beare to execute Águila's plan. But it seems more likely that none of the Irish leaders was enthusiastic about the idea, while acknowledging that they could not break faith with their ally.

On the night of December 23 (by the old-style Julian calendar then still used by the English), the Irish began their approach march in two divisions, O'Neill in the van and O'Donnell trailing. The Spanish from Castelhaven along with the troops under Captain Richard Tyrell made up a flying squadron that O'Neill might use to maneuver with once the fight was joined. Guiding on the well-worn Cork-Kinsale road and having only two miles to travel, the Irish managed to get themselves to the base of the Ardmartin ridgeline atop which Mountjoy had his main camp. The Irish march also threatened the secondary camp of the Earl of Thomond at the west end of the ridge. Alert to the Irish advance, Mountjoy sounded the call to arms.

No sooner had the English trumpets rung out than O'Neill began to withdraw his formation to the west. The Spanish were furious, for Águila's plan depended upon Mountjoy dividing his forces. Later Spanish accounts hinted at betrayal: "If they stood and faced them there, there could not be but a good outcome, and this would have been very true if the Earls had done this, but from what one could see they had only intended to make that appearance."[71] O'Neill's retreat, in fact, did have the intended effect and further drew Mountjoy well out of his fortifications. Fearing a Spanish sortie from Kinsale, he left Carew in command at the main camp and pursued the Irish with about twelve hundred infantry and several hundred cavalry under Wingfield.

It seems probable that this may be just what O'Neill intended, for when he reformed his squares on a second rise a mile away, which was done in reasonable order, he was placing the bulk of his troops against a portion of Mountjoy's. Further, he enjoyed the protection of a bog to his immediate front, from which skirmishers began to harass the approaching English. Yet this was hardly a prepared defense as had been the case in his previous victories. O'Neill's main body was in the center, flanked by O'Donnell on his left, or north, and the Spanish and the mercenaries under Tyrell forming the southern flank. The line was also bolstered by the small body of Irish horse screening O'Neill's main "battle." O'Neill's position was not a bad one, but it did invite the prospect of a more open-field fight.

Mountjoy advanced cautiously, happy to shoo O'Neill away from his camp but still worried that a strong sally by Águila would have sorely tested his divided force. Approaching the new Irish position, Mountjoy had Wingfield and a mixed infantry-cavalry force of several hundred in the vanguard to develop the situation. After several attempts, he drove in the Irish skirmishers and seized a causeway across the bog. The way was opened to come to grips with O'Neill, even if the causeway acted as a bottleneck channeling the English approach. To hold the corridor, Wingfield immediately passed his cavalry over—about two hundred horse altogether—and charged O'Neill's pikemen, testing their mettle but veering off at the last minute. In response the Irish cavalry countercharged, shouting defiance but similarly reluctant to close with their more heavily horsed and armed English counterparts; as one Spanish commander later wrote, "There was no desire to fight on our side and these people have no order."[72]

But Mountjoy had already sensed an opportunity. Watching the scene unfold from a hilltop and seeing Wingfield's men clear the bog, he sent forward the rest of his cavalry and his own flying squadron of infantry under Sir Henry Power. Wingfield and his deputy Richard de Burgh, Earl of Clanrickarde, met with Sir Henry Danvers and the new troops of English horse. They smelled blood. Despite O'Neill's improvements, the English cavalry, on larger horses that could carry a heavier saddle with stirrups, had an immense advantage over Irish horsemen; for the Irish, cavalry were a light, scouting force, but English cavalry could fight. Against a broken, disorganized, or open enemy formation—as the Irish horse now were—the combination of mobility and power of English horsemen was irresistible. The English in Ireland had waited decades for such a moment.

Wingfield aimed his blow well and struck with all the strength he could muster. His four hundred cavalry with supporting infantry first targeted the Irish horse, driving it into O'Neill's main formation, breaking and confusing it, and further driving it northward into O'Donnell's troops. These, in their turn, panicked and fled. Danvers recounted that the attack "broke the gross which consisted of 1500 men, they were all of the country of Tyrone, this being such a fearful thing to the rest, that they all broke and shifted for themselves."[73] The army that O'Neill had painstakingly designed, built, and nurtured through the years was shattered in a few minutes. Wingfield's attack had also split the Irish right wing, isolating Tyrell's regiment and the Spanish. Mountjoy pushed forward the remainder of his infantry, engaging them directly and then flanking them. Tyrell's men melted away to leave the Spaniards making a hilltop last stand. In the end, Captain Alonso de Ocampo and fewer than fifty of his men survived to surrender. Mountjoy's victory was complete. The elated commander knighted Clanrickarde—who would later marry the widow of the executed Earl of Essex, Frances Walsingham, only child of Elizabeth's secretary—on the spot for his conspicuous bravery.

Wingfield's cavalry pursued the Irish as far as his exhausted horses would go. In his report to London, Mountjoy estimated the rebel dead at one thousand and claimed that, but for their own starving mounts, the slaughter might have been double that. Another eight hundred Irish were wounded but subsequently died of exposure; the English took no prisoners save the Spanish. English losses were perhaps only one cornet in a cavalry troop—although deaths from disease would continue in Mountjoy's camp. Águila sat tight in Kinsale, only sending out a small party late in the day when he mistook the *volée de joie* fired in celebration as Mountjoy's men returned to camp for the long-awaited attack by O'Neill. The Spanish commander had no word about the battle until the courier Bustamente returned from Castelhaven a week later to explain that the Irish were giving up for good:

> After arriving at their quarters . . . on the evening of the fourth of January, they wrote to Don Juan del Águila telling him that they could not help him. And though the Spanish captains, who were present, told them that that was a cruel decision, and that it was possible to renew the siege by returning to the first quarters, the earls would not do so. Instead they replied that if they waited for the same friends there, they [the friends, probably the Munster lords] would hand them [O'Neill and O'Donnell] to the enemy. Thus, on the morning of Friday the fifth of January all the earls' army was formed up and in less than an hour everything was undone from top to bottom.[74]

With but five hundred followers, O'Neill had to ensure his grip on power in Ulster. O'Donnell, with little to return to in Tyrconnell, would make for Spain, presaging the larger "flight of the earls" that would come in 1607. Upon receiving word of the Irish withdrawal, Águila asked for terms. Within a few days, the capitulation was signed and Águila came to dine with Mountjoy.

THE O'NEILL'S END

The English understood their triumph in providential terms. Writing to Robert Cecil, Sir George Carew explained, "This miraculous victory, for so I well term it, no man can yield reason for it, God only did give it us, casting into their hearts a needless fear having six hands for one to fight against us." Mountjoy's dispatch the next day said simply, "God hath given the Queen the greatest victory she ever obtained in this country."[75] That may have been a low standard, but after almost a decade's dealing with Tyrone and the direct intervention of the Spanish, to say nothing of helping to keep the Dutch revolt alive and repelling Philip II's periodic armadas, Elizabeth had many reasons for relief and to feel blessed. And with her parliament restive under the burden of taxes to pay for her wars, the government looked to spin this victory in much the traditional manner, as a triumph of a plucky Protestant army over the coalition of Catholics arrayed against it. The caution and moderation of the mid-1580s had been set aside, and with the still-cloudy prospect of succession now looming larger than ever, the regime returned to its imperial, ideological roots; the propaganda mill again began to grind. Early the following year, a "discourse" was published, comprised of a theological rebuttal of Catholicism and a versified celebration of Kinsale and its aftermath. The author, Ralph Birkenshaw, echoed the themes of the early 1570s, including a justification—verging on a celebration—of the bloodletting involved. Birkenshaw was the comptroller to Sir Ralph Lane, the muster-master of English forces in Ireland and someone who had come in for criticism from Mountjoy for lax administration, so Birkenshaw may well have had a flattering purpose, not only in regard of Mountjoy but of the government as a whole. At any rate, his *Discourse occasioned upon the defeat, given to the Arch-rebels, Tyrone and Odonnell, by the right Honourable the Lord Mountjoy, Lord Deputie of Ireland, the 24. Of December, 1601, being Christs Eave: And the yielding up of Kinsale shortly after by Don John to his lordshippe* concluded in the manner of *Cold Pye for Papists*:

> Now sith Jehova of his mercie great,
> Wondrously hath fought in his owne cause,
> And given now Mountjoy for to see,
> That counsel, horse, and men get not the field:
> But whom God loves, and those who serve him still,
> Are sure to conquer as their ownselves will.
>
> Then let ELIZA rest still on Gods strong hand,
> Obey his laws, advance his Cospell pure,
> Roote out blind Papists, Priests, and filthie Friers,
> Bring all degrees to heare Gods holy word:
> Cherish the good, snub such as wicked are,
> And then ELIZA shall prosper in the war.[76]

While Mountjoy, too, reported his version of events, he still had work to do to translate his battlefield successes into something more lasting. O'Neill's northward march was a catastrophe, an increasingly panicked flight that saw hundreds drown in river crossings; by the time it returned to Ulster, the earl's army was a shadow of its former self. The retreat also exposed Munster to reconquest. By early spring, Mountjoy's force had recovered sufficiently to begin the systematic reduction of the remaining rebels. His first moves were to dispatch Carew and the Earl of Ormond to intimidate and bribe the fence-sitting lords of western Cork and to eliminate the last pockets of resistance—in particular the stronghold of Philip O'Sullivan Beare at Dunboy. O'Sullivan Beare himself escaped to Spain, there to publish a famous lament for the rebellion and lionization of the "last stand" of his one hundred fifty or so followers at Dunboy, killed to a man in the castle basement.

In June 1602, Mountjoy returned to Ulster with his main force and began an orchestrated scorched earth campaign to finish off Tyrone once and for all. From Carrickfergus in the eastern part of the province, Sir Arthur Chichester pushed toward Lough Neagh. Sir Henry Dowcra led a force southward along the Foyle as Mountjoy crossed the Blackwater from the south. The three English pincers methodically closed on O'Neill's fortress at Dungannon, building garrisons along the way both for security and to carry the destruction deep into the countryside, at last hacking at the real roots of the Irish insurgency. As Vincent Carey has argued, the campaign was unprecedented in scale and system. Like a modern firefighter, Chichester described a giant "back burn" of the country surrounding Dungannon.[77] By just the third week of June, O'Neill burned his own stronghold down and fled. Indeed, the English had so thoroughly ravished Ulster that they could not subsist their own forces. For the people of Ulster, the result was a famine so horrible that, through the following winter, it produced instances of cannibalism. Mountjoy was not insensible to the suffering—Fynes Morryson, his secretary, recorded vivid and horrid scenes in his account—but concluded they were necessary to end the rebellion. So, too, it was thought, was the grisly propaganda.

With her own death approaching, Elizabeth in February 1603 gave Mountjoy leave to enter to into one final negotiation with Tyrone, offering to let the earl keep his head in return for his submission; she preferred a humbled O'Neil to a martyred one. Indeed, the day before Mountjoy could send a messenger to the open talks with O'Neill, the last of the Tudors passed away, and word had barely reached the English commander when, on the afternoon of March 30, the Irish leader entered Mountjoy's headquarters at Mellifont Abbey, halfway between Dublin and Dundalk. Kneeling for over an hour, O'Neill declared his loyalty and desire for forgiveness, and the next day, once again on his knees, presented and signed a written version of his vow and request for clemency. A few days later he rode with Mountjoy to Drogheda then on to Dublin, where the surrender was proclaimed publicly and O'Neill was informed of Elizabeth's death and that James Stuart had become James VI of Scotland and James I in England and Ireland. The Irishman wept on the news. "There needed no Oedipus to find out the true cause of his tears," declared Fynes Morryson, for his "most humble submission" had "eclipsed" his past "vainglory."[78] Mountjoy also made the most of O'Neill's surrender, parading him through parts of Ireland and even escorting him to London, where he made such a favorable impression on King James that he was restored as Earl of Tyrone.

More even than the sea war against Spain, the conquest of Ireland had solidified a strategic consensus among the Elizabethans. It required a level of sustained effort and expense that dwarfed even the repulse of the *Gran Armada*. And it required a level of military competence and governmental organization that, in previous endeavors, the English state could not manage; Mountjoy may have been a sometime "favorite" at court, but more importantly he was also a student of military affairs, if not a "professional" in the modern or mercenary sense. He managed a complex set of campaigns and worked well with the Royal Navy. The long-running effort also reflected a hard-won maturation of the political nation. Elizabeth at last found a commander she could trust. The parliament provided sufficient finance with little grumbling. The last postern gate to the British Isles was closed, if not permanently latched; the regime was at least secure enough to be transferred to a new ruling family without fear of British civil war. New strategic initiatives were possible, and indeed James would soon make an honorable cease-fire, if not a permanent peace, with Philip III. Finally, Tyrone's embrace of the Catholic cause, along with Spain's intervention, also cemented Britain's place as the rightful leaders of the Protestant cause; what would undo the Stuarts—twice—was their failure to accept this strategic responsibility. In the end, not even the cautious Elizabeth could suppress the mounting confessional character of the British understanding of international politics and power. Wisely, she chose to ride the tiger of imperial ideology, harnessing the energy of the growing English political nation and guiding it where it longed to go: westward.

6

THE ROANOKE COLONY

In the spring of 1588, Sir Richard Grenville, one of the foremost sailors of the Elizabethan age and close associate of Francis Drake and Sir Walter Ralegh, readied a small fleet of seven ships, including the queen's twenty-two-gun *Tiger*, for the reinforcement and provisioning of the first English permanent colony in North America, at Roanoke on the barrier islands of what today is North Carolina. Grenville's preparations were nearing completion at the end of March, when the privy council intervened and ordered Grenville "to forebeare to go his intended voyage." In the season of the Spanish *Gran Armada*, "Her Majesty dothe receave dayly advertisement of the preparations of the King of Spayne to increase, whereupon it is also thought necessary her Navyes on the seas should be reinforced and strengthened, and to that end order is given bothe for the staye of all shippes in the port townes of the Realme, and to the said townes to furnish a certain number of vessels, &c." Grenville, lord of the manor of Bideford in north Devon, was "to have shippes so by him prepared to be in readynes to ioyne with her Majesties Navye as shalbe directed hereafter."[1]

Thus was the Roanoke colony, established the previous year, "lost," or, as Kenneth Andrews mordantly put it, "effectively sentenced to death."[2] The Roanoke effort was a product of the developing war with Spain and finally the victim of it: intended, first of all, as a potential haven for English privateers hoping to intercept King Philip's treasure fleets, a forward base in the New World, Roanoke had to be sacrificed to defend the home waters from the threat of the *Gran Armada*. The colony was an expression of the expanding scope of English strategists but also of the limits of English military, economic, and other means. It would not be until the cessation of hostilities—and the suppression of the Spanish-fueled revolt in Ireland—under Elizabeth's successor that Englishmen would return to the North American coast to stay.

At the same time, the colony marked the beginning of a long and complex strategic interaction with the indigenous peoples of North America, or "Indians" as Europeans called them. In the colonists' conception, this would be an anti-Spanish (and later, an anti-French) strategic partnership and in this regard seemed to promise a more decisive outcome than the plantation of Ireland or weaning the Scots from their previous attachments to the "auld alliance" with France. England's strategic purpose in Scotland and Ireland was primarily defensive, to close the postern gates to continental European powers and suppress local insurrections. By contrast, colonizing North America was a turning of the table, prying open the gateway to global power in the New World. Such a strategy also underscored the need to navigate the shallow and treacherous waters of indigenous politics; in America as in Ireland and Scotland—or even in the north of England—it was not simply the case that every enemy of an enemy would be a natural and permanent friend. Calculating the new and often kaleidoscopic balance of power began to involve a new set of players with their own and often opaque interests and agendas and indeed a game played by a different set of cultural rules entirely. Building outposts in the New World would add new layers of complexity to British strategy-making, require new institutions of government, and, in particular, change the nature of military forces, especially the army. As the colonies grew, so grew the strategic conundrum; in the end, of course, the contradictions became insurmountable and the main American colonies lost.

DISCOURSES ON WESTERN PLANTING

Through the course of Elizabeth's reign, establishing an enduring presence in the New World had become a commonly accepted principle among English strategists, one springing from a common understanding that the immediate European balance of power and Spain's position as aspiring hegemon was the fruit of its global power and, especially, its American empire. It was Philip's "Indian gold," said Ralegh, "that endangereth and disturbeth all the nations of Europe, it purchaseth intelligence, creepeth into the councils, and setteth bound loyalty at liberty in the greatest monarchies of Europe."[3] The balance of Europe's great powers and England's place among them was London's primary concern, but it was the treasures and ores of the Aztecs and the Incas that tipped the scales.

Further, it had dawned on even the most enthusiastic navalists and promoters of a blue-water strategy that maritime power alone was an intermittent and perhaps inadequate means; intercepting a treasure fleet as it sailed for Spain was very difficult to do, for a host of reasons. And while scoring a one-time jackpot might be an alluring prospect, even to a queen, no raiding strategy could produce a lasting strategic effect. Thus Drake in his circumnavigation and in his other forays into the Caribbean had become enamored of the idea of creating a kind of alliance or strategic partnership with indigenous tribes, or *cimarrones*, of Panama who had escaped from Spanish colonies. Advancing English interests demanded not just striking power but staying power. Again Ralegh put the conundrum clearly and pithily: "The king of Spain is not so impoverished by taking three or four port towns in America as we suppose, neither are the riches of Peru or Nueva España so left by the seaside, as it can be easily washed away, with a great flood, or spring tide, or left dry upon the sand in a low ebb."[4]

At the same time, there was a growing recognition that, while the Spanish position in America was durable and profitable, there were also substantial gaps both north and south of the Caribbean and, as Drake had found, in the Pacific. Philip had been relatively tolerant of English privateers through the late 1560s, and Elizabeth's attenuated diplomacy during the late 1570s and her reluctance to become too deeply involved in the Dutch war—which had become Spain's primary military effort in the wake of the victory at Lepanto and the subsequent stabilization of the Mediterranean—deprived English adventurers of both royal backing and assets. Nor were London's merchants, for whom trade with Spain and with the Spanish Netherlands was critical, in a mood to exchange steady commerce for a chance at riches through plunder. However, as tensions mounted through the early 1580s, so did interest in claiming a larger and more permanent English stake in the western hemisphere.

Finally, there was a powerful ideological and confessional component to the English colonial impulse toward America. West Country gentry, in particular, tended to be nautical, profoundly Puritan, and rabidly anti-Spanish. Drake's zealotry was apparent throughout his circumnavigation; Grenville ended his life as an English and Protestant martyr, leading the queen's ship *Revenge* alone against fifty-one Spanish ships of the armada of 1591. Grenville's heroism was rapidly spread through Ralegh's *A Report of the Truth of the Fight About the Isles of the Azores This Last Summer Betwixt the* Revenge, *One of Her Majesty's Ships, and an Armada of the King of Spain.* Despite its ungainly title, Ralegh's propaganda was hugely effective, giving Grenville a mythic proportion even unto Alfred, Lord Tennyson's day:

> And the sick men down in the hold were most of them
>   stark and cold,
> And the pikes were all broken or bent, and the powder
>   was all of it spent;
> And the masts and the rigging were lying over the side;
> But Sir Richard cried in his English pride,
> "We have fought such a fight for a day and a night
> As may never be fought again!
> We have won great glory, my men!
> And a day less or more
> At sea or ashore,
> We die—does it matter when?
> Sink me the ship, Master Gunner—sink her, split her in
>   twain!
> Fall into the hands of God, not into the hands of Spain!"[5]

One of the first expressions of royal interest in an American colony was a patent issued in June 1578 to Sir Humphrey Gilbert, yet another Devon adventurer and Ralegh's half-brother. The patent was both wide-ranging and open-ended; Gilbert obtained "free libertie and license from time to time, and at all times for ever hereafter, to discover, finde, search out and view," but also "to have, hold, occupy and enjoy to him, his heirs and assignee forever" any "remote, heathen and barbarous lands, countreys and territories not actually possessed of any Christian prince or people."[6] This was a very blank check; for a period of six years, Gilbert was free to pick his spot and do with it as he pleased, as long as the Spanish or Portuguese weren't already there. Gilbert's initial attempts to cash the queen's writ foundered on court rivalries, storms at sea, doubts about Gilbert's seamanship, and a spell of duty in Ireland. It was not until the summer of 1583 that Gilbert got across the Atlantic, first taking possession of Newfoundland and then intending to work his way southward. In the process, he lost one of his few ships in a wreck off Sable Island, just east of the Canso Peninsula of Nova Scotia, and turned for home. Gilbert himself went down off the Azores.

Gilbert's one lasting success was to enlist his half-brother in the colonial project. Inheriting the patent in March 1584, Ralegh was already a rising star at court, firmly established as Elizabeth's principal favorite. A young London man-about-town observed that Ralegh "was in high favor with the Queen's Majesty. . . . Neither [Robert Dudley] my lord of Leicester nor master Vice-Chamberlain [Sir Francis Knollys] in so short a time was ever the like, which special favor hath been within this two months. I have heard it credibly reported that Master Rawley hath spent this half year above 3000 pounds. . . . The whole court doth follow him."[7]

In sum, Ralegh had the kind of access, influence, money, and power that that few could match. He was also the embodiment of the Elizabethan strategic mind. Ralegh had long been dedicated to the geopolitical "Protestant interest," having in the late 1560s joined a group of Devonshire volunteers who fought with the French Huguenots. Returning to Oxford and then London and the Inns of Chancery, where he likely came to know the elder Richard Hakluyt, a lawyer and older cousin to the author of the *Discourse of Western Planting* but also an enthusiastic colonialist. Working his way at court, he gravitated to the Leicester-Walsingham circle and was sent to Ireland in 1580 to help quell the second Desmond Rebellion in Munster. Ralegh won the trust of the English commander, Lord Grey de Wilton, and also took part in the siege of Smerwick at the tip on the Dingle peninsula. There, six hundred reinforcements sent by Pope Gregory XIII, mostly Spanish and Italian troops, were slaughtered along with an unknown number of Irish when the castle surrendered. Ralegh returned to court the next year, rapidly catching the queen's eye and accumulating the favors that were to make him a wealthy man.

Upon inheriting Gilbert's patent, Ralegh took two steps. The first was to send out a reconnaissance force of two ships under Philip Amadas and Arthur Barlowe; this will be discussed in greater detail below. The second was equally if not more important: he set about building a case at court and for Elizabeth that such a colonial adventure would be in the national interest, an element of a strategy for containing Spain and thus an effort worthy of both public and private support. In this effort, he had a close ally in Sir Francis Walsingham. Walsingham had become an admirer of the younger Hakluyt's writings, especially his just-published

Divers Voyages touching the discoverie of America, and the Ilands adjacent, a compendium of travel writings about the New World, drawing on a variety of continental sources. Urging Hakluyt to "turn not only to your owne good in private, but to the publicke benefite of the Realme"—in other words, the benefit of Walsingham's understanding of the Spanish position in America—the secretary sponsored the young academic's sojourn in Paris, where he could find access to a wider world of sources to contribute to Walsingham's intelligence network.[8]

Hakluyt provided Walsingham with periodic assessments during his time in Paris, pressing the case for colonization as a matter of urgency, lest the two Catholic powers—in addition to Spain's empire, the French had established not just a position in Canada but had built toeholds in Florida—finally exclude the lackadaisical English from the continent entirely. Learning of Gilbert's failures, Hakluyt feared the English interest in colonization would "waxe cold and fall to the ground."[9] He volunteered to cross the Atlantic himself, but more importantly, threw himself into writing his *Discourse on Western Planting* (hereafter, the *Discourse*) as a memorandum for the queen, Walsingham, and her other close advisers. It was, as Hakluyt's modern biographer Peter Mancall put it, "a grammar of colonization . . . the language and logic that would guide the English colonization of North America."[10]

The project also benefitted from the rising sense of crisis at court. In the summer of 1584, the Duc D'Alencon, brother to the French king Henri III and the focus of so much English diplomatic, dynastic, and matrimonial intrigue, died. Almost immediately thereafter, William the Silent, Prince of Orange and the leader of the fractious Dutch rebels, was assassinated by a Catholic retainer, Balthasar Gerard, allegedly at the behest of Philip II and with the aid of Jesuit plotters. Elizabeth's attempt to keep England at a distance, to sustain a favorable balance of power by pulling strings from afar, had collapsed completely. Increasingly, it appeared that only direct military steps could forestall Spain's bid for European hegemony and the extirpation of Protestantism.

Thus Hakluyt's tract was part scholarly discourse but larger part propaganda, an argument for decision and action. He reaffirmed that the English had "juste Title" originating in Sebastian Cabot's voyages for Henry VII and that the lands north of Florida, a vast expanse from 30° to 63° north latitude, was not possessed by any Christian prince or people but by idolatrous heathens. Having established that fact, he began his case for English action with a moral argument that was both religious and confessional but also geopolitical in effect: it was the task of "the Kinges and Queenes of England," as the leaders of the Protestant interest, not just to evangelize the indigenous tribes but to save them from Catholicism, and especially from its rapacious Iberian expressions. The Spanish and Portuguese boasted of having built more than two hundred churches in five decades of American colonization, but this was merely a "vain ostentation," a pretense that masked their lust for "filthie lucre." Thus "the people of America crye out unto us their nexte neighbors to comme and helpe them"—again, anticipating the language of the Great Seal of Massachusetts—"and bring unto them the gladd tidings of the gospel."[11] The centrality of this argument in a tract of this sort—written, above all, to persuade a cautious and conservative queen, allegedly averse to ideologically driven strategies—is striking. It is unthinkable that Walsingham or Burghley would permit the *Discourse* to be presented to Elizabeth without their careful scrutiny. That this should be the opening shot in the salvo of arguments Hakluyt would present is a measure of how deeply held such beliefs were among the Elizabethan elites.

The prospect of economic prosperity provided a second rationale. In the course of the Dutch war, the European markets for English trade had become increasingly limited, not to say dangerous; it was imperative to find new outlets. Hakluyt's economic arguments were comprehensive and sophisticated, balancing the opportunities for long-term development and the social stability that would entail with the usual prospects—or dreams—of resource exploitation. In addition to the better-known Atlantic coast, Hakluyt touted the "commodities of the Inlande," summarizing the corpus of European writing on exploration of the western hemisphere, including source materials in Italian and Latin as well as English. To be sure, he listed a spectacular array of get-rich-quick resources: gold, silver, emeralds, pearls; "spices and drugs" such as cinnamon, cloves, and musk from beavers; "exceeding quantitie of all kynde or precious furres" which Hakluyt had seen dressed by the royal skinners of Paris. But he also emphasized the mild, supposedly Mediterranean climate and the prospects for agriculture and, especially important to Englishmen, naval stores that would require labor and husbandry, not simple extraction. Thus, he continued, American colonies would also address the problems of rising unemployment and underemployment in England. Beyond finding a way to make use of excess labor—and solve the criminal and social problems that created—the colonists would soon provide a booming export market for English goods, especially woolens. "Cappers, knitters, clothiers, woolmen, carders, spynners, weavers, fullers, sheremen, dyers, drapers, hatters and such like"—the tradesmen who had suffered the most from the constriction of markets in northern Europe—would prosper. Indeed, Hakluyt could barely control himself in imagining the economic benefits that would ensue from successful colonization: even "olde folks, lame persons, women, and younge children" would be "kepte from idleness, and be made able by their owne honest and easie labor to finde themselves w[i]thoute surchardinge others." Not until John Locke, a century later, would such an argument again be made so forcefully. "I may well and truly conclude with reason and authoritie," Hakluyt declared, "that all the commodities of all our olde decayed and dangerous trades in Europe, Africa, and Asia" could be had in America, for a fraction of the cost—but only if prompt action were taken.[12]

At its core, the *Discourse* was a strategic argument that put America in the global and European context. The assassination of the Prince of Orange was a timely reminder of what Philip's American treasure bought, not only on the continent but in Ireland, in Scotland, and from the "unnaturall rebelles" in England itself. The Spanish king had also funded seminaries for English Catholics "to be thornes in the side of their owne commonwealths." In sum, American treasure made Philip a proximate and existential threat as well as an aspiring universal monarch.[13]

Spain's strength was also its weakness. Her American possessions were "farr distante from one another," as Drake and other privateers had made clear. And the indigenous peoples chafed at Spain's tyrannical rule, ready to rise up: "The Ilands there abounde with people and nations that rejecte the rude and bluddy governmente of the Spaniarde, and that doo mortally hate the Spaniarde. . . . Some of [Philip's] Countries are dispeopled, somme barren, somme are so far asunder also held by Tyranie, that indeede upon the due consideracion of the matter, his mighte and greatnes is not such as prima facie yt may seme to be."[14]

Philip's weakness in America made the entire Spanish empire vulnerable. "If you touche him in the Indies," Hakluyt asserted, "you touche the apple of his eye. . . . For take away his treasure which is nervus belli, and which he hath almoste oute of his west Indies, his olde bandes of souldiers will soone be dissolved, his purposes defeated, his power and strengthe diminished, his pride abated, his tyranie utterly suppressed."[15] This house-of-cards argument was a common one in English strategic thought—because it was a powerful one. What distinguished the *Dis-*

course was the admission that pithing the Spanish snake would require not just immediate but also sustained effort. The opportunity would not last forever; the French and the Dutch had begun to intrude in North America. But to seize the day demanded more than haphazard privateering for profit, more than a one-time raid; only a more durable form of power projection and settlement would do. Thus the last chapters of the *Discourse* included an extensive discussion of the stores, provisions, and mix of skills needed to found a durable colony. Mancall's summary of the tract is apt: "The *Discourse* reflected Hakluyt's understanding of England. Twin dangers faced the nation: Catholic Europe and domestic poverty. Henry VII's lack of vision a century earlier had effectively excluded England from the wealth of the Indies. . . . Hakluyt distilled the most up-to-date information about the western hemisphere into one document. He took scattered ideas and gave them a shape. Once he assembled the pieces, the conclusion was inescapable. England had to embrace western expansion. Failure to do so would guarantee ruin at home."[16]

Hackluyt presented the *Discourse* to Elizabeth on October 5, 1584, along with his analysis of Aristotle's *Politics*, giving the queen much to think about. Two days later, he began his journey back to Paris. Passing the threshold of open war with Spain and all that might entail, Elizabeth and her advisers would soon have to decide what Ralegh's colonial enterprise was worth.

RECONNAISSANCE

The issue took on further urgency with the return of the Amadas-Barlowe scouting mission two weeks previously. The two ships had left England in late April, heading south as Drake had done along the western coast of Europe and northwest Africa, swinging westward at the Canaries to ride the trade winds and current toward Puerto Rico and the Caribbean, arriving on June 10. They spent almost two weeks there, taking on fresh water and food, then began working their way northward, coasting along eastern Florida under the guidance of their Portuguese pilot, whose name has been Anglicized as Simon Fernandes. Very few Englishmen were experienced pilots in these waters, and having to rely on Iberians— including those taken captive—was often problematic; Fernandes appears to have been a Protestant, but even so his trustworthiness was thought to be in doubt. Land was spotted on July 4, and they worked their way northward from Cape Fear. This was their primary mission: to find an appropriate spot to locate a privateering base, a sally port from which to strike at Spanish shipping repeatedly and decisively.

The challenge, once they reached the Outer Banks, was to find a channel that could accommodate deeper-draft warships. The barrier was then perhaps a mile wider than it is now, and the best opening appeared to be at the northern tip of what was then Hatarask Island, near modern Nags Head, but the channel was a mere twelve feet deep at high tide. The land itself however, seemed bountiful, as Barlowe reported: "We viewed the land about us, being whereas we first landed, very sandy and low towards the water side, but so full of grapes as the very beating and surge of the sea overflowed them . . . I think in all the world the like abundance is not to be found. . . . This island hath many goodly woods and full of deer, conies, hares, and fowl, even in the midst of summer, in incredible abundance. The woods are . . . the highest and reddest cedars of the world."[17]

The reconnaissance parties were closely observed by the Algonkian natives of Roanoke Island, which lay just to the west inside Albemarle Sound. When it began to look as if the English were not simply passing through, three Indians rowed across to the barrier, and one came ashore, calling to the English in their ships and making friendly gestures to come and parlay. In reply, the English landed a party and beckoned the Indian to come aboard, where he was given a hat, a shirt, other gifts, and a taste of wine. He was then put back ashore, but now the three Indians brought back a load of fish in return. The initial contact between the English and the Roanokes had been a peaceful and successful one.

The next day, a flotilla of canoes returned with a party of about forty to fifty men, including an imposing figure named Granganimeo, brother to the *weroance*, the "chief" or "king" of the Roanokes, Wingina. At the time, Wingina was recovering from wounds suffered in battle against another nearby village, Pomeiooc, lying to the south. The people of Ossomocomuck—the loose league of villages of which the Roanoke settlement was a part—lived in a region where the local balance of power was in flux; indigenous peoples had already had substantial experience of Europeans and understood that the power of the English newcomers was great but potentially dangerous and, if they were to remain, the English could be valuable allies.[18] Granganimeo staged a traditional ceremonial exchange that formally established good relations, including trade relations. While the English would not part with the swords that the Indians so valued, a pattern of continual trade was established and, as important from the English point of view, a sense of sufficient security to allow for further exploration. The first stop was Granganimeo's palisaded village at the north end of Roanoke Island, where Barlowe and seven of his men were feasted in style: "We were entertained with all love and kindness, and with as much bounty, after their manner, as they could possible devise. We found the people most gentle, loving and faithful, void of all guile and treason, and such as lived after the manner of the Golden Age."[19] Nonetheless, even this successful encounter had moments of tension; Barlowe also paid close attention to Roanoke weaponry and continued his exploration of the region.

Barlowe took a small party in his pinnace—small craft that accompanied large ships, better suited to maneuvering in shallow waters and with oars as well as sails, and that were used in European naval combat to deliver boarding parties—up the Albemarle Sound and the surrounding waters while Amadas continued on with the larger ship, probably to probe the Chesapeake Bay. In addition to recording the lay of the land, Barlowe made a study of the politics of the native tribes, not only the internal structure of the Ossomocomuck villages but their relations with the surrounding peoples; the English experience in Ireland made plain the need to know the basis of the indigenous political power structure, as any initial colony would site an inevitably small and vulnerable party of English in an Algonkian land. At some point, he took on board two Indians, Manteo and Wanchese, who would return to England with him. Manteo was a Croatan, whose village was near today's Cape Hatteras, and was as smitten with the English as Barlowe was with the natives. Wanchese was a Roanoke who would prove himself a true subject of Wingina and less enthusiastic about the colonists.

After a month of exploration, Barlowe made for England and arrived there in mid-September. Ralegh set to work editing Barlowe's report of the trip as part of his efforts to raise money and interest at court for a serious attempt at colonization in 1585; the Barlowe report would add on-the-spot and anecdotal narrative to complement Hakluyt's *Discourse*. Ralegh's publicity campaign may have taken on additional urgency once Amadas returned, probably about mid-November. Although Amadas endorsed and signed the Barlowe report, it contains no record of what is most likely to have been a disappointing voyage, first to the Chesapeake, the most likely locale for a permanent naval base that could accommodate large warships, but where the powerful Powhatans were known to be hostile to Europeans, having wiped out a Spanish Jesuit mission. Hearsay had it that a number of Amadas's men had been also killed. On his way home, Amadas intended to make a final pass through the Caribbean in search of prizes, but he was caught in a storm and limped back to England via the Azores.[20] Beyond the bad headlines Amadas's troubles would have generated, they underscored the tensions between the long-term colonizing mission and the need to turn an immediate profit to lure private investors. The weaknesses and poverty of the Elizabethan state—and the compromises and contradictions that resulted from the primacy of private means over public ends—were again on display.

Ralegh threw himself into every aspect of preparation. One critical step was to develop Manteo and Wanchese as translators, sources of intelligence, and featured figures in public promotion. In this effort, Ralegh was both wise and fortunate to be able to assign Thomas Harriot to the task. Harriot was, in addition to being part of Ralegh's household, a true Renaissance man of science—later celebrated as the "Tycho Brahe of optics and the English Galileo"—and a meticulous observer of the indigenous peoples of Roanoke.[21] By mid-winter, Harriot had learned some Algonkian and Manteo and Wanchese some English; Harriot also gained a better understanding of the political geography of the region and the character of Algonkian religion. Ralegh took the two Indians into his household as well, dressed them in English fashion, and made them part of his propaganda campaign. They must have been impressive physically and carried themselves with dignity, appearing quite capable of becoming "civilized," becoming Christians, and becoming Anglicized—models of what Elizabethans wanted their colonizing efforts to achieve. As Hakluyt's elder cousin—also, confusingly, named Richard, but a prominent lawyer and promoter of colonization—put it: "The people be well proportioned in their limbs, well favoured, gentle, of a mild and tractable disposition, apt to submit themselves to good government and ready to embrace the Christian faith."[22] Manteo and Wanchese were paraded, to positive effect, before the parliament. Londoners saw what they hoped to see.

Ralegh also endeavored to transform Elizabeth's patent into a broader form of support, introducing a bill into parliament to confirm his privileges. The bill passed the House of Commons and failed in the House of Lords, which thought it redundant to the queen's patent. But Ralegh achieved his larger purpose; the committee designated to review the bill included Walsingham, Christopher Hatton, Philip Sydney, Drake, and Grenville. This was a powerful line-up and one dedicated to the pursuit of the Protestant interest and the war with Spain as well as a measure of Ralegh's standing at court. Elizabeth knighted him on January 6, 1585; in return, Ralegh requested the honor of calling his new colony "Virginia"—hardly an act of political virginity.

But, as so often, although the queen was willing to confer authority and her blessing, she was reluctant to commit significant state resources to the enterprise. She did allow Ralegh 2,400 pounds of gunpowder and the use of her two-hundred-ton galleass *Tiger* (although she may have charged him for it). Perhaps more important, she released Colonel Ralph Lane, the deeply experienced soldier, from his command in Ireland to serve as the governor of the colony, while continuing to pay his salary.[23] In all, Ralegh assembled a fleet of seven ships. The *Tiger* was to be the flagship or "admiral," commanded by Grenville and with Fernandes as the chief pilot. Other ships included the *Roebuck*, a one-hundred-forty-ton flyboat (a broad-beamed design perfected by the Dutch for use in their coastal waters as well as having oceangoing qualities) and the one-hundred-ton *Red Lion*. The ships' complements, including the soldiers and others who would establish the colony, totaled six hundred. By every measure this was a large and serious effort. It might have been larger, too; some advisers wanted to increase the force to eight hundred, but Ralegh was unable to recruit so many in such a short time. The task force was also well supplied with armaments of all sorts and tools, including a forge, to start the colony. Most of the bulky supplies, including the food, were carried aboard the *Tiger*. The favorite Ralegh, too dear to Elizabeth to be risked on such a venture, would have to remain in England; he set about preparing a follow-on supply mission to sail later in the summer and to synchronize plans with Sir Francis Drake, who was plotting a massive raid on the Spanish Caribbean. Although Drake's effort would dwarf Ralegh's, they were in some measure the opening twin offensives in Elizabeth's war against Spain at sea and in the Americas; in concert with the coming commitment to the Dutch, the summer and fall of 1585 would mark the impressive beginning of an expansive and long-running global effort that reflected England's global view of the contest with Spain and the sources of power. For more than a decade Elizabeth had preferred diplomacy to war, but the time for half measures was over, and the remaining two decades of her reign were a continuous struggle.

THE COLONY OF 1585

Despite the queen's approbation and indirect participation, Grenville's expedition was a private venture and a tertiary strategic concern. His fleet sailed from Plymouth on April 9 and, despite a storm that scattered it, the *Tiger* made the crossing to the Caribbean in less than a month, dropping its anchor on May 11 off the southwest coast of Puerto Rico, at what was apparently a prearranged rendezvous point.[24] Here Grenville debarked Lane's men, built a new pinnace to replace the one they had lost in the storm, and waited to reassemble his flotilla. Only the *Elizabeth*, one of his smaller ships, made it; others including the *Red Lion* are likely to have gone privateering. Grenville himself took two smaller Spanish ships and began his northward journey at the end of May, pausing briefly on Hispaniola to trade with a Spanish outpost that was either none too particular about business matters or intimidated by the *Tiger's* firepower. Grenville also deposited his Spanish prisoners and made no secret of his onward mission. The other significant development of the sojourn in the Caribbean was the eruption of an argument between Grenville and Lane. Both were men with strong personalities; Lane was a noted disciplinarian and Grenville something of a hothead who, in his youth, had killed a man in a London street brawl. The quarrel cannot be said to have had a material effect on the mission, except that it suggests something of the pressure that Lane felt himself to be under—his beef was that Grenville had put him in a risky position by sending him in search of salt supplies in Spanish-held territory. Though a skilled military commander, Lane was not always at his best in uncertain or ambiguous situations.[25]

The *Tiger* and her escorts arrived off the Outer Banks after about two weeks at sea and on June 26 attempted to thread their way through an inlet into the sound. But what appeared to Grenville and Simon Fernandes to be a deep-water harbor was in fact shallow; the ships all ran aground. The smaller ones freed themselves relatively quickly, but the larger *Tiger* took a pounding. As Ralph Lane put it: "The *Tiger* lying beating upon the shoal for the space of two hours by the dial, we were all in extreme hazard of being cast away, but in the end, by the mere work of God, floating off, we ran her aground hard to the shore, and with so great spoil of our provisions saved ourselves and the noble ship also, with her back whole, which all the mariners aboard thought could not possibly but have been broken in sunder, having abiden by just

Figure 6.1. Ralegh's Virginia.

tally above 89 strokes upon the ground."[26] Though the *Tiger's* essential structure was intact, the pounding had caused great leaks that spoiled much of the supplies, leaving the colonists with little food. The colony did not get off to a good start.

A second bad omen came on July 3. As the crew began repairs to the battered ship, Grenville sent a small party to reestablish contact with the Roanokes and Wingina; with food supplies largely gone, the colonists would have to depend even more on good relations with the Indians. As a Roanoke, Wanchese was naturally selected to act as interpreter, but shortly after the party reached the island, Wanchese disappeared, making his way across the sound to the mainland and to Wingina's central village of Dasemunkepeuc. Wingina took him in and sheltered him from the English who came in search of a man they had tried to befriend and upon whom they depended. As would soon become apparent, Wanchese's time in England had heightened his fear and hardened his hatred of the English. While they commanded superior resources and technology that would empower the Roanokes against their rivals, the English were also very inherently threatening. Their power could also be used for evil—or at least uniquely English—purposes.

Wanchese's betrayal also heightened anxieties in Grenville and Lane. Far from home, the bulk of their provisions lost, a tiny and vulnerable band in an unknown environment, with only Manteo to speak for them among the local people, their position was tenuous, to put it mildly. From the start, Lane's approach—for it was he who would stay behind to lead the colony once Grenville departed with his ships—appears to have been to hedge against the prospects of hostility on the part of Wingina, both by showing a strong front and by looking for other Indian allies. Perhaps not surprisingly in light of Wanchese's defection, one of Grenville's next moves was to visit the village of Pomeiooc, from whence Wingina had received the wound that had laid him up the previous year. They also moved farther south and up the Pamlico River to the village of Secotan and up the Pungo River inlet to Aquascogoc. All went well at Secotan, but when Philip Amadas, in charge of one of the boats, discovered that a silver cup had been stolen at Asquacogoc, he returned to retrieve it. The *weroance* at Aquascogoc did not give immediate satisfaction, and as he drew out the negotiations, Amadas saw the women and young children fleeing the village. Perhaps fearing treachery and an ambush, he acted preemptively, burning the town and the fields and driving the entire populace into the woods.[27]

In profound ways, these initial encounters set the pattern for what was to follow. The essential purposes of the colony were strategic and European—to establish a secure base and supply site for increasing both raids on the Spanish in the Caribbean and the odds of snagging the treasure fleet. Though America seemed to abound with the products and prospects for an ordered, agrarian, Anglicized society, that would remain a goal for the future. When Lane set about fortifying the colony—one of the reasons he had been chosen as commander and governor was his expertise in fortification—he faced it toward the sea, against the Spanish whom he assumed would be searching for him. By contrast, the colonists would live in huts outside the perimeter, on the assumption that the local tribes would either be natural allies, as was emphasized by Ralegh, Hakluyt, and others in London, or that the local balance of power could be manipulated to English ends. When Indian politics proved harder to read or control, the English became nervous and felt the need to demonstrate their strength. In all, the colony included just 108 men—and they were all men—including about sixty soldiers. Roanoke was the tiniest outpost at the farthest reach of English power.

It took the better part of two months to prepare the colony, repair the *Tiger,* and complete these initial local scouting missions. As the ships prepared to return to England, Lane wrote an initial assessment, "from the new Fort in Virginia," for the Hakluyts, including the results of their forays onto the mainland. Perhaps not surprisingly, Lane painted a rosy picture: "We have discovered the maine to bee the goodliest soile under the cope of heaven, so abounding with sweete trees, that bring such sundry rich and most pleasant gummes, grapes of such greatness, yet wild, as France, Spaine nor Italy hath no greater, so many sorts of Apothecarie drugs, such severall kinds of flaxe, and kind like silke. . . . The people naturally most courteous, & very desirous to have clothese, but especially of course cloth rather than silke, course canvas they also like wel of, but copper carieth ye price of all, so it be made red."[28]

These natural resources, however, were not immediately exploitable, as the Aztec treasures, Inca mines, or beaver pelts of Canada could be. They wanted development, English development. If "Virginia had but horses and kine [that is, cattle] in some reasonable proportion," he concluded, and were "inhabited with English, no realm in Christendome were comparable to it," but the natives, lacking the knowledge to properly "use" the land, could not do it.[29] This was, in addition to being an economic observation, one with strategic and moral implications. Because the Indians did not properly "use" or develop the land, they had no legitimate title to it, no real "dominion." This was a great convenience to the English: they could, with clear conscience, dispossess the Indians from the land. Nor would they have to assert—as the Spanish had done—a right of "conquest." Lane's report had both material and ideological motives.

But neither could Lane's colonists immediately make "use" of Virginia. As noted above, more than half the complement of colonists was soldiers. There were a number of "gentlemen," lesser aristocracy who may have lent social cache to the venture but men who did not expect to work to feed or house themselves; they also expected their serving boys to attend to them, not to the general welfare. The scientist Thomas Harriot, who would later doubt the wisdom of Ralph Lane's leadership, was openly critical these adventure-seekers: "Some were of a nice bringing up only in cities and towns, or such as never had seen the world before. Because there were not to be found any English cities, nor such fair houses, nor at their own wish any of their old accustomed dainty food or any soft beds of down or feathers, the country was to them miserable and their reports thereof according."[30] And so Lane had to worry about the inadequacies and vulnerabilities of his own men as well as the possibilities for Indian treachery—two intertwined problems.

In addition to his work cataloguing the natural world of "Virginia" and its people, Harriot also was the day-to-day English liaison with Wingina. Given the multiple uncertainties the *weroance* had about the newcomers and the anti-English line coming from Wanchese, Harriot won a good deal of access to the Roanokes' villages and lives. This was certainly a two-way exchange, with Harriot learning much about Algonkian systems of religious beliefs and in turn introducing the Indians to Protestant Christianity, for Harriot's faith was strong. But Harriot and his small parties are also likely to have done much to spread the infections, most probably the flu, that had such devastating effects on indigenous populations that lacked immunities. Twice Wingina became ill, lying "languishing, doubting of any helpe by his owne priests." Whatever the exact virus was, it struck quickly and with fierce lethality. Even a passing visit by Harriot and his party could be decimating: "Within a few dayes after our departure from evrie such towne, the people began to die very fast," he wrote perplexed, "in one [village] six score, which in trueth was very manie in respect of their numbers."[31]

In sum, relations between the Lane colony and Wingina's people were complex and volatile from the start. The colonists could not support themselves—would starve—without help from the Roanokes yet maintained the many military advantages their modern weaponry and Lane's experience gave them. Yet the Indians were potentially treacherous; English fears reflected fact as well as prejudice. It seemed they could turn without warning, as Wanchese had done. To the Roanokes, the lethal power of Englishmen was also evident in their viral "invisible bullets" that could kill scores who simply came into the presence of this mysterious force. Employed to Wingina's ends, English power could protect his people and indeed make them a dominating local force. But it seemed that the English, too, could turn without warning. It was a brittle formula for building a lasting strategic alliance; both sides had high hopes, great needs, and deep fears.

Near the end of August, Grenville and the *Tiger* set sail for England; one of the smaller ships had been sent back earlier to report, and the last, the *Roebuck*, left at the end of the first week of September, carrying another optimistic report from Lane to Walsingham. Grenville docked at Plymouth in early October, having taken a Spanish prize on the way home, and *Roebuck* was close behind. But in the interim, the larger strategic picture had darkened. In May, Philip II had placed an embargo on all English ships in his harbors and in short order seized them. The war had begun in earnest, and Elizabeth responded by issuing letters of marque, transforming piracy into privateering and increasing the incentives for action. This had immediate consequences for the Roanoke colonists. Ralegh had organized a force in June that was, in addition to conducting raids on Spanish shipping, also to bring reinforcements and resupply to Roanoke. Instead, it was sent to the Newfoundland fisheries and to warn English ships not to go to Spain with their catch, but rather to take Spanish and Portuguese fishing vessels and then to return home. The Roanoke mission was scrapped.[32]

Given the loss of supplies when the *Tiger* ran aground, this was to leave the small colony even more dependent on its relations with Wingina's people. Lane, the fortifications expert and disciplinarian, was energetic in establishing the physical colony. By the time Greenville had sailed for home, a fort of sorts—a trench and earthworks—had been completed, as had cottages for the colonists. Lane was also zealous in enforcing sanitation; of the 108 colonists, only four would die in the coming ten months. But this small company was only a quarter to a third of what the manpower of the colony was intended to be. And if the men were healthy, the gentlemen adventurers were quickly discontented. Beyond the rough living, it was soon apparent that there were no precious metals or other high-value items to be had easily or in quantity. The amount of arable land on the island was limited, and the colonists had lost their seed corn, could not master the Indian technique of trapping fish in weirs, and soon found themselves trading their copper and goods for Roanoke-grown corn. Together with the game they hunted, the colonists acquired enough corn and fish from Wingina to make it through the winter. However, the Roanoke economy did not produce a lot of surplus food, and thus the season was hard on both the English and the Indians and the scarcities slowly soured relations. English firepower and technology made the colonists strong; their inability to feed or otherwise sustain themselves made them weak.

There is no surviving contemporaneous narrative of the events of that winter, but beyond the simple effort to survive, Lane's prime purpose was to explore northward and inland. This strongly suggests that, despite his happy-talk report to Walsingham, he had quickly decided that the Outer Banks were the wrong place to site a permanent colony. The combination of a lack of a deep-water anchorage, the challenges of subsistence, and the ambiguities of relations with Roanokes counted three strikes against the spot, and it seems almost certain that Lane was looking to relocate in the coming year, when reinforced and resupplied, probably to the Chesapeake Bay, and despite the likely hostility and warlike reputation of the Powhatans. Lane also deepened his knowledge of Algonkian political geography, in particular the Chowanoacs tribe, its powerful chief Menatonon, and an even greater people of the interior, the Mangoaks. The winter of 1585–86 was also marked by two events among the Roanokes. One was the death of Granganimeo, the leader of the pro-English faction among the tribe. The other is that Wingina changed his name to Pemisapan. While the meaning of the name is unclear, it was not uncommon for Algonkian individuals to change names when the felt that they were entering a new phase of life. As Michael Leroy Oberg puts it: "Wingina's adoption of a new name probably was related closely to Algonquian spirituality and the *weroance*'s developing understanding of the English. He had arrived at an important conclusion, a seminal moment in his life, and what followed from this point was going to be very different from all that came before. . . . [He] had concluded that his people's survival depended upon separating themselves from the English, whose arrival . . . had initiated drastic and devastating changes in his community."[33]

Thus it is perhaps little surprise that Lane's account of the colony reads like one part promotional pamphlet cataloguing the wonders of the New World and one part after-action report of the events of the spring of

1586; it is a small classic of the military "official report" genre: one participant's self-interested and self-justifying view, a not necessarily false but certainly selective account. At the same time, Lane's actions had a logic born from a rising sense of threat, a recognition that the position of the colony was extremely tenuous, and that he had very little insight into the Indians' intentions. And Lane preferred preemption to waiting on events.

Formally, Lane and Pemisapan (as he shall be called henceforth) remained on speaking terms. In the early spring of 1586, Lane consulted with the Roanoke chief about his plan for further westward exploration, hoping to enlist native guides for the effort. Pemisapan encouraged the idea but warned that Menatonon was holding a council of inland tribes, perhaps totaling three thousand warriors and including the Mangoaks as well as the Chowanoacs, to debate what to do about the colony. Whether this was true or not, Lane felt he could not afford to ignore the risk. He moved a substantial force up the Chowan River, surprising Menatonon and capturing him. In the subsequent interrogation, Menatonon maintained that it had in fact been Pemisapan who was behind the plan to attack the colonists and that the Roanoke leader had informed the inland tribes of Lane's coming.[34]

Menatonon's testimony convinced Lane that he had been double-crossed by Pemisapan, who may have hoped that Lane's party would be killed on their journey, the Chowanoac confederacy doing what the Roanokes feared to do themselves. Menatonon also offered guides and support to Lane's return journey, his son Skiko as a hostage to ensure his bona fides, and valuable information about possible places to relocate the colony nearer to the Chesapeake Bay as well as, perhaps prized the most, about a "marveilous and most strange Minerall" to be mined along the rivers to the west in a region known as "Chaunis Temoatan. The mineral they say is Wassador, which is copper, but they call by the name of Wassador every metal whatsoever." But, in comparison to English copper, "that of Chaunis Temoatan is very soft and pale."[35]

Thus, despite the growing threat from the Roanokes, Lane and a party of forty men agreed to go in search of what might be gold. But as they went upriver, the local Indians withdrew, taking their corn supplies with them. In the one case, they encountered a party of Indians, who called out to Manteo and promptly unleashed a volley of arrows. By Lane's reckoning, they were now 160 miles from the colony; without Indian support in the form of food and guidance, they would never make it to where the mines might be. It was time to turn for home and to reckon with Pemisapan. Lane saw the failure of his mission as clear evidence of betrayal; the Roanoke leader had conspired "of purpose drawen foorth . . . upon the vaine hope [that Lane's men would] be in the ende starved."[36] When Lane returned to Roanoke, he found what he expected, that Pemisapan and his followers had "raised a bruite among themselves that I and my company were part slayne and part starved." Worse, the *weroance* now insisted that the English God "was not God, since hee suffered us [that is, the English] to sustaine much hunger, and also to be killed" by the Indians upriver.[37] Pemisapan's assertion was not only specific—that Lane's men had been defeated and killed—but general—that English power was not supreme, could be successfully resisted, and indeed should be resisted; the costs of cooperating with the colonists were too high to be sustained. In this conclusion, Pemisapan anticipated a process and came to a point that would characterize future English and Indian conflicts: in the beginning, high—if differing—hopes for cooperation based on mutual humanity and political or military interest; in the end, a bitter recognition that the only lasting solution would be the total dominion, if not elimination, of the other, that peaceful coexistence was an impossibility.

The first order of business for Lane's little band was simply to survive. Indeed, to eliminate the Roanokes would be suicidal, for the colonists could not even feed themselves until the relief due to come from England in the late spring or early summer. And simply by surviving the trap that Pemisapan had set for him during the trip toward the interior, Lane had gained a critical, if evanescent advantage over the Roanoke leader: claims of English weakness had been badly discredited. Lane felt that he could at least intimidate the Indians for the next few months until reinforcements arrived, and then the whole colony might be relocated to a better harbor and a more stable relationship with the natives, perhaps in the Chesapeake. Lane's hand was strengthened further when a party from the inland chieftain, Menatonon, arrived at Roanoke, ostensibly to visit the hostage Skiko but also to establish a direct relationship with the English. The principal emissary, Okisco, came to "yelde himself servant, and homager, to the great Weroanza of England"—that is, Queen Elizabeth—"and after her Sir Walter Ralegh." Speaking on behalf of Menatonon, Okisco explained to Lane "that from time forward hee, and his successours, were to acknowledge her Majestie their onely Soveraigne." As Michael Leroy Oberg speculates, Menatonon seems to have beaten Pemisapan at his own game, elbowing the Roanokes aside as the middlemen between the English and the peoples of the interior and, no doubt, ready to exploit the advantages of such a position. This, too, was to prove a recurrent pattern of relations between colonists and natives, but it also signaled that Pemisapan was losing control of events.[38]

Indeed, the Roanokes were split about what to do. But when the leader of the "appeasement" faction, an elder named Ensenore whom Pemisapan acknowledged as his "father," succumbed to disease, the internal tribal political balance tipped permanently in Pemisapan's favor. Ensenore's death reinforced Pemisapan's claim that encounters with the English inevitably came to a bad end. The power of the English might be great, but it was too great a problem for the Roanoke community. Pemisapan convinced his followers, likely a majority but not the entire tribe, to leave the island for the mainland, not only moving their corn-fields but destroying the fish weirs left behind.

Lane, suspicious of the Roanokes and constantly collecting intelligence from disaffected members of the tribe and Skiko, believed Pemisapan not only meant to starve the English but that this was a preliminary move presaging an outright attack. In Lane's account, once Pemisapan had moved clear of Roanoke Island, he sent a large gift of copper to inland tribes to bring together a large force to overwhelm the English, first targeting the leadership—not just Lane but Thomas Harriot and "all thee rest of our better sort, all our houses at one instant being set on fire." The remaining colonists, "both dismayed and dispersed abroade in the Islande seeking of crabs and fish to live withal," could be disposed of at leisure. Lane concluded that Pemisapan intended to attack in the second week of June 1586.[39]

Lane moved to preempt Pemisapan. He put out that he was preparing to remove the colony to Croatan, that the English fleet would soon arrive, and that Lane would come to the village at Dasemunkepeuc to ask for help for the move. Pemisapan responded that he would come to Roanoke rather than have Lane come to the mainland, but he remained hunkered down in his village; Skiko told Lane that Pemisapan was waiting to assemble his large force and would not come until he meant to attack. On the last day of May, Lane tried to sever communications between the island and the mainland. After dark, he sent out a small boat to prevent any Roanoke canoes from returning to their village. Intercepting one, Lane's men overturned the canoe and in the subsequent struggle decapitated two Indians; other Roanokes still on the island, witnessing the attack, began a skirmish with the English.

Luckily for Lane, Pemisapan in distant Dasemunkepeuc did not hear the sounds of the fight, and thus the next morning when Lane, with two boats and about twenty-five men, approached the village, the cover story of the move to Croatan remained credible. Pemisapan, in Lane's telling, "did abide my coming to him."[40] Once in the chief's inner circle, Lane cried out, "Christ our Victory!" His men opened fire, Philip Amadas striking Pemisapan in the first volley. But as Lane's men moved through the village, they tried to distinguish Manteo's friends and Croatans more generally—Lane intended his attack to target just the anti-English faction. In the melee, however, such distinctions became lost; the slaughter became indiscriminate. This, too, was a pattern that would be repeated in years to come. The confusions also allowed Pemisapan—who either had merely been wounded or not hit at all—to attempt to steal away. In his desperate dash, the *weroance* was wounded twice, once in the buttocks, but, though bleeding profusely, he made it into the underbrush. Edward Nugent, an Irishman with whom Lane had served in Kerry, led the pursuit. "Lane," writes Michael Leroy Oberg, "was worried. Nugent had been gone too long and Lane feared that 'we had lost both the king and my man by our owne negligence to have been intercepted by the Savages.' The Englishmen prepared to follow Nugent's path out of Dasemunkepeuc, expecting that their friend had run into an ambush. They marched a short distance before they met Nugent alive. They found him "returning out of the woods with Pemisapan's head in his hand. The English returned to Roanoke. Once there they impaled Pemisapan's head on a pole."[41]

Lane's attack may have been a tactical success, but it marked a larger strategic failure. The Outer Banks was no place to found any sort of colony; both the waters and the natives were unfathomable and treacherous to the English. It could not serve as a forward base to prey on Spanish shipping; making lasting Indian alliances had nothing to do with the Spanish but everything to do with Algonkian politics and at any rate were made nearly impossible by microbes that neither side understood; there were no precious metals or other high-value resources waiting for easy harvest; and the mission to "civilize" and bring Christianity would, at the very best, take a long time. Lane, the thoroughgoing professional and Irish veteran, was defeated and dispirited. His iron discipline and preemptive tactics had brought his company intact through a challenging year, but he wanted no more.

Just a week after the attack, Lane's outpost on Croatan reported "a great fleet of 23 sails" just offshore.[42] This proved to be a flotilla commanded by Sir Francis Drake fresh from raids on Santo Domingo and Cartagena in the Caribbean and the sack of the Spanish outpost at Saint Augustine; Drake expected to be the first privateer to use the Roanoke colony as a place to refit. And he had rescued and carried off a large number of slaves and Indians from his Caribbean raids to help build the Roanoke colony. Drake offered Lane two choices. In addition to the new manpower, Drake would supply food, clothing, and other supplies, as well as a pair of pinnaces suitable for reconnoitering the region so that Lane could resume the effort to locate a good deep-water port. Drake also promised to leave enough supplies, the seventy-ton bark *Francis*, and a cadre of seasoned navigators so that the colonists could return to England at any point if they so decided. The second choice was to embark the embattled colonists for England then and there.

Drake's offer was bountiful, and Lane and his men genuinely grateful for the lavish and very timely help. But all he could promise in return was to remain throughout the summer. The deal was struck on June 12, but the next day Drake's fleet was struck by a huge storm and driven against the shore of the Outer Banks. The winds reached hurricane force and forced the *Francis* well out to sea. Although Drake renewed the offer with another ship, the bark *Bonner* was more than twice the size of the *Francis* and not well suited to shallow-water operations. Lane and his men—Drake required Lane to hold a council of his colony—had reached their limit. "Considering the case that we stood in," wrote Lane,

> the weakness of our company, the small number of the same, the carrying away of our first appointed bark, with those two special [sailing] masters, with our principal provisions in the same, by the very hand of God as it seemed, stretched out to take us from thence: considering also that [Drake's offer of the *Bonner*], though most honorable of his part, yet of ours not to be taken, insomuch as there was no possibility for [the ship] to be brought into the harbor: Seeing furthermore, our hope for supply with Sir Richard Grenville [whose relief expedition had not yet arrived at Roanoke], so undoubtedly promised us before Easter, not yet come, neither then likely to come this year considering the doings in England for Flanders, and also for America, that therefore I would resolve myself, with my company to go into England in [Drake's] Fleet.[43]

Drake weighed anchor for England on June 18, carrying the exhausted Lane and his men. If Lane was relieved to see the Outer Banks sink below the horizon, he must also have dreaded what awaited him in England.

THE LOST COLONY

Lane's failures were a bitter disappointment to the promoters of colonization. Where Lane had seen the hand of God in his troubles—and thus his decision to return to England could hardly be criticized—Hakluyt saw the actions of providence in a rather different light. God's wrath had been brought upon them "for the cruelty, and outrages committed by some of them against the native inhabitants of that country."[44] Thomas Harriot, too, was critical of Lane's aggressive posture toward the Indians. "Some of our companie, towards the ende of yeare" he wrote, "shewed themselves too fierce, in slaying some of the people, in some towns, upon causes that on our part, might easily have bene borne withall."[45] Whether Lane and his men had acted reasonably under difficult circumstances—and, because his narrative is the only direct account of the action, it is difficult to second-guess his command decisions from centuries' distance—they certainly revealed the difficulties of long-term cooperation between the colonies and the natives. Indeed, diseases comprehended by neither colonist nor native made an almost insurmountable problem for relations; it was often lethal simply for Algonkians to be in the same place as Englishmen.

But even had Lane's year at Roanoke been a happier one, the growing conflict with Spain was absorbing increasing amounts of Elizabeth's attention and limited resources. The Dutch war was not going well; the Earl of Leicester's expedition was causing more headaches to the Dutch and his queen than the Duke of Parma, and the prospects of a Spanish invasion of England were great. Critically, Sir Francis Walsingham withdrew from the colonizing effort, taking with him the courtiers who had so enthusiastically contributed to the venture. Drake had started plotting to conduct direct descents on maritime Spain, leading up to his spectacular raid on Cadiz. Even Ralegh was beginning to turn his attention more toward Ireland, where profitable land acquisitions were in prospect, than America. He had spent perhaps as much as £30,000 on various North American ventures, and while privateering had been profitable, Roanoke was almost a total write-off. Moreover, his position as Elizabeth's great favorite was now being challenged by the appearance at court of the young Robert Devereux, Earl of Essex.

Through the winter of 1586, Ralegh weighed the information and reports provided by Lane, Thomas Harriot, and mapmaker John White. He shared summaries with Hakluyt, now back at his post in Paris, where he was gathering fresh intelligence about Spain's plans for North America, especially in response to Roanoke. Importantly, Hakluyt weighed in on the matter of the proper site for future efforts: "If you proceed," he wrote Ralegh, "in your enterprise of Virginia, your best planting will be about the bay of the Chesepians."[46] Ralegh also had to contend with the news that Sir Richard Grenville, at last returned from a voyage which neither sustained Lane's colony nor returned much in the way of plunder, had no interest in a return trip in 1587; like Ralegh, Grenville had more immediate prospects in Ireland.

John White, however, was enthusiastic about returning to Virginia. The New World seemed a promised land to White, and he was willing to organize a new colony, not of soldiers or gentlemen adventurers and their servants, but of craftsmen of the "middling sort," capable of developing a self-sustaining community. They would also be self-financing. By the sale of their accumulated property in England, the new colonists would acquire what they needed to seize opportunity in America. The colony could then become the locus of a naval base, but rather than being a drain on the royal—or Ralegh's—purse, it would serve as a new market for English trade. Once the colony was an economic success, it could become a strategic resource. From Ralegh's point of view, this was an attractive prospect: his colonial claims could be sustained for a much more affordable price; all White's people would need was transport and means of defense.

To attract the kind of colonists envisioned required a different kind of organizational structure. Thus Ralegh incorporated the Assistants of the City of Ralegh under himself as governor. There were to be twelve "assistants," a kind of board of directors. This syndicate provided a vehicle for raising money, distributing land—Ralegh was prepared to give grants up to five hundred acres—and proffering social status; a coat of arms was created. John White, who was to be the governor of the city, received one as well. Equally important, the venture needed good publicity, especially since Lane had returned under a cloud of grumbling. Thomas Harriot took up the task, producing what was to become known as A briefe and true report of the new found land of Virginia. This brilliant propaganda pamphlet, which will be discussed in greater detail below, proved a profound influence on future English colonization of Virginia and beyond, and is still a reflection of how American colonists understood their endeavor, but Harriot could not complete it in time to help White. Nevertheless, the description of a fertile land of plenty, ready and open for "use," was the kind of appeal White must have made to reach the audience he aimed to attract.

In short, Ralegh, White, and Harriot looked to bring English thinking about America into line with received wisdom about "plantations" in general and then—in the late 1580s—again in focus as part of the effort to resettle Munster in Ireland. That is, the City of Ralegh and the colony of Virginia were reconceived not simply as a military outpost but as a "new England," a replication, even an exaggeration, of the virtues of English economy, society, and politics. The City of Ralegh was established by formal and explicit contract, a private arrangement—only the queen could issue a charter—between the governors and the governed. To be sure, the new colony would eventually still serve the traditional strategic purpose of "annoying" Philip II "in his Indies," but there was a further intent to build a new element in the imagined empire, something valuable in itself. Karen Ordahl Kupperman well summarized this attitude: "England had no need to remain parasitical on the great Spanish empire" by simply attempting to feast off the treasure fleet. The commodities to be developed in Virginia "would build a greater English empire, one that would last because it would be based on self-renewing resources."[47]

With just a few months to prepare for this effort, and facing stiff competition with the Munster plantation for recruits, White was unable to meet his target of one hundred fifty colonists, though he did manage to draw in a combination of men, women, and children—a potential community of families, not a company of soldiers. The Croatan Manteo and another Indian, Towaye, accompanied the party, and Manteo was to be made the indigenous ruler in the name of Ralegh and the queen. In April, the final roster assembled to board three ships—the *Lion*, with White as captain and Simon Fernandes again the pilot; an accompanying flyboat carrying most of the supplies; and a pinnace, to be left with the colonists, under Captain Edward Stafford, commander of the Chesapeake expedition conducted previously under Lane. From Portsmouth they made their way slowly down the Channel, calling at Plymouth before finally beginning the crossing on May 8. Hopes were high, expectations not unreasonable.

While at Portsmouth, some of the party went over to the Isle of Wight to meet with Sir George Carey, who was about to receive permission to put out a squadron of privateers; even before the colonists put to sea, it was clear that their interests might well be subordinated to those of the sea war against Spain. Richard Grenville, too—his Irish interests notwithstanding—would receive a similar privateering commission for 1587. But the sea war was becoming public as well as private business: while White was making his crossing, Sir Francis Drake would be leading his famous descent on Cadiz, including four Royal Navy ships of the line in his fleet. The ambitions of English colonizers may have risen, but the attention of the government and the political nation was fixated on Europe and on the naval contest in European waters.

John White's journal is the only original narrative of what would become the "Lost Colony" of Roanoke.[48] It is a terse account, but one that reveals an ever-growing frustration. White had dedicated himself to this vision of a new England in America and, despite challenging circumstances, had worked tirelessly to launch the effort in a very short time. But the visionary and the energetic organizer was not a strong commander. He fell almost instantly into conflict with Fernandes, and not for the first time. White had faulted Fernandes for the grounding of the *Tiger* in 1585—and on May 16 complained to his journal that the pilot had "lewdly"—that is, maliciously—"forsook our Flie boate, leauing her distressed in the Baye of Portingall."[49] The strong-willed sailing master Fernandes was the real commander of the little fleet and did not want the colonists to interfere too much with his principal interest, privateering.

Despite the conflict between White and Fernandes and the oil-and-water mix of civilians and sailors, the real troubles began to emerge only after a quick and easy crossing of the open Atlantic. Stopping at St. Croix to rest, the colonists ate the first fruits they found, "like greene appales," which proved poisonous and left them violently ill, with "a sudden burning in their mouthes, and swelling of their tongues so bigge, that some of them could not speake."[50] Finding no fresh water, they drank from a standing pond, whose water also poisoned them; even those who only washed found their faces so swollen they could not see for almost a week. Eventually, search parties found fresh water and some giant island tortoises to eat, but they also caught sight of Indians. These were no threat, but White reports that Fernandes had assured him the island was uninhabited. What little trust White had in Fernandes was evaporating rapidly.

The differences in purpose became even clearer as the small fleet made a leisurely cruise through the Caribbean. The next stop was Puerto Rico, where fresh water was easily found, but the colonists drank more in beer than they took on in water, and two colonists who were Irish Catholics deserted. A second stop on the island, at Rojo Bay, to take on salt, was aborted at the last minute by Fernandes, who claimed the landing was not safe. The Portuguese pilot also insisted that they overshot their intended landing spot on Hispaniola, where White had planned to pick up young orange, pineapple, and other plants for the new colony. A last and also unlucky try at salt was made at Caicos Island. In all, Fernandes had tarried three weeks in the Caribbean, to no reward: "About the 16. Of Iuly, we fell in with the maine of Virginia, which Simon Fernando tooke to be the island of Croatan, where we came to anker, and rode there two or three daies: but finding himself deceaued, he waited, and bare along the coast, where in the night, had not Captaine Stafford bene more carefull in looking out, then our Simon Fernando, wee had beene all cast away vpon the beache, called the Cape of Feare, for wee were come within two cables length vpon it: such was the carelessness, and ignorance of our Master."[51]

White's fears were about to be realized in full. When on 22 July, the ships at last found Roanoke, White readied forty men to go ashore to search for a small party left the previous year by Grenville and also to install Manteo in his semifeudal position as overlord of the region. This was only to be a brief visit prior to continuing on to the Chesapeake, the intended site of the new colony. But just as the party cast off from the *Lion* in its accompanying pinnace, one of the sailors aboard the larger ship called out to the pinnace crew to leave most of the men at Roanoke and that only White and few others would be allowed back on board. This mutinous act against White was sparked by the conflict in interest between colonists and privateers; "the Summer was farre spent" with no prizes yet taken and a trip to the Chesapeake might add further weeks. It "booted not" Governor White to contend with Fernandes and his crews—all of whom backed their sailing master. Despite the fact that when he went ashore and discovered that the Grenville party had all been killed—White no doubt remembered how relations with the Indians had deteriorated at the end of Lane's time—and that Roanoke fort had been "rased downe," White swallowed Fernandes's *diktat*; Fernandes would not even bring his ships across the Outer Banks, remaining at anchor off Hatorask Island. The arrival of the missing flyboat on July

25, containing a majority of the colonists' stores, may have frustrated Fernandes's attempt at a quick getaway. "God disappointed his wicked pretenses," gloated White.[52]

Historians, even those critical of Lane's approach to colonizing, are united in concluding that John White was a weak leader.[53] His bare-bones account gives little indication of the reasoning behind the decision to remain at Roanoke. The negatives were obvious: the island lacked the natural resources to sustain much of a colony, and the major planting season had passed. Lane had all but destroyed relations with the local Indians; in the aftermath of the attack that had killed Wingina, Wanchese had claimed the leadership at Dasemunkepeuc. The colonists were only beginning to unload their ships and make repairs to the huts on Roanoke when a party from the village had slipped over to Roanoke on 28 July and, coming upon George Howe, one of the twelve "assistants" of the City of Roanoke and a White confidant, "wading in the water alone, almost naked, without any weapon, saue only a small forked sticke, catching Crabs therewithall, and also being strayed two miles from his companie, shotte at him in the water, where they gaue him sixteen wounds with their arrows: and after they had slaine him with their wooden swords, beat his head in peeces, and fled ouer the water to the maine."[54]

Things were hardly better on Croatan. Two days after Howe was butchered, White and Manteo sailed off to restore what had been the friendliest relations for the Lane colony. The reception on Croatan was frosty: only after being reassured that they would not have to feed the newcomers from their small stocks of food and establishing a kind of friend-or-foe recognition system—the Croatans previously had paid the price of Englishmen's inability to see the difference between "friendly" and "hostile" Indians—was there any move to indulge in the feasting rituals that marked indigenous diplomacy. White asked the Croatans to spread the word among the Algoquian settlements that his colony was of a very different sort than Lane's had been, and not a threat; White had come to live together in peace. He summoned the local *weroances* to Roanoke to work out a pact for coexistence.

None came. By August 8, White resolved that it was time to exact vengeance on Dasemunkepeuc for Howe's killing; it was an outrage that must be punished, lest it encourage others. Shortly after midnight on August 9, Manteo "very secretly conveyed" a raiding party across the sound in search of Wanchese and his followers. It was still dark, but "hauing espied their fire, and some sitting about it, we presently sette on them." Most fled into the surrounding woods, but a few were killed before it became clear that "wee were deceaued, for those Sauages were our friendes, and were come from Croatan, to gather the corne, and fruite of that place, for they vnderstoode our enemies were fledde imme-diately after they had slain George Howe."[55] White's good intentions had made no difference: not only had Wanchese's people slipped away, but the Croatans had acted faster. Without the food supplies, it would be hard for Wanchese to return to Dasemunkepeuc; the Croatans were not only increasing their own stocks against the likelihood that the new colonists would need help but improving the common security against their enemies—only to run afoul of trigger-happy Englishmen.

White had little choice but to remain at Roanoke and make the best of it; the options to go to the Chesapeake or even to take the colony home to England had vanished. On August 13, Manteo was baptized and made England's representative and lord among the Algonkians. On August 18, White's daughter Elenora, wife to Roanoke assistant Ananias Dare, gave birth to "the first Christian borne in Virginia, [and so] she was named Virginia." On August 21, a nor'easter blew up that forced Fernandes to cut the mooring cables on the *Lion* and the flyboat and to stand off at sea for six days, "so that wee feared he had been cast away" since most of the crews were ashore.[56]

The prospect of losing this lifeline also seems to have brought out a controversy between White and the colonists, for whom little had ever gone right and who must by now have lost some confidence in White's ability to lead them. The day after the storm, a delegation led by the two surviving and present assistants petitioned White, should the ships not be lost, to return to England "for the better and sooner obtaining of supplies" to sustain a colony now operating under very different cir-cumstances than intended. The governor's greater value to the colony, in the eyes of the governed, lay in London, not Roanoke. White initially refused, pleading a combination of honor and worry about his personal possessions, not making official mention of his granddaughter or his own dream of the project. Desperately, the next day a larger group, "not onely the Assistants, but diuers others, as well woman as men," renewed their entreaties.[57] On August 27, after being in Roanoke again barely a month and with just six hours to pack his bags, White embarked on the flyboat, and his nemesis Fernandes weighed his anchors for England.

White's odyssey was far from over. From the start, when one of the bars that controlled the flyboat's capstan broke and caused the wheel to whip the other bars into most of the crew, injuring them badly, the return voyage home was a nightmare. When they made the Azores, Fernandes at last left them behind, going in search of prizes. The flyboat slowly limped northward from there, drifting for almost three weeks of "scarse and variable windes, our fresh water also by leaking almost consumed." Then "there arose a storme at Northeast, which for 6. Dayes ceased not to blowe so exceeding, that we were driuen further in those 6. Days than we could recouer in thirteene days." Only on October 16 did the ship sight land, "but we knew not what land it was."[58] It was Ireland. Meeting a small ship, the flyboat took on emergency provisions, but of the small crew remaining another three died and another three were too sick to continue and went ashore. In desperation to get home, so did White, transferring to the *Monkey*, bound for Southampton.

White did not get to see Ralegh until November. He convinced his patron to prepare a pinnace for emergency relief until a major effort could be mounted under Grenville in the summer of 1588. The pinnace mission was scrubbed, and in the spring the privy council ordered Grenville to "forbear" and, like all English shipping, prepare to defend against the Spanish armada. White would not give up and was granted two other pinnaces to attempt a relief or rescue voyage. This expedition, too, ran afoul of the privateering priorities of the ship pilots, who also failed in their attempt to take prizes. In the pursuit of a larger French ship, White was wounded twice in the head and once in the buttocks and was lucky to get back to England alive.

Still White would not relent. Even though he could not organize a relief effort in 1589, he struck a bargain with Ralegh and a new group of nineteen associates headed by Thomas Smythe and William Sanderson, both of whom had lent money to Ralegh and financed New World exploration generally, "for the continuance of the City of Ralegh Venture."[59] In 1590, White finally made a return journey, although only after he was forced to conclude a bargain with John Watts, the leading entrepreneur of privateering. In return for the queen's license to plunder, Watts's ships would be required to escort supply ships to Roanoke. But when it came time to sail, Watts's raiders, with White aboard, went straight for the Canaries and thence to the Caribbean. There, a ship of William Sanderson's, the *Moonlight*, joined them, but the privateering cruise continued through July. It was not until the middle of August that *Moonlight* and Watts's ship *Hopewell* reached the Roanoke shore. White must have felt his faith rewarded when "we espied towards the North end of the Iland," where the settlement had been, the "light of a great fire thorow the woods." Putting strength to oar, a party rowed toward the light, and "we let fall our Grapnel neere the shore, & sounded with a trumpet a Call, & afterwards many familiar English tunes of Song, and called to them friendly." But they heard no answer, and so at daybreak on August 18, 1590, White led a party ashore.

> Comming to the fire, we found the grasse & sundry rotten trees burning about the place. From hence we went thorow the woods to that part of the Iland directly ouer against [Wanchese's village] Dasamongwepeuk, & from thence we returned by the water side, round about the Northpoint of the Iland, until we came to the place where I left our Colony. . . . In all this way we saw in the sand the print of the Sauages feet of 2 or 3 sorts troaden [at] night, and as we entered vp the sandy banke vpon a tree, in the very browe thereof curiously carued these faire Romane letters C R O.[60]

A BRIEFE AND TRUE ACCOUNT

With those three carved letters began the legend of the lost colony of Roanoke, but also ended the first English attempt to establish a self-sustaining colony and mid-Atlantic outpost in North America. White did not yet finally despair, however; the carving was an agreed signal, and, had they meant to communicate that the colony was in danger, were to have been accompanied by the sign of the cross. White assumed that the colonists had relocated to Croatan, the most likely refuge and source of sustainment. He convinced the pilots of Moonlight and Hopewell to sail back southward in search of his wandering tribe.

Fittingly, the unpredictable Outer Banks weather played havoc one last time with White's hopes. With a tempest brewing, the ships were loaded hurriedly and with limited supplies of fresh water. As the storm broke, so did cables securing Hopewell's anchor and it was decided to make for the Caribbean for the winter; Moonlight had become so leak-prone that it sailed directly for England. As the gale increased in intensity, it blew the Hopewell into the open Atlantic, forcing its sailing master to decide that the Azores would be the most immediate refuge. There the ship fell in with an English fleet headed for the coasts of Spain and

Portugal, hunting the annual treasure fleet. For the final, fatal time, the sea war against Spain had trumped the needs of the colonists at Roanoke. It was also the final straw for White, who retreated into a quiet life, first in Plymouth, then in Ireland on one of Ralegh's estates. He thus remained a kind of colonist, though in Newtown, County Cork, rather than the City of Ralegh, Virginia.

White's granddaughter, Virginia Dare, and the rest of the lost Roanoke colony passed into the realm of myth. Never seen again by Englishmen or other Europeans—the Spanish learned of the Roanoke colonies and, though taking the threat seriously, had no better luck in actually reaching the spot—they remained a ghostly presence in the minds of future English colonizers. As leader of the Jamestown colony two decades later, Captain John Smith heard tales from Indians and sent several parties in search of Roanoke survivors, only to learn in 1608 that they had been killed. Modern scholars believe it likely that the Roanoke party moved to the Chesapeake, where they may have lived peaceably for several decades.[61] And it is perhaps credible that their end may have coincided with the arrival of a permanent English colony in the region; the coming of Europeans could only be destabilizing to the local Indian balance of power.

But if the Roanoke efforts were a practical failure, they were nonetheless an important proof of principle: with proper backing, structure, and commitment, the English now knew they had what it took to create and build a self-sustaining colony along the middle North American coast. In other words, Roanoke was a tactical defeat that would lead—once the royal succession was secured, the threat from Spain contained, and the Tyrone revolt in Ireland suppressed—to a future strategic success. Such colonies could not be get-rich-quick schemes like Spain's treasure troves to the south, but they could fulfill the kind of longer-term, more durable, and "developmental" role, becoming the "new Englands" integrated into the growing economic, social, cultural, and political British empire, as imagined by Hakluyt and others. America could and would be put to good "use," though this would, almost inevitably, transform any prospective indigenous "ally" into an adversary and embroil Englishmen deeply in Indian politics and power struggles they would struggle to understand.

Thus perhaps the lasting effect of the Roanoke adventures was to be found in the publication of Thomas Harriott's *A briefe and true report of the new found land of Virginia*. As noted, the manuscript was whipped into shape and into circulation to try to generate support for White's 1587 colony, but the fastidious Harriott—who in the future found his true calling in important science and mathematics—did not quite get the job done in time. The report was printed first in 1588 but more importantly, reprinted by Hakluyt in 1589 and, in four languages, in 1590 by the Flemish printer Theodore de Bry. As Peter Mancall observes, this was "perhaps the most important work demarcating the emphases of the times," capturing the New-World dimension of the Elizabethan strategic zeitgeist.[62]

As might be expected from someone with a very modern and scientific sensibility, Harriott's tract was in fact a remarkably true report of Virginia's natural life and its indigenous inhabitants, notable for its lack of exaggeration. Indeed, its very observational accuracy and rhetorical restraint also made it extraordinarily convincing propaganda, for it reflected back to Elizabethan elites their best beliefs about colonization. The Briefe and true report is worth examining at some length. Reflecting its original role as a recruiting tool for White's 1587 effort, Harriot's account begins by debunking the "slaunderous and shamefull speeches bruited abroad by many" who had returned from Lane's 1585 colony, who "not onely [had] spoken ill their Governours, for but their sakes slaundered the country itself." These were lies by those who "have spoken of more than they ever sawe, or otherwise knew to be there." In particular, these were the laziest gentlemen adventurers who, when they discovered "that after golde and silver was not so soone found, as it was by them looked for, had little or no care of any thing but to pamper their bellies," behavior fit for a dissipated Spanish conquistador, but not a striving Protestant Englishman.[63]

To set the record straight, Harriott offered his report in three parts. The first was a review of "merchantable" commodities that would befit the English economy and help establish an imperial economic system that would dovetail with the home economy, the second of commodities "for victual and sustenance of mans life." But it was the third, the "briefe description of the nature and manners of the people of the country," that was most critical strategically and politically.[64] The indigenous societies, too, could be made to dovetail into a British system. That this effort had thus far failed did not matter, and colonists would cling to this belief for decades to come.

To begin with, Harriott asserted that the Indians "are not to be feared, but that they shall have cause both to feare and love us that shall inhabite among them." Militarily, the advantages were entirely with the English. His description would have struck veterans of the Irish wars as familiar:

> Those weapons that they have, are onely bows made of Witchhazle, and arrows of reedes, flat edged truncheons also of wood about a yard long, neither have they any thing to defend themselves but targets made of barks, and some armours made of sticks wickered together with thread. . . . Their manner of warres amongst themselves, is either by sudden surprising one an other most commonly about the dawning of the day, or moone light, or els by ambushes, or some subtile devises. Set battels are very rare, except it fall out where there are many trees, after the deliverie of every arrowe, in leaping behind some or other.[65]

Beyond these tactical and operational matters, Harriott saw that indigenous societies and political structures were loose and dispersed, not well organized to resist a proper colonizing effort. The Algonkian towns were small, only a few near the seacoast, and containing on average ten to twelve houses. Nor, apparently, was there much higher-level organization. "In some places of the Countrey," Harriott observed, "one onely towne belongeth to the government of a Wiroans or chiefe Lord . . . [and] the greatest Wiroans that yet we had dealing with, had but eighteen townes in his government & able to make not above seven or eight hundredth fighting men at most."[66] This localism, too, was like Ireland.

If these weaknesses allayed English fears, they also raised English hopes: "By so much the more is it probable that they shoulde desire our friendships and love, and have the greater respect for pleasing and obeying us." This also perfectly fit the English model of colonizing. "Whereby it may be hoped," Harriott concluded, "if by meanes of good government be used, that they may be in short time be brought to civilitie, and the embracing of true religion."[67] This was the British imperial, expansionist approach in sum: establishing security through military supremacy, pacifying and integrating the locals into the empire by first civilizing and then Christianizing them as good Protestants, for the salvation of their souls and to make them allies in the Protestant geopolitical cause. By such means could the peoples of disparate cultures, politics, and faiths be made "new English."

Harriott saw the Algonkians as essentially human. "Some religion they have already," he wrote, and "though they believe that there are many Gods," there was "one onely cheefe and great God, which hath been from all eternitie." The Indians, so to speak, were on the path to monotheism. They also believed in the immortality of the soul. Moreover, the social and political order, though on a small scale, had the making of civility in it. They had "great respect to their Governours, and also great care what they doe," lest they suffer the "punishment ordained for malefactours, as stealers, whoremongers, and other sorts of wicked doers, some punished with death, some with forfeitures, some with beating, according to the greatenesse of the facts."[68] And the Algonkians were clearly impressed with the power of English Protestantism. "If they knewe not the trueth of God and religion already, it was rather to be had from us," although the Indians did not quite grasp the distinction between the word of God and the physical Bible: "Although I tolde them the booke materially and of it selfe was not of any such virtue . . . yet woulde many bee glad to touche it, to embrace it, to kisse it, to holde it to their breastes and heads, and stroke all over their body with it."[69]

Harriott concluded his sketch of Algonkian society by repeating his warning that success depended upon the quality of British rule; hegemony was only sustainable if it was benign and perceived to be just. He had wished to make it plain "that there is good hope [the Indians] may be brought through discreete dealing and government to the imbracing of the trueth, and consequently to honour, obey, feare and love us." But he also warned that "some of our companie towards the end of the yeere" had unecessarily "shewed themselves to fierce, in slaying some of the people, in some townes." Perhaps the killings were "justly deserved," but they were strategically risky and might better have been avoided. Strict martial law and unbending military rule, Harriott hinted—even though his tract was written partly to defend Ralph Lane's reputation—would not be sufficient to build self-sustaining colonies or a durable empire.

Harriott's terse tract was a powerful summation of the prospects and purposes for English colonization. But what gave the *Briefe and true report* special force was the accompanying drawings by John White, particularly as translated into prints in the more widely circulated de Bry editions. White's illustrations of Algonkian figures and societies made Harriott's words even more vivid, making the exotic seem more familiar, and he was as scrupulous and meticulous in drawing as Harriott was in prose. White's figures were further "Europeanized," indigenous facial and other features softened and "classicized" as they were worked by de Bry's engravers. And, to make the point even plainer, the de Bry editions included woodcuts of Picts—pre-Roman Britons—all but indistinguishable from Algonkians. The distance from savage to civility was not so far, and it was a road the British themselves had travelled; indeed, in de Bry, the Pict appeared more savage than the Algonkian.

In attempting to settle in the Middle Atlantic, Ralegh's colonists had pushed the boundaries of Britain to a new frontier. For the moment, it was a frontier too far, and the danger from Spain was pounding on England's front door. Yet even in failure, the effort reaffirmed the soundness of the overall strategy to achieve great-power status and security through western expansion and empire. The matter of succession to Elizabeth loomed, as ever, but the regime was no longer immediately challenged internally. Scotland was far from won, but it was no longer a source of immediate vulnerability, not only because of the more or less friendly regime in Edinburgh but because France, the traditional source of mischief, was itself divided. By the turn of the century, Ireland, too, would appear reasonably stable and a good prospect for colonization. On the continent, and by the skin of their teeth, the Dutch had all but proved their de facto independence from Spain, helping to ameliorate the threat of invasion. And on the high seas, Englishmen had showed themselves the equal of the Spanish and more; around the globe, they sailed where they pleased.

In forty-five years on the throne, Elizabeth had achieved much. She did not pass from the scene without issue, either, for she had given birth to a tradition in strategy-making that provided guidance and inspiration to her successors both in London and in the New World. But one of the characteristics that has given this tradition such longevity is that from the start it had many parents, not just the queen, nor her advisers or her courtiers. As much as the poetry or plays of the era, the English approach to strategy was an emanation from an extraordinarily rich and broadly shared culture, from a vital and growing political nation whose discourse was charged with disputatious energy.

7

THE ELIZABETHAN
STRATEGIC DISCOURSE

With a global view of the balance of power, memories of past glory and pressures of present weakness, a drive to defend the "true religion" against the encroachments of Rome and Spain, a large and literate political class, and decades of unresolved internal and external conflict, it is hardly surprising that Elizabethans were forever debating questions of geopolitical purpose, military means, and, above all, ways to employ the latter to achieve the former. The conversation about strategy was continuous, vigorous, and frequently had consequences.

Over the course of Elizabeth's long reign, something like a consensus had jelled from out of contingent decisions, trial and error, ideological and confessional fervor, military and diplomatic experience, learned debate, political faction, bureaucratic habit, profit motives, and a hundred other factors. First of all, it was necessary that England become an empire, encompassing large areas and diverse peoples; domestic—England and Wales made a "composite monarchy" already—and international politics alike demanded it. The sixteenth century was a period of globalization, and isolationism was simply impossible—or at least unlikely to be survivable let alone successful. Second, it had to be an empire with a larger purpose, securing a space for the practice of Protestantism. This would not only serve God's transcendent purpose but secure justice and thus stability in the world. Nor could English nationalism alone make a coherent imperial polity. Kingdoms that shared a common basic religious faith—and a common fear of Catholic Counter-Reformation—would have less reason to quarrel.

But how and where to build a modern empire? Through the Elizabethan period, the political nation fumbled its way toward a number of
rough strategic rules of thumb. The first imperative was to assert English
control across the isle of Britain itself, beginning with the centralization
of power in England and the continuation of the Tudor order and regime
if not the House of Tudor itself. And if—after the failures of Henry VIII's
"rough wooing"—Scotland could not be conquered nor yet joined in a
union, neither could it be permitted strategic independence, particularly
to ally with France. Rule number two applied to continental Europe,
and despite the Norman roots of the English crown, a series of holding
actions would have to suffice. England was not strong enough to do
more than hope that diplomacy, maritime descents, Protestant allies and
proxies—assured and stiffened with British contingents on occasion—
could chain down Spain, France, or, heaven forbid, a combination of
Catholic powers. The third rule, the one that might in the longer term
realize England's great-power ambitions, mandated colonial and imperial
expansion to the West. Here, too, the English conceived unique strategic
ends, as we have seen, meant in contrast to what they perceived to be
the Spanish model. Ireland would be colonized, civilized, Protestantized,
and take a stake in a shared, "British" imperial project; so would colonies
in North America be modeled as "new Englands." The Atlantic would
not, like the English Channel, be a moat for defense but, secured on the
far European and North American shores, an internal sea across which
to project military power and develop a powerful trading economy that
might at least balance, if not surpass, Spain's harvests of bullion. Thus,
the ultimate purpose of English sea power was not simply to secure an
"international commons" open to all but to make possible the building
of a transatlantic "greater Britain" that could compete with Spain.

The Tudor conception of an imperial Britain as a framework for
the reassertion of English power was a widely shared and also shaped
as an increasingly powerful idea across an expanding political nation;
indeed, there was something inherently plastic in the thing. Nevertheless,
three broad strands wove themselves into a powerful cord. The first of
these was the "Galfridian" myth of an Arthurian British empire, which
found its voice in the 1570s through the writings of John Dee, a Welsh
mathematician, astronomer and astrologist, occultist, and public intellectual who had an uncanny influence with the queen and court—not
least with the supposed *politique* William Cecil—despite his many quirks.
This conception had great emotive power, in that it recalled not only

the greatness of an Arthurian past but, indirectly, England's recently lost continental outposts. At the same time, the current continental balance and the problems of Spanish power and English weakness made it impractical and all but unrealizable. The second, and more powerful, was a Protestant, Renaissance-humanist vision of Britain as a neo-Roman res publica, an idea developed powerfully by Sir Thomas Smith, perhaps the leading light of the Cambridge humanists, who was the first Regius Professor of Civil Law and then vice-chancellor of the university, and tutor to the young William Cecil. Smith also was a politically influential figure in his own right and had a strong hand in shaping a younger generation. With its roots in classical thought and fully informed of other Renaissance and humanist political theory and debate, this second strand of British empire-imagining exercised a far more profound and practical influence over Elizabethan policy. The third strand, equally powerful, had its origins in the defense of the Protestant Reformation. It is useful to think of this aggressively Protestant strand as an overlay on the humanist strand; William Cecil, as we have seen, was, for all his caution, relentlessly and powerfully committed to the Protestant cause described above, and Elizabeth's many Protestant champions were steeped in Renaissance political thought. Thus any differences between the camps of courtiers had more to do with priorities and personalities than principles. But, as the mix made for policy differences, the distinction remains a useful one.

Intertwined with these political principles were two other, "functional" strands that originated from the growing and increasingly professional military class, sailors and soldiers alike. Just as English minds absorbed and contributed to the political thought of the late Renaissance, so, too, did they absorb and adapt to the rapidly changing paradigms of warfare on the European continent, at sea, and, most critically, at the colonial perimeter that was becoming so central to the overall balance of power. The late sixteenth century is often thought to be a period of "military revolution," with the proliferation of easily carried firearms, innovations in fortification, developments in oceangoing warships, and the logistical and tactical puzzles these new inventions created. But even as they became alert to new ways of war, Englishmen also understood that not every continental innovation was as useful or applicable to their particular strategic circumstances—in Ireland, there was little to besiege or to fortify to a European degree. Finally, England was a slowly developing and centralizing state but lacked the resources of Spain or France. The result was that a cadre of thoughtful and experienced officers, ranging from Francis Drake and Walter Ralegh to John Norris, Lord Mountjoy and Ralph Lane (and sometimes including courtiers like the Earls of Leicester and Essex), who were familiar both with cutting-edge military developments but also with the ways these trends mattered for English purpose. These experts played a substantial role in shaping English strategy, both in London and abroad, especially in the colonial context. In building this composite sketch of the English strategic debate, Sir John Norris will speak for this class. He also reflects the aspirations of his class: Elizabeth's military men—much like her close civilian advisers—were almost exclusively "middling sorts" on the make, ambitious to better themselves socially and economically, "meritocrats" and "technocrats" displacing the feudal aristocrats who heretofore had dominated the English military caste.

There was, finally, a fifth element in the strategic discourse, a new but powerful strain: the voice of English colonists and their advocates. As with the military men, colonists had immediate and practical concerns that shaped their interpretation of basic political and strategic experience. What might appear at Cambridge or court as the niceties of policy or strategy seemed more like necessities of survival out along the imperial frontier. Civilizing indigenous "Indians" or revealing the truths of reformed religion were less pressing than conquest. Security came first, and the lack of it tempered ambition with anxiety; it was these pioneers who felt the weaknesses of the Elizabethan state most keenly and directly.

Thus, the Elizabeth strategic discourse was a continuous debate. Yet looked at in the whole, it was one that lurched toward a remarkably strong consensus that would provide a yardstick against which subsequent policy would be measured. As will be shown in the following volumes of this series, this consensus took a beating through much of the seventeenth century, only to return during the Revolution of 1688 and the reigns of William III and Anne. In these snapshots of the men whose writings and actions did so much to forge that consensus, we see the outlines of what would prove to be a deeply embedded strategic culture.

JOHN DEE'S IMAGINED EMPIRE

By the late 1570s, Elizabeth's via media—in international and confessional affairs alike—began to break down. Charting a middle course between

Protestants and Catholics on the continent and at home was proving increasingly difficult; as Spain stepped up its efforts to crush the Dutch revolt, so did the queen's councilors step up their pressure on Elizabeth to intervene. Whether she would or no, her people declared that "Elizabeth now Queen of England is ordained of God to be Queen of Jerusalem."[1]

The politician in Elizabeth had little interest in assuming such an apocalyptic role. Yet the dynastic international order she desired—where monarchs ruled absolutely, without interference from either religion or popular politics—could not be revived. A durable strategy could not rest simply upon containing France and Spain; it had to be based upon something greater. The queen could not just stand *against*, she had to stand *for*—that is, for an order that gave meaning to the world and purpose to her people's trials. Indeed, even Elizabeth and her courtiers lived in a larger world, where a transcendent order stood just in the shadows:

> In that almost alien universe, Queen Elizabeth I pores over her alchemical manuscripts and then applies their methods in her laboratory, seeking incessantly for the philosopher's stone that will purify decaying bodies and society alike. In that world, the Queen's most influential adviser, Lord Burghley, pleads for a fragment of that stone to help build a navy against the Spanish Armada, and the Queen's favorite, Lord Robert Dudley, believes that Christians can legitimately conjure angels to reveal the political future. It is where experienced politicians wonder what the appearance of comets signals for the future of war in the Netherlands, where ancient prophecies are applied to Elizabeth as the Last World Empress before Christ's imminent Second Coming.[2]

John Dee was, particularly in the years when Elizabeth and her principal advisors defined the role that they wished to play on the stage of empires, the man who conjured a vision of English greatness, of a British empire—for it was Dee who gave the term its currency. Dee was a magus, not only to the alchemical queen but to an idea of British power. Indeed, Dee did not so much invent the idea of a global British empire; he channeled it. Glyn Parry, in his enthusiastic, profoundly sophisticated biography, asserts that Dee's "imperial" writings "would determine English history for centuries to come."[3] If a strategic culture is something that coheres around a shared meaning in the exercise of power, then John Dee has a fair claim as the original source of the Anglo-American tradition.

An extraordinary claim, but Dee was an extraordinary character in an extraordinary time. He sought nothing less than a comprehensive understanding of all of creation, which he was sure God had vouch-safed to elevated minds. In applying his wide-ranging learning and fertile mind to imagining a British empire, Dee looked primarily to the Arthurian past—a realm that encompassed not only the British Isles but extended to northwest Europe (and thus made the English Channel and the North Sea an internal sea, or, in international legal terms, a mare clausum subject to English dominion) and North America. As a direct descendant of Arthur and the Plantagenets, Elizabeth's claims could be extraordinarily expansive. This European Arthurian legend lent legiti-macy to the forward-leaning Protestant element at court, and the Earl of Leicester embraced it enthusiastically: during the summer of 1575, when the debate over intervention in the Netherlands began to peak, the earl "staged elaborate Arthurian pageants for Elizabeth at [his castle at] Kenilworth." Similarly, in The Faerie Queene, the Arthurian rescue of Belge—as directed by the Elizabeth-figure Mercilla—is a central trope for Edmund Spenser, from whom we shall shortly hear more.[4]

But Dee's Arthur served to advance claims not only in Britain and Europe but in the New World as well, and in many ways it was this element in Dee's thought that had the greatest and most lasting effect, if only because English claims in Europe were no longer within the grasp of English monarchs. London might see the European great-power balance as its most pressing strategic concern, but it could not practically realize any territorial dream. Thus, with time, the maritime dimension of Dee's British empire "became the defining feature of the empire itself."[5] But while the "continental dimension" of Dee's conception became incon-venient and unrealizable, it never became irrelevant: Elizabethan, later British and Anglo-American strategy-making might encompass the entire world, but its balance-of-power bottom line was in western Europe. Dee's greatest impact was to weave these two strands together.

Dee's ideas were developed and redeveloped throughout his life, and he was not afraid to tailor them for political or personal expediency; he made his living from his wits and worked tirelessly to shimmy up the Elizabethan social and economic poles. Nor were confessional niceties too much of a problem for Dee—except when he ran afoul of either committed Catholics or Protestants—and he looked for advancement as energetically under Edward VI and Mary Tudor as under Elizabeth. Nonetheless, it was by applying his academic and alchemical skills to advance the cause of geopolitical Protestantism in the late 1570s and early 1580s that he enjoyed his greatest successes. Three works encapsulate Dee at his most influential: *General and Rare Memorials Pertaining to the Perfect Art of Navigation*, which appeared in 1577 after numerous revisions; and two manuscripts widely circulated at court, *On the Limits of the British Empire* and *Of Famous and Rich Discoveries*.

When *Memorials* appeared in September 1577, it provided both justification for the assertion of English power in northwest Europe and a military plan for fulfilling its providential predictions. Dee "believed in the centuries-old vision of a reformed world, unified politically and religiously under a Last World Emperor [and] saw Arthur as part of his search 'for the pure verity, understanding and recovering of divers secret, ancient and weighty matters' of universal knowledge."[6] Dee's angels had convinced him that, particularly in the context of Spain's troubles in the Netherlands, Elizabeth was designated to be this universal monarch. The moment was "a little lock of Lady Occasion, Flickering in the Air, by our hands, to catch hold on: whereby, we may, yet once more (before, all, be utterly past, and for ever) discreetly, and valiantly recover, and enjoy, if not all our Ancient and due Appurtenances, to this British Monarchy, Yet, at the least, some such Notable Portion thereof, As . . . this may be the most Peaceable, most Rich, most Puissant, and most Flourishing Monarchy of all else (this day) in Christendom."[7]

Dee also drew the title page illustration for *Memorials*, depicting Elizabeth at the helm of the ship of Christendom, supported by Britain, "to arm ourselves with a war machine." That war machine would be a "Petty Navy Royal," not oceangoing galleons but a fleet meant to rule the waves of the northern mare clausum. Its purposes were to prevent an invasion; suppress piracy and smuggling, particularly of military stores and arms; protect English trade and fishing industries; and train more navigators and seamen—traditional arguments made previously and continuously by English advocates of a maritime strategy. This British "Narrow Seas Fleet" would secure "the Royalty and Sovereignty of the Seas . . . environing this Monarchy of England, Ireland, and (by right) Scotland, and the Orkneys also."[8]

In typically Elizabethan manner, Dee declared that this fleet would be self-financing, "maintained, without any Cost or Charge to the Queene."[9] However, beyond customs revenue or booty reclaimed from pirates, Dee proposed a tax scheme—what would one day be known as "ship money"—that, despite involving what Dee claimed were very low rates of assessment, was both impolitic and impractical. Even more controversially, the fleet was intended to be an instrument of the Earl of Leicester's ambitions for the Netherlands, and as such it ran afoul of the queen's changing policies and attitudes toward the European balance of power. Dee's powerful statement of a forward strategy of support for Protestants and enmity toward Spain was too rich for Elizabeth, and she forbade wider distribution of *Memorials*.

Nonetheless, *Memorials* expressed and shaped the Elizabethan strategic imagination in the year that Drake put to sea and long after; its effects were larger and perhaps beyond what the author directly intended. Two months after the manuscript began to circulate, Sir Humphrey Gilbert visited Dee at his house at Mortlake, from which he is likely to have sent two "discourses" on "how her Majestie may annoy the king of Spain," not simply by closing off the sea approaches to the Netherlands and dominating the waters of northwest Europe but operating in the open Atlantic: "[The] way to worke the feate is to sett forth under such like colour of which place they shall . . . meete in effecte all the great shipping of Freaunce, Spayne, and Portyngall, where I would have take and bring awaye with fraygthes and ladings, the best of those shippes and burn the worst."[10] Gilbert and Drake are sometimes dismissed as little more than state-sanctioned pirates, but if so it was at least piracy with a strategic purpose. In sum, *Memorials* and Dee's work more broadly helped to solidify the link made by Elizabethans between projecting power into and across the Atlantic and the balance of power on the continent. This was neither strictly a blue-water approach nor an exclusively continental one but a marriage of the two that came from a larger, global appreciation of the balance of power. The security of the Tudor regime, the safety of the "British" realm, and England's interests in the European "near abroad" were inextricably tied to the ability to conduct military operations on an expanding scale.

At the same time he was producing *Memorials*, Dee also wrote the extensive manuscript *Of Famous and Rich Discoveries*, in support of the "Cathay Campaign," or search for a northwest passage. William Sherman writes that Dee was likely hired either by the court insider Sir William Dyer or by the Muscovy Company directly to be "the voice of scholarly persuasion" in support of the project, "but the frame of the argument transcended the question of Cathay and contained the elements of

Elizabethan expansionism as a whole."[11] Over the sprawling manuscript's two hundred fifty folios, Dee summoned the full panoply of his claims, beginning with the idea that these would be voyages of recovery—again, recovery of a lost Arthurian British empire—rather than discovery. On the way to the northwest passage to the east lay a hemisphere of islands and regions "fully appertinent to the Crown of this Brytish Impire" that would make England "the Incomparable Island of the Whole World."[12] In short, Dee's rationale and support for the search for a northwest passage was a piece of his larger vision of and argument for a British empire, a commercial expression of the larger imperial vision.

During this period Dee also composed a third elaboration of his ideal, *Brytanici Imperii Limites*, the *Limits of the British Empire*—and very expansive "limits" they were. They included extensive claims to the North American coast, justified by both human and divine law, essentially everywhere north of Spain's possessions in the Caribbean: "Of a great parte of the sea Coastes of Atlantis (otherwise called *America*) next unto us, and of all the Iles nere unto the same, from Florida northerly, and Chieflie of all the Ilands Septentroniall [that is, northern], great and small, the Tytle Royall and supreme government is due, and appropriate unto yo[ur] most Gratious Ma[jesty] and that partlie Iure Gentium, partlie Iure Civilis, and partlie Iure Divino, No other Prince or Potentate els, in the whole world being able to allege therto Clayme the like."[13]

Dee seems to have begun work on *Limits* even before the other two titles, though not completed it until 1578. This was also the period when he had the greatest access to Elizabeth and the greatest credibility, so it is likely that the manuscript served as a kind of briefing paper for discussions at court. Dee notes in his diary that he carried the manuscript with him on his visits, particularly in the summer of 1578.[14] The apogee of Dee's career came during a series of conversations, arranged by Leicester, with the queen and Burghley at which he presented Elizabeth with a variety of papers, including a draft of *Limits*. The interviews began in the late morning of Monday, October 3, 1580, with the queen in her gardens at Richmond Palace and continued that afternoon when Burghley, no doubt wary of Leicester's motives and anxious to monitor the potential policy implications of Dee's claims, joined the session.

William Cecil was himself deeply knowledgeable about the genealogy of European royalty. He continued his examination of Dee on both Tuesday and Wednesday, taking copious notes from *Limits*, and Dee noted that "he used me very honorably on his behalf." Yet by Friday, October

7, Burghley must have come to the conclusion that Dee's arguments were both substantively weak and politically inconvenient, for "being told of my being without [Burghley's chambers], and also I standing before him at his coming forth," Elizabeth's principal strategist brusquely brushed past and "would not speak to me." On October 10, the queen visited Dee at Mortlake to make amends, assuring him of Burghley's praise of his scholarship. But in fact the geopolitical developments of late 1580, and particularly the news that Philip II had annexed Portugal, made British assertions of European or oceanic sovereignty seem not only empty but dangerous. Moreover, the Leicester-Walsingham faction was forced to move the hopes of its "forward" policy to France and the person of the Duke of Anjou as the counterweight to Spanish power in northwest Europe.[15] Even the most aggressive advisers felt it was time for England to mark time strategically, wringing what could be got from dynastic diplomacy rather than direct military means.

As Glyn Parry observes, thus passed the "high-water mark of Dee's imperial advice to Elizabeth," and thereafter the courtly "tide went out, taking Dee with it."[16] Though his personal fortunes ebbed, his imperial and strategic vision endured. He would remain a source and inspiration for trans-Atlantic exploration and colonization. And, by the late 1580s, when the situation in northern Europe was at its most perilous and the Dutch begged Elizabeth to become their sovereign, Burghley revived the very arguments he dismissed in 1580; his notes to *Limits* eventually served his view of the national interest. But perhaps Dee's most significant contribution was to synthesize the westward-looking, blue-water, colonizing strain of British strategic culture with the eastward-looking, continental, power-balancing strain into one coherent, historically and divinely legitimate, and long-lived global imperial vision. This best suited the expansionist impulse that coursed through the hearts of both "cautious" *politiques* like Burghley and Elizabeth and aggressive "geopolitical Protestants" like Leicester and Walsingham. This balance would prove difficult to maintain, but it also proved to be the point of equilibrium to which later British strategy-makers would return.

THOMAS SMITH AND THE
MISSION CIVILIZATRICE

Ireland lay at the heart of English imperial thought, and putting down Tyrone's rebellion provoked the greatest, most sustained, and most costly military effort of Elizabeth's five decades on the throne. In combination with the consolidation of the regime in England and the exclusion of France from Scotland, the conquest of Ulster marked a final transition from an older "English" approach to strategy-making to a fully British perspective; it was still a long way from a "united kingdom," but it was undoubtedly an empire—encompassing many peoples of many faiths, including a diverse and contentious collections of Protestant sects and various regional, economic, and social interests—engaged in a global struggle for power.

Thus, in the early 1570s Sir Thomas Smith, one of the leading political and intellectual figures of the time, a member of the Leicester-Walsingham circle and a man devoted to the larger "Protestant interest," was given a grant of 360,000 acres in east Ulster to plant a new English colony. Smith was the very model of the English humanist, rising from modest origins to become earl, along with John Cheke, one of Henry VIII's King's Scholars at Cambridge and, in 1533, taken on as a university lecturer in Greek and Greek philosophy. By 1540, his learning and eloquence had so dazzled Cambridge—and students such as a young and impressionable William Cecil—that he was appointed to one of five new, royally sponsored Regius chairs, holding the position in civil law. Three years later, at age thirty, he became vice president of Queens' College.[17]

Smith made the jump from college to court under the reign of Edward VI and through the ascendency of the young king's uncle, Edward Seymour, Earl of Somerset, who had recruited a group of young Cambridge scholars, such as Cheke to tutor the king and Cecil to help buttress Seymour's household establishment. Smith was made clerk of the privy council, a lucrative post that also meant insider access at court. Within a year, Smith was raised to become second secretary to the king. Another formative experience was Somerset's renewal of Henry VIII's "rough wooing" campaigns to force the joining of the English and Scottish thrones through the marriage of Edward and Mary, then the infant Queen of Scots; illness prevented Smith from taking part militarily, but the campaign was a seminal moment for the young, ambitious scholars from Cambridge, especially Cecil and Smith. In sum, Smith had joined a new kind of elite: the men whose learning, particularly in political philosophy, put them at the heart of late Tudor strategy-making and whose first thoughts were how to secure the regime and consolidate power throughout Britain—in large degree by rolling back the French "auld alliance" to Scotland but more generally to suppress Catholic and continental influence across the British Isles. Although Smith expressed his commitment to Protestantism of the times in humanist, seemingly secular terms, he could work comfortably and closely with Thomas Cranmer, the energetic Archbishop of Canterbury, and very much shared the ideology of geopolitical Protestantism, the drive to secure a "greater Britain" that would be a bastion of English reformed Christianity.

In early 1547, Smith became a member of the household of Edward Seymour, Earl of Somerset, a close advisor to Henry VIII and brother to Jane Seymour, the king's third wife. Upon Henry's death, Somerset was named to the Council of Regency for his ten-year-old nephew Edward VI; he soon dominated the council, designating himself "Lord Protector of the Realm" and receiving a dukedom. Though Somerset is often portrayed as a power-mad autocrat, the duke confronted a daunting challenge: as a minor, Edward was a king wanting in legitimacy, a condition exacerbated by the reformation of traditional religion. The response—a "monarchy of counsel"—anticipated Cecil's "mixed monarchy," and indeed Cecil drew deeply on his experience of Edward's reign during Elizabeth's early years. For his part, Smith was very much a public face of the new order, serving as a lead examiner in the case of Edmund Bonner, the soon-to-be-deposed bishop of London for his attacks on the council and Somerset and his resistance to reform of church and state. As Anne McLaren observes, Smith made the case "presenting government policy as both consensual within the Council and as the king's will, pressing patriotism into the service of godliness."[18] Smith would return to these issues and arguments during his service under Elizabeth.

The fall of Somerset, Edward's very short reign, and the coming of the Catholic Mary Tudor to the throne drove Smith into the political wilderness, but through his second wife he acquired a manor house, Hill Hall, redesigning it as a Renaissance palace in the French style, and acquired one of the largest libraries in the country, collecting not only classical texts but modern works of political philosophy such as Castiglione's *Book of the Courtier*. "Most significant of all, Smith may have used Hill Hall as an alternative university, encouraging scholars to meet and discuss important issues and problems in order to advise politicians."[19] These sessions included military and strategic discussions. Gabriel Harvey, himself an ambitious young Cambridge scholar and frequent participant in such discussions, recorded one Hill Hall conversation about strategy for Ireland framed around Livy's history of the Roman Republic:

Thomas Smith junior [Smith's son] and Sir Humphrey Gilbert [debated] for Marcellus, Thomas Smith senior and Doctor Walter Haddon for Fabius Maximus. Before an audience at Hill Hall consisting at that very time of myself, John Wood and several others of gentle birth. At length the son and Sir Humphrey yielded to the distinguished Secretary: perhaps Marcellus yielded to Fabius. Both of them worthy men, and judicious. Marcellus the more powerful; Fabius the more cunning. Neither was the latter unprepared, nor the former imprudent: each was as indispensable as the other in his place. There are times when I would rather be Marcellus, times when Fabius.[20]

Smith did not immediately resume a role at court with Elizabeth's ascension to the throne in 1558. He had fallen out with Cecil and sought to "write himself back into favor" by taking part in the raging debate about Elizabeth's marriage, producing a "Dialogue on the Queen's Marriage" that rehearsed the case both for and against a foreign match, but playing to the advantage of Robert Dudley, not yet the Earl of Leicester but very much the queen's favorite and the most likely substitute English match. Despite this, Smith eventually reconciled with Cecil and was rewarded with the punishing but plum role at the French court as an emissary explaining Elizabeth's reasons for supporting the Huguenots, not an easy assignment in an environment dominated by the aggressively Catholic Guise family faction. Smith was skewered both by the contradictions in Elizabeth's policy and his need to cover for the actions of Nicholas Throckmorton, another court favorite who was in the field with the French Protestant forces. After several years of frustration and increasing illness, Smith moved to Toulouse, again seeking solace through his pen, producing the constitutional treatise *De Republica Anglorum: a Discourse on the Commonwealth of England*, now regarded as Smith's most famous work.[21] It was both the most important contemporary explication of the practical workings of the Tudor government and, at the same time and perhaps more importantly, an apologetic for a godly, conciliar—and thus with more than a hint of republicanism—yet still absolute form of monarchy.[22]

This was also a politics of "association," a term of political philosophy and a concept that would periodically resurface, not only in Elizabeth's time but throughout the trial of the Stuart century to follow; the problems of a monarch of constrained capacity—a minor male, a woman, or one under the spell of an especial court "favorite"—remained a constant challenge. The answers—and, by contrast to the problems of unchained absolutism as evidenced in Spain or France, relatively successful answers— lay in the essential godly virtue of a Protestant political nation and the structure of mixed, conciliar monarchy. *De Republica Anglorum* described both the perfected form and actual practice of English government, offering a kind of contracted model for a British empire: "A common wealth is called a society or common doing of a multitude of free men collected together and united by a common accord and covenants among themselves, for the conservation of the themselves as well in peace and is in war." In the context of widely shared and thoroughly reformed religion, the dangers of disorder and classical republicanism were mitigated—the bigger the political nation, the better. As were the yeoman of the countryside, so might the tradesmen of the towns might "be commonly made Church-wardens, alecunners (i.e., ensuring the purity of ale and beer), and many times Constables."[23] The British Empire was to be made by and for the "middling sort" as well as the monarch and the nobility.

It was in France also that he began to think more systematically about the challenges of colonization and Ireland—of how to integrate the periphery into this godly, orderly commonwealth. He wrote to Cecil in June 1565, "For this two hundred years not one hath taken the right way to make that country either subject or profitable," arguing that more thorough conquest would be "the most honourable and princely enterprise that Her Majesty might take in hand." In the fall, he continued: "In my mind it needeth nothing more than to have colonies. To augment our tongue, our laws, our religion in that Isle, which three be the true bands of the commonwealth whereby the Romans conquered and kept long time a great part of the world."[24] Smith focused ever more on the Irish question upon his return from France to Hill Hall in the late 1560s. In 1571, Throckmorton died, Cecil was elevated to become Lord Burghley, and Francis Walsingham dispatched to Paris as ambassador. Needing a steady hand, Cecil turned to his old teacher; Thomas Smith returned to the privy council and, after performing stalwart duty in the case against the Duke of Norfolk, was chosen to become secretary in Cecil's place.

Smith seized upon his elevation to promote a colonization scheme for Ireland, petitioning the queen for a grant of lands in eastern Ulster. Appealing to Elizabeth's parsimony as well as her strategic ambitions, he proposed to form a company that would undertake the conquest and colonization "at their own charges and perils" to "to make the same civil and peopled with natural Englishmen born." In support and to recruit fellow investors and adventurers, Smith produced a pair of "startling modern" propaganda pamphlets that introduced themes that would become staples of British colonial rhetoric.[25] To begin with, Smith shared the general English view of the Irish, including the Anglo-Norman elites. He noted "the idle following of herds as the Tartarians, Arabians, and Irishmen do." Smith contended that England was overpopulated, "with few dwellings empty." Ireland, in contrast, was an underdeveloped, "vacant," and desolate "waste." His was a "noble and honorable enterprise of inhabiting the wastes of Ireland." Once again, the English views of proper husbandry and economic and social development provided material reason and moral legitimacy for a colonial project. He therefore strenuously contended that—in marked contrast to Spanish colonization of the Americas—his project was no "conquest except they will call inhabiting of waste and desolate grounds a conquest." Appealing to the incumbent lord lieutenant in Dublin, Sir William FitzWilliam, Smith wrote: "It is the best conquest that is done by amity, benefits and quietness. I would have [his son, who would actually lead the colony] a defender, no invader, and maintainer of ploughs and tillage, not a chaser away of them, a people of houses and towns, not a desolater . . . they come to enrich the country with corn and other provision whereof they shall also reap more benefit, not to impoverish it."[26]

As Hiram Morgan observes, Smith hoped to provide his colonists with conditions that would not only allow them to settle peacefully and develop Ireland economically, but provide the basis for a civilized political order. Development and security would walk hand in hand. Eventually, argued Smith, this Ulster colonial inkspot would spread into a mixed commonwealth along English lines, of the sort sketched in *De Republica Anglorum*: "Nothing doth more to people the country with men, maketh men more civil nor bringeth more commodities to the sustenance of man than the plough." In sum, Smith's view was entirely in the mainstream of London's thinking about economic and social development. Alas, like traditional northern English lords, this is not how the indigenous Irish saw it; Sir Brian MacPhelim O'Neill—heretofore an O'Neill loyal to the crown—got hold of a copy of the pamphlet and saw in it nothing but threat. Writing separately to Fitzwilliam and to the English court, he complained that it was a usurpation of his power and a poor reward for his past services fighting for Elizabeth. But he also complained that Ireland was too poor to support an increased population, in essence turning Smith's development argument on its head. Wastes were wastes, in Sir Brian's reckoning; Smith's enterprise was not a win-win proposition but a zero-sum game, and change would undermine the O'Neill machine. Unable to prevent the enterprise from going forward, the Irish chief resorted to a mixture of irregular war and diplomacy, following tradition and foreshadowing the tactics that were to be perfected by Tyrone. Smith's first colonizing attempt came to a bad end when his son was shot and killed in October 1573.[27]

The failure was an especially bitter one for Smith: just prior to the expedition, he was assigned again to duty in France, negotiating the Treaty of Blois. He could not run the Ireland expedition by remote control, and his son was weak, corrupt, and fatally unlucky. Yet Smith resolved to try his colonization plan once more, now admitting that it must be a more straightforward and state-sponsored plan of conquest, occupation, and only eventual civilization. In December 1574, he completed a minutely detailed plan—one that would find echoes in later plans for English colonies in North America. Smith's modern biographer, Mary Dewar, described it as "nothing less than a complete blueprint for the organization and government of a colony."[28] All colonists were expected to be soldiers as well as settlers, and the colonial government would be military government; the executive would hold a colonel's rank. Smith made it clear that security was the first order of governmental business, before development could begin. In specifying "Offices Necessary in the Colony of the Ardes [of Ulster] and Orders Agreed Upon," he wrote: "First, until the colony be settled that you have quietness for the artificers to work in the town, husbandmen in the fields, and the merchant to fairs and markets within the territories of the colony, it must be understood that you are either wholly in the war or half in the war and half in peace. And because you must begin as you were all in war, these offices be necessary."[29]

The first objective was to establish a fortified capital. "The chief strength to fortify a colony is to have a principal city or town of strength well walled and defended."[30] Although Smith's Ulster capital was to be called "Elizabetha," his plan drew heavily on his knowledge of Roman history. He first conceived it as a "Castra colonelli"—a colonel's camp. Military defense trumped all else; no scattered settlements or farmsteads— inviting targets for Irish raiders—were allowed. "This [form of] habitation together engendereth civility, policy, acquaintance, consultation and a firm and sure seat." The town or camp was to be laid out in a grid with a central market.

Forecasting what would be the long-term pattern of English strategy-making, the get-rich-quick scheming of the publicly sanctioned but privately funded 1571 expedition had given way to a more sober, state-directed enterprise. Technically, this was still a private venture, but this time Lord Burghley led a group of aristocratic and politically connected backers. The queen herself also took something of a directing interest, not only in Smith's colony but also in one mounted by the Walter Devereux, first Earl of Essex. Alas, although the plan was sound, the resources were wanting. Initial successes were not enough to resist an Irish rising that drove the settlers out of the Ardes, squabbles among the on-the-ground commanders crippled attempts at a coherent military response, and Elizabeth was still decades away from acquiescing to the kind of investment that Ireland demanded.

Thomas Smith was better at philosophy than policy and a better adviser than executive. Nonetheless, his influence on the course of English political thought and colonial strategy was profound and durable. He had gone a long way toward producing a framework that would one day yield more successful results not only in Ireland but in the New World. He established that English colonies should be "new Englands," with English governments, English law, English trading economies, English societies; they should be part of the larger, British imperial commonwealth. He thought that the Irish natives—be they Gaelic or "Old English"—could be incorporated and eventually even integrated and assimilated, though he had few illusions about the military measures that would require. But it would fall to one of his Hill Hall acolytes, Edmund Spenser, to spell out how brutal those measures might be.

THE CAREER OF SIR JOHN NORRIS

Concluding his portrait of *Sir John Norreys and the Elizabethan Military World*, John Nolan recalls the advice of a fellow historian upon embarking on the project: "a biography of Norreys would have to be a 'career' rather than a 'life.' "[31] But not only is there very little record of Norris's—to use the regularized version of the name—"private" life, it is also the case that Norris was perhaps the foremost "professional" soldier of the time, not a courtier nor a gentleman adventurer nor even simply a tradesman who had mastered a set of tactical or logistical skills. What distinguished Norris from many of his contemporaries was his political savvy, his understanding of the use of military power as a tool of statecraft. And, despite a prickly personality, he could frame military matters in a way Elizabeth could understand and came to trust. So did Lord Burghley. Indeed, his very crankiness made Norris a kind of counterweight to the zealousness of the aggressive Protestants who dominated the "war party" at court. Norris could be relied upon to see the difficulties in any course of action, a valuable perspective to an inherently cautious queen and her principal strategist.

And no understanding of the influences on Elizabethan strategy-making would be complete without a consideration of the rising class of career soldiers and sailors that marked the slow but steady centralization, professionalization, and militarization of the Tudor state. As always, strategy-making reflects a negotiation of ends and means, a balancing of what is desirable and what is practicable. Despite the overall trend toward centralization, the previous chapters all make plain the eternal truth that the on-the-ground military officer often had a stronger hand in shaping the course of events than did the queen, her senior counselors, or any London investors. This proved especially so when it came to colonization campaigns like Ireland or Roanoke, where the decisions to be made were as much political—international, imperial, and local—as narrowly military. Despite being deeply involved in the major strategic decisions of his day, John Norris has faded from view. "Had he been a mariner like Drake, Hawkins, or even Frobisher," writes Nolan, "his name would be much more commonly known."[32]

Yet Norris's career is, in many ways, more instructive than those who lived more colorful lives. The Elizabethan period is notable for the birth of this "class of captains," the professional soldiers who, from Tudor times onward, increasingly served as Britain's lords lieutenant and governors general.[33] These were frequently imperial proconsuls whose missions were civil as well as strictly military; they fully expected that their duties included what is commonly known today as "nation-building." In this way, the ethos of the English and later British army differed significantly from that of the Royal Navy, often exacerbating the constant contest between the blue-water and continental strains in Anglo-American strategic culture. To simplify but clarify: in the "maritime" reckoning, colonies were places to plunder or bases whose purpose it was to serve the global operations of the fleet. Yet as colonies became frontiers to be defended and advanced, and "wastes" to be developed, the governor general stepped to the forefront. Thus, somewhat counterintuitively, soldier-centric "continentalism" became the preferred strategy of the commercial and, in time, Whiggish element in British politics, whereas the Tory-style country-gentleman "squire-archy" tended to embrace the sailor-centric and allegedly cheaper maritime approach.

The professionalism of this new class of military men was born of necessity, from the deepening Elizabethan commitment to the Dutch rebellion. In the Netherlands, English officers learned, often the hard way, the evolving arts of modern conventional warfare in confronting the Spanish *tercios*. "The connection with the Dutch army also provided the English 'army' with a tactical system used in a more or less standard fashion for decades," according to Nolan. "Young Englishmen of military bent swarmed to [the English regiments in the Low Countries], which nearly became an academy for the training of officers."[34] Ireland was also a school for soldiers, though that curriculum was quite different. Many of the same officers learned to adapt, albeit slowly and painfully, to an innovative insurgent enemy employing equally sophisticated weaponry while at the same time working with a variety of Irish allies and proxies from kerne to clan chief. In both cases, English captains learned how to raise, equip, feed, and otherwise sustain forces for extended periods and at great distance—both in space and time—from London. In addition to tactical, logistical, and operational lessons, they learned the arts of "garrison government." From Berwick near the Scottish border to the "cautionary towns" of the Low Countries to Dundalk, Newry, and Kinsale in Ireland, English garrisons became what Stephen Saunders Webb described as the breeding ground of "the soldier-executives of British cities and American colonies."[35]

These officers were both the tool of Elizabethan centralization and a forge for it. They were men of middling rank, for the most part, and while they arrayed themselves with the various factions in Elizabeth's court—especially with those favorites like the Earls of Leicester and Essex, who strove to establish political and personal reputations built upon the martial virtues—they reflected the trend to subordinate the great nobility to royal will. In fact, it was Norris's family ambitions that most often got him into trouble; the queen both relied upon his professional judgment yet feared what looked like a drive to replicate the independent power of the "marcher barons" that had long been the plague of English monarchs. And the failed Essex coup counted a number of disgruntled military professional strivers in its disorganized ranks. But the attitudes of the professional class were better reflected in the behavior of Lord Mountjoy, who went to great lengths to distance himself from Essex despite their former close relations. Indeed, it was something of a compliment to Mountjoy—one lost on Essex—when, in 1599, he was passed over for command in Ireland for being studious and measured where Essex was charismatic and boisterous. The queen's confidence in Mountjoy proved to be well placed, and when he came to command in Ireland, she deferred to him in a way she could not with Essex. At the end of her reign, Elizabeth seems to have found a general she could trust tactically, operationally, and financially, but most of all politically.

No one individual makes a perfect prototype of the professional Elizabethan soldier-executive, and the historical record is less than complete.[36] The prickly Norris, whom we have met in several previous chapters, however, captures many of the essential traits of the type and is all the more interesting in that he seems to have been an especially quarrelsome personality. No Elizabethan "favorite"—although his mother Marjorie was on intimate terms with the queen—Norris was retained and advanced in spite of himself. The historian Emmanuel van Meteren summed up the Dutch view of Norris: "manly and brave but much too arrogant."[37] Many of Norris's countrymen held similar opinions.

Finally, it should be emphasized that Elizabethan "professionalism," not entirely unlike its modern counterpart, was interwoven with factionalism, patronage networks, and the personal loyalties that came from shared service. Men like Norris sought shelter under the protection of the mighty at court and likewise offered shelter to loyal subordinates. Periods of organizational retrenchment were frequent, for Elizabeth and Burghley were forever seeking both strategic and budgetary economies. Senior commanders like Norris often invested their own money to recruit and retain junior commanders and men, and to supply their forces. Even the most scrupulous had "overhead" costs they needed to amortize during periods of inactivity, which inevitably appeared to outsiders as waste, fraud, and abuse. The queen and her treasurer had a quite modern preference for well-defined contracts and their own pet contractors, who were often competitors to Norris and his networks. Parliament, too, whose job it frequently was to come up with money to fund England's forces, echoed with expressions of outrage, particularly when things went wrong in the field. While the government may have had good reasons to be suspicious of corruption—reasons that grew as the pace and scope of the overall military effort increased with the years—its guilty-until-proven-innocent attitudes made a difficult situation worse. The Elizabethans, in the process of modernizing their military, were likewise inventing new forms of civil-military relations. Sir John Norris was undoubtedly a touchy personality, but he often had good reason to be touchy.

Norris was probably born in 1547, to a family that had long been a part of the Tudor military establishment; his great-great-grandfather fought at Bosworth. He was the sixth child of Marjorie and Sir Henry Norris, England's ambassador to France from 1566 to 1572, when he was succeeded by Sir Francis Walsingham. Young John accompanied his father to France, where he got his first exposure to serious soldiering, and perhaps also to Calvinism, with the troops of Admiral Gaspard de Coligny, the Huguenot leader. Norris also formed a close tie to Walsingham, who "for the next decade and a half consistently directed John Norris to the places where aspiring Protestant soldiers were needed most."[38] He also managed to stay in the good graces of William Cecil, but famously and loudly split with the Earl of Leicester in the Netherlands in 1586 and did not get along either with Sir Francis Drake or the young Earl of Essex during the Portugal expedition. Importantly, after his service as ambassador to France, Sir Henry Norris was elevated to the peerage as Baron Norris of Rycote, and, though in his sixties, became lord lieutenant for two counties, a post that greatly aided the careers of his sons—several of John's brothers also became professional soldiers and colonists—by linking them to the domestic Elizabethan military establishment, which was undergoing substantial reform. "As a Lord Lieutenant, Henry Norris could recruit replacements for [his sons'] companies, making sure that promising men were chosen and properly equipped. Lord Norris was also in a good position to assess candidates for junior officers in his sons' commands. . . . Given this, it is not surprising that a large proportion of John Norris' subordinates were drawn from the gentry of Oxfordshire and Berkshire. . . . Likewise Lord Henry Norris' network of servants, friends and clients provided a natural pool of associates who accompanied John Norris' armies."[39]

John Norris's military career almost precisely traces the period of England's military transformation, when both its land and naval forces were professionalized and brought increasingly under central control of the crown. The reforms of the army began with the organization of local militias into more regular Trained Bands in 1572—the year that

Norris returned from service in France under Coligny and was fortunate to avoid the St. Bartholomew's Day Massacre that killed the admiral— and continued "to the late 1590s, by which time Mountjoy's army in Ireland and [Sir Richard] Vere's forces in the Netherlands displayed a level of modern professionalism roughly equivalent to their continental competitors." Nolan's biography of Norris makes a convincing case that, during those years, "Sir John became Queen Elizabeth's all-purpose troubleshooter, inevitably on the scene wherever the Queen's interest was fixed."[40] Respect for his tactical and organizational skill gave Norris a strong hand in the making of strategy:

> When he was involved in extended policy debate, Norris' ideas usually won out. His opinion that Munster must be resettled with an English population ultimately shaped English policy there, though he himself did not stay on the scene to carry it out. His belief that only a full-scale war with Spain could keep the Netherlands revolt alive became Crown policy in 1585 after extended debate on the subject. His constant arguments that Brittany needed to be the focus of English efforts in France became royal policy in early 1592 after his personal lobbying on the subject. . . . Likewise, his belief that a conciliatory policy toward [the Earl of Tyrone, Hugh] O'Neill in Ulster was necessary in the short run tended to win out in Privy Council debate even as events in Ireland undermined it.[41]

In sum, from the time in the mid-1580s when Elizabeth committed to pursuing a strategy of direct military engagement on the European continent and colonial expansion in Ireland, Sir John Norris served in every theater and helped establish strategic priorities.

Over the course of his varied career and deployments, Norris did three tours in Ireland. The first, beginning in 1573, was a successor to the failed colonization attempts of Sir Thomas Smith, though this time with better resources, leadership, and finance from Walter Devereux, the first Earl of Essex, and a contingent of six hundred royal troops. The queen also lent Essex £10,000. Over the next two years, crown expenses totaled almost £90,000 on what was supposed to be a mostly private enterprise, one that also revealed the complexities of colonization. Among his officers were John Norris and his brother William.

The Essex "plantation" in Antrim was, like Smith's before it, shaped as much by English humanist political thought as by experience of Ireland. There was a power vacuum in Ulster at the time. Shane, the energetic O'Neill of the 1560s, had been killed by Scottish MacDonnell mercenaries, and these "Redshanks," following their own charismatic leader, Sorley Boy MacDonnell, were challenging the weaker O'Neill successor in the eastern part of the province. Essex intended likewise to exploit the situation, allying his forces with the younger Baron of Dungannon—and future Earl of Tyrone—Hugh O'Neill, to evict the Scots. In sum, this was no mere campaign of conquest but one intended to bring English political civility to a chaotic situation by cooperation with and support for like-minded locals.

At first, things seemed to go well. The local O'Neill warlord, Sir Brian MacPhelim, who had caused such problems for the Smith colony, made his submission. But Essex exacted a high price, including taking ten thousand of Sir Brian's cattle as hostage and placing him under guard. MacPhelim soon escaped inland, and Essex sent a column from Carrickfergus to run him down. It was William Norris's cavalry troop that rode into the inevitable ambush. William's horse was killed beneath him and he was on the verge of being hacked to pieces when John rode to his rescue, snatching him up on the rear of his horse and beating his way back to English lines. The engagement was a rude awakening for Essex. Faced with a much tougher task than the one he had imagined, he wrote to Elizabeth to request reinforcements. Having been singled out for bravery, John Norris made the perfect messenger.

Whether Norris played a role in convincing the queen to double down on her investment in Essex is not known, though hanging the earl out to dry in Ulster would have risked alienating a powerful noble supporter at home and undermined English authority in Ireland. The net result, however, was that Essex was made governor of Ulster, over the protests of Lord Deputy Sir William FitzWilliam, and reinforced with an additional three hundred veterans from the Low Countries and a levy of another three hundred troops, including John Norris's first company command. In the meantime, Essex shifted his base southward to Drogheda—plague had broken out in the Carrickfergus camp, killing fifteen men a day—and prepared, in early 1574, to invade Ulster from the south. Once again, Essex focused first on Brian MacPhelim O'Neill in eastern Ulster before turning to the larger forces being mounted by the O'Neill's paramount chief, Turlough Luineach, in central Ulster.

And again Essex enjoyed initial success, establishing a post on the Blackwater River that cut Ulster in two and forcing Brian MacPhelim to submit after a short skirmish. Essex exacted a lesser price in cattle but also took possession of Belfast, with John Norris, now clearly a trusted lieutenant, installed as constable. With his operational rear and line of communication with England safely secured, Essex turned north and west to tackle the rest of Ulster. He brushed aside a small covering force, but failing to bring Turlough Luineach to battle, Essex went on a rampage through the Tyrone countryside, destroying crops and seizing herds, but also wearing down his own forces. John Nolan concludes that this raiding impressed Norris as fruitless, giving him an aversion to Ireland and a professional's aversion to irregular warfare that he would retain most of his life and share with many of his contemporaries. Norris "later expressed the belief that expeditions into [Irish insurgents'] territory were useless unless followed up by military occupation, an application of brute force which the English Crown could not afford."[42]

The failures of the 1574 campaign also drove Essex to harsher methods. These failures must also have made an impression on Norris, who now became the earl's enforcer. In October, Essex invited Sir Brian MacPhelim O'Neill to Belfast. The Irish chieftain returned the favor by throwing a three-day feast for Essex, but at the end of the celebration, Essex, fearing treachery, arrested O'Neill. Next Norris led a slaughter of more than two hundred of O'Neill's followers, including "men, women, youths and maidens."[43] Sir Brian, his wife, and his leading subordinates were hauled off to Dublin, where they were summarily executed. Back in Belfast, Norris tried to exploit his emerging reputation to terrify Sir Brian's successors into submission; many of the Irish believed Norris was "in league with the devil."[44]

The final year of Norris initial Irish deployment was a repeat. In 1575, Essex tried again to subdue Ulster, invading Tyrone with a force of about one thousand. Once across the Blackwater, his enemies at last came to meet him, Turlough Luineach O'Neill bringing a force of about two thousand along with fourteen hundred Redshanks under Sorley Boy MacDonnell. Essex convinced the Scots to withdraw, but the Ulstermen then made a ferocious attack. It was driven off with a loss of cattle and Turlough Luineach's cloak, but Essex contented himself with reinforcing the Blackwater crossing and building, with Hugh O'Neill's help, a small fort. Refitting himself in Belfast, Essex then went after Sorley Boy MacDonnell in northeast Ulster. What resulted was a vicious but indecisive engagement along the River Bann, in which Norris was wounded through the shoulder. Essex, declaring his mission accomplished, returned to Carrickfergus while pillaging the surrounding country, writing to the queen that he had "left all the county desolate and without people." As Nolan observes, English colonizers "believed such tactics were effective because they deprived the Irish of the means to live in selected areas, in effect creating protective zones of devastation around the population."[45]

Norris's service concluded with one final act of this extreme form of counterinsurgency, conducted jointly with a three-ship squadron under Francis Drake. Elizabeth had tired of the great expense and small return of Essex's colonizing campaign. Without government support, the earl could not maintain his army at Carrickfergus, and so he decided to return to England. His final orders were to Norris and Drake to attack Rathlin Island, a staging base for the Scottish mercenaries off the northeast corner of Ireland. On July 22, Norris, with four hundred men in makeshift transports, rendezvoused with Drake at Rathlin, surprising the garrison and penning it inside a small castle. Drake unloaded two cannon and three days later, Norris's men assaulted the breach. The assault was driven off, but the commander asked for terms, which Norris and Drake were ready to accept as Sorley Boy's main force was massing on the mainland. Sparing the lives of the constable and his wife and daughter, Norris demanded that the remaining Scots must "stand upon the courtesy of the soldiers."[46] As the garrison marched out, two hundred Scots were slain. Over the next several days, follow-on operations around the island killed several hundred more hiding in caves and along cliffs.

Shortly after the Rathlin massacre, Norris left Ireland for England, recuperating on his family's estates. Though English direct involvement in the Dutch resistance to Philip II was still years away, by the spring of 1578 plans were afoot to offer English troops in service to the States General of the Netherlands. It was in this context that Norris built a military reputation as a senior battlefield commander, a careful logistician and organizer, and, ultimately, a trusted strategic adviser to the queen. In the early and middle 1580s, Norris's position was even more delicate; as the Dutch situation worsened under the relentless pressure from the Duke of Parma's careful offensives, the States General and Elizabeth looked for help from the French Duke of Anjou, beginning the complex dance of diplomacy that held out the prospect of matrimony and created such a domestic political storm in England. Norris often found himself as the man on the spot in the Netherlands and in Flanders, in the end taking the strategic responsibility on his shoulders for standing firm with the Dutch and turning against the duplicitous Duke. Elizabeth accepted the wisdom of Norris's actions and advice. In the end, in 1584, he would return from the Low Countries to England with a personal recommendation from William the Silent of Orange and an appeal for a greater commitment of English forces, to be led by Norris, to the Dutch war.

Elizabeth acknowledged the strategic logic of Norris's recommendations, reinforced by the steady urgings of the Earl of Leicester and Sir Francis Walsingham, but the queen was not yet ready for open war with Philip. As a kind of consolation prize, Norris was offered the post as lord president of Munster. In the wake of the second Desmond Rebellion and the attainder of the rebels' lands, the English were ready to attempt another "plantation" in Ireland. While he did not receive the command he desired in the Netherlands and, after his previous experience in Ireland, may have harbored misgivings in returning, the Munster opportunity was a good one. The southern province was lush and, prior to the rebellion, relatively well developed, although the heavy soil made the idea of tillage agriculture—a central pillar of the scheme for colonization and civilization along English lines—an impractical substitute for the pasturing of cattle.[47] Still, Munster seemed a pleasing contrast to Ulster, and at least the rebellion had removed the political obstacles to power. Moreover, the plantation scheme, carefully developed by Burghley, carried the chance for riches and patronage for Norris, his brother Thomas, and his military family as well. Munster, Norris reported upon his arrival in August 1584, was "like well tempered wax, apt to take such form as her majesty will put upon it."[48] Norris would have a good degree of latitude in Munster, too: Sir John Perrot, possibly a more vitriolic character than Norris, was the new lord deputy. The messy business of governing Ireland and subduing Ulster—where the situation had barely changed in the decade since Norris left—was supposed to be Perrot's, though Norris spent much time in east Ulster helping the lord lieutenant make yet another attempt to suppress Sorley Boy MacDonnell and in Dublin helping to get the legislation establishing the Munster plantation through the parliament.

Norris's Munster interlude lasted but a year and, but for a brief pause to oversee the fortification of the Munster coast in 1590, he would spend the next decade in the forefront of the war against Spain. On May 12, 1585, Sir Francis Walsingham ordered Norris to return to England to prepare to lead an English expeditionary force to the Low

Countries. The Duke of Parma had pushed the Dutch rebels to the brink, besieging Antwerp, and all English ships in Spanish ports were to be seized. It seemed that, at last, Elizabeth could no longer avoid direct commitment to the war. When she finally did so, signing the Treaty of Nonesuch in August, she named Norris the general to lead a complement of five thousand infantry and one thousand cavalry. This confirmed Norris's position as the foremost English military professional of the era, but his position was immediately complicated by the arrival of the Earl of Leicester as Elizabeth's political "representative" to the Dutch States General—the Dutch had offered the queen another crown, which she refused—and commanding general of the overall anti-Spanish coalition. Still the queen's favorite, the charismatic leader of the forward faction at court, and a man with military expertise and ambition, Leicester's appointment put Norris in an impossible position. Though the two got on well at first, Leicester brought over a flock of gentlemen followers to whom he had promised commands. Norris would not have a free hand in running his army.

Nor did things go well in the field in 1586. Though Norris distinguished himself tactically, as did the English troops, the combination of Elizabeth's diplomacy—she was negotiating with Parma all the while—and the disparities of strength between the Spanish and Dutch forces also put Norris in an exposed position. As the costs of operations increased, defeats mounted, and Leicester's allocations of commands and troops factionalized the English contingent, Sir John made a convenient scapegoat. Leicester's charges of corruption were taken with a grain of salt by Elizabeth and Burghley, but there was little they could do to salve the rising bitterness between Norris, the proud professional, and the earl, the haughty aristocrat. Leicester took the quarrel back to court over the winter and, perhaps inevitably, the queen decided the matter for her favorite. Norris was recalled.

In retrospect, however, this loss of position may have worked to Norris's advantage. Leicester's campaign for 1587 collapsed. It soon became "clear that Leicester's lack of leadership ability, sensitivity to personal honor and paranoiac belief that everyone was against him were the real causes of the failure. Defeating Parma would have been difficult difficult without these handicaps, but with them Elizabeth's army was doomed to impotency. . . . In October it was decided to engineer Leicester's graceful return to England."[49] The support of Walsingham, Burghley and others at court helped to validate Norris's position and revive his reputation. In particular, Burghley was coming to trust the general and became something of a patron. The military professional and the prudent statesman made a kind of natural pair, perhaps drawn by a mutual sense of England's strategic and military limits. This growing trust was reflected the following year, the year of the *Gran Armada*. Norris was given command of the most forward English force in Kent, the most likely landing place for the Duke of Parma's troops had the Spanish made good their invasion plans. Norris was to buy time while Leicester massed the main army at Tillbury, where, as the invasion threat receded, the queen came to address her men on August 18, 1588, with Norris among her small personal escort.

Norris's military preeminence made him the natural choice to lead the expedition to Portugal the following year. To be sure, Norris made major mistakes of judgment in the campaign, the most debilitating being the decision to lay siege to Coruña. However, without his organizational skills the expedition would never have happened, and the fractured command structure—further complicated by the recklessness of the young Earl of Essex, who was abetted by Sir Roger Williams, one of Norris's lieutenants but also a man of surpassing personal ambitions—was an accident waiting to happen. In the end, the shortcomings of the expedition are best understood as reflecting shortcomings in the structures and finances of the Elizabethan state, which, despite improvements and experience, remained an ad hoc and improvised thing. Thus, despite the expedition's dodgy finances—which, again, can be seen as an expression of the "overhead" costs of the off-the-books military that the queen could not officially afford—Sir John's reputation survived the fiasco.

The Portugal expedition marked the zenith of Norris's influence on policy and strategy. As he waited for the queen's displeasure to dissipate, others came to the fore, a measure of the growing professionalization of the English military and Norris's role in that process. Francis Vere was now the leading English general in the Netherlands, still the most coveted command, and Sir Roger Williams, once an officer in Norris's regiment, had graduated to become the principal military adviser to the Earl of Essex, in the wake of Leicester's death both the queen's new favorite at court and the leader of the war party in the government. And so, before his final posting to Ireland, most of Norris's remaining efforts would be devoted to economy-of-force campaigning in Brittany.

On August 1, 1589, while Norris and Drake were being called to account for the Portugal expedition, Jacques Clément, a fanatic devotee of the Catholic League in France, disguised himself as a priest in order to stab the last Valois king, Henri III, to death. Next in line for the French throne was Henry of Navarre, a Protestant and leader of the Bourbon family. Henry represented a tremendous opportunity to Elizabeth, who had long worked to enlist the French as allies in the struggle against Spain. But while he had a legitimate claim on the French throne, it was the Catholic League that held Paris and much of France. Moreover, the League enjoyed Spanish support, and the Duke of Parma quickly led troops from the Netherlands to lift Henry's siege of the French capital. Henry's cause, like that of the Dutch, thus was also a liability to the English. Henry's weakness was underscored the next year when Charles Emmanuel, Duke of Savoy and married to one of Philip II's daughters, invaded Provence. A third front opened in October 1590 when Spanish forces landed at the port of Blavet, on the southern coast of Brittany. This was also a direct threat to English interests, as the north Breton ports could serve as embarkation points for a cross-Channel invasion.

Once again, Elizabeth found herself dragged into a continental conflict propping up an ally whose strategic interests diverged significantly. Moreover, the conflict was first and foremost a French civil war. The challenge threw English strategists into a tizzy; though they grasped the danger posed by a Spanish assault on Brittany, English forces—and thinking—were already stretched tight. In a memorandum for the queen, Sir Roger Williams captured the dilemma, arguing, essentially, that Brittany was a sideshow that would consume resources without producing decisive result. "Believe me unless you can give great blows," he lectured the privy council,

> Either on the Indian navy [that is, the treasure fleet] or in those countries where [Philip's] treasure comes or on the disciplined army, I mean on the Duke of Parma, or in the main of Spain or Portugal, be assured that all the rest is but consuming of little fires. Do what you can without putting the Spanish King in hazard of one of the three, Your Lordships shall never bring him to any reason. . . . Let him be thoroughly warned in any of the three [main] actions, be assured his own estate will force him to any peace or condition you can desire, for necessity hath no law.[50]

Norris, with a force of several thousand, was already in Brittany when Williams made his case. The queen, who hated to bend to the supposed necessities of professional military advice, nevertheless sent yet another English expeditionary force under Williams to campaign in Normandy—Williams had cleverly argued that, if the port of Rouen were seized, the customs revenues would more than pay for the effort; he knew what would appeal to the parsimonious queen and Burghley. In the event, it would be the Earl of Essex who would lead the expanded English effort in France, with Norris in Brittany playing a secondary role.

For the next two years, it required all of Norris's tactical and political skills—including his willingness to take independent decisions in hopes that Elizabeth would ultimately sanction them—simply to fight to a stalemate in Brittany. He also worked hard, though with little result, to coax what support he could out of the French, even to the extent of moving his troops to the border between Brittany and Maine, well away from the Spanish or the Channel ports. This move also helped him quarter his forces through the winter, since supply from England was not reliable. The futility of the campaign, however, began to tell on Norris, as did the continuous complaints about the cost from London. Elizabeth began to demand the withdrawal of Norris and his troops, but, reluctant to admit failure, Sir John played for time in hopes that a battlefield victory could redeem the effort. In the summer of 1593, it appeared that Norris's mulish stance was paying off: the French at last began to send troops to southern Brittany to threaten the Spanish stronghold at Blavet, and Burghley wrote that the queen was coming around. But the bottom dropped out in July when Henry, famously deciding that "Paris was worth a mass," converted to Catholicism and concluded a truce with the Catholic League. Even though Henry vowed to keep fighting the Spanish, the prospect of two Catholic great powers on the continent again flummoxed English strategists. Ordered to bring his troops home by way of the Channel Islands, Norris moved slowly across Brittany through 1594 and even snatched an important victory by taking the Spanish fortress at Crozon, which guarded the harbor at Brest. But that was in mid-November, too late to shift even the mercurial Elizabeth: Norris and two thousand veterans from the Low Countries were earmarked for Ulster.

English soldiers, like English diplomats and aristocrats, regarded service in Ireland more as punishment than opportunity. And, after Brittany, writes John Nolan, Norris's "finances"—despite the complaints from the treasury, Norris had paid for a good portion of the Brittany effort from his own pocket—"his career and his once-mighty reputation had all been ruined."[51] And Norris, exhausted by the Brittany campaign, tried to avoid the Ireland assignment. It is not fanciful to suppose that Norris foresaw that the Irish mission and the Irish climate would kill him—which, in 1596, it did. He was also well aware of the confused strategy toward the Tyrone Rebellion, as described above. The queen and Burghley delayed the branding of the O'Neill as an outlaw until Norris's arrival in Dublin, but his mission was more political and symbolic, an effort to convince the Irish of the seriousness of English intent. The effect was undercut by Norris's quarrels with Lord Deputy Sir William Russell, and the forces at Norris's disposal were woefully inadequate to the task of extending English writ throughout Ulster, let alone Ireland as a whole. Norris's "reputation seemed to signal that Queen Elizabeth had decided on war, but was really intended to intimidate" the rebels.[52] It was left to Mountjoy—who learned his trade in Brittany under Norris—to finish the job.

In his final posting, as so often before, the best Norris could do was to prevent a bad situation from deteriorating. John Nolan, Norris's biographer and a scholar of Elizabethan military reforms as a whole, concludes that Sir John's "relegation to [history's] footnote can be attributed to the fact that his career was primarily related to land warfare: "The great legends of Elizabeth I's war with Spain were made at sea, sacking Cadiz (twice), raiding the West Indies, challenging hopeless odds in the *Revenge* and defending the coasts of England from the 1588 armada. These famous naval actions have become the subject of both popular histories and more detailed academic studies debating the importance of Elizabeth's navy in the foundation of England's long age of naval mastery. The Elizabethan army, by contrast, has received relatively short shrift."[53]

There is much truth in Nolan's lament, but perhaps more to the story: the navalist focus on the sea war with Spain omits too much that was central to Elizabethan strategy-making: the stabilization of the Tudor regime at home, securing the British isles as a whole, preventing a coalition of Catholic great powers, supporting Dutch independence and the global Protestant cause, and the planting of new Englands in Ireland and America. None of these tasks could be accomplished without the professionalization of the Tudor military, the transformation of Trained Bands of militia into a force that could both square off with Spanish *tercios* in the open field, provide the glue to diverse coalitions, and match wits with Irish insurgents. Sir John Norris's lugubrious "career" may lack the dash and verve of more colorful contemporaries, but it reflects how Elizabeth's "imagined empire" was to be made real.

THE SPENSERIAN STYLE
IN ELIZABETHAN STRATEGY

In the November 1964 issue of *Harper's Magazine*, historian Richard Hofstadter identified what he described as "The Paranoid Style in American Politics." The article was first and foremost a polemic against the presidential candidacy of Senator Barry Goldwater, but in its search for "political psychology through [an analysis of] political rhetoric," Hofstadter's method was partially akin to that employed in the present study. Hopscotching through history even more lightly and rapidly, Hofstadter identified a long-running, conspiracy-minded strain in American political thought that saw human history "in apocalyptic terms." His "paranoid spokesman . . . traffics in the birth and death of whole worlds, whole political orders, whole human values. He is always manning the barricades of civilization. He constantly lives at a turning point."[54]

These kinds of anxieties were widely shared even among the supposedly seasoned and *politique* elements of the Elizabethan political nation. Indeed, Hofstadter was wrong to relegate the barricade-manning, civilization-defending, epoch-defining impulse in Anglo-American political thought to the fringes. As we have seen, the Elizabethans understood themselves to be at the forefront of a global struggle, not simply against a dominating Hapsburg dynasty or a would-be hegemonic European great power, but also an end-of-days contest to reform Christianity and save humankind, or at least the godly Protestant minority. Hofstadter's definition of the paranoid's enemy—"a perfect model of malice, a kind of amoral superman—sinister, ubiquitous, powerful, cruel, sensual, luxury-loving"[55]—was how Elizabethans imagined Philip II. To reduce the Elizabethans' geopolitical anxieties to the terminology of modern political science, they lacked any sense of strategic depth. Even as the Tudor regime endured, prospered, and expanded, the enemy remained both at the gates and within the walls. Whether in northwest Europe or in Ireland or on the seven seas, the front lines felt close to home and under threat. The English imperial project was an exceptional one—it promoted "liberties" and the true faith—but therefore one that was particularly risky. The Elizabethans deeply believed they were the last, best hope of earth, and the course of history was theirs to be nobly won or meanly lost.

The anxieties rose to a more feverish pitch in the context of colonization. Ralph Lane was as experienced and hardened a military professional as the Elizabethan era produced, but it is hard to avoid the conclusion that, abandoned at the edge of empire on Roanoke, he slowly began to panic; the weight of carrying an apocalyptic cause and a *mission civilatrice* into a howling wilderness and an alien if not necessarily hostile culture was a heavy burden. The hopes and fears—and, perhaps, the contradictions thus entailed—that shaped Elizabethan and subsequent Anglo-American attitudes to strategy-making were on fullest display in Ireland. Until the arrival of Mountjoy—and not even his "scorched earth" victories would prove enduringly decisive—English strategies for Ireland had failed. Indeed, from the initial "surrender and regrant" efforts of the 1540s to the Ulster colonization schemes of the early Elizabethan period to the Desmond and then the Tyrone Rebellions, the situation had gone from bad to worse. Both the underlying Gaelic order and the grasping "Old English" Catholic nobility had proved resistant to political stabilization, social improvement, and civilization, let alone to religious reformation of the sort Englishmen felt necessary to their imperial project. The failure to "Anglicize" Ireland left the island, and thus England and the idea of a British empire, vulnerable to Spanish and Catholic meddling. It was a crippling failure.

Both the aspirations and anxieties found their most powerful expressions in the works of Edmund Spenser, the genius "poet historicall" of the age. They run through almost all of his work, including his greatest poetry; it is an oversimplification but yet broadly true that the more pastoral and allegorically complex compositions of his earlier years give voice to English aspirations while his later work, particularly the last books of *The Faerie Queene* and the dialogue *View of the Present State of Ireland* is darker, more direct, and deeply anxiety-ridden. Spenser's rhetorical gift, his channeling of widely held attitudes, and his own starkly unique expression of these attitudes combine to make him a kind of id of the Elizabethan strategic mind. In Spenser, the best angels of the Protestant Reformation and the English Renaissance collide with a very bleak view of human nature—or at least of Irish culture—and the necessity for violence and the use of famine as a weapon of war. Spenser gave Englishmen a preview of the dilemmas they would come to face as they pushed their imperial frontiers westward across the Atlantic. The problems of adding new Englands to the empire remained militarily and morally intractable.

Beyond the differences of Elizabethan and modern English, reading Spenser is a challenge, not simply as literature—even his seemingly straightforward allegories can have multiple meanings—but as political commentary. The vexing question, particularly as it relates to Ireland and the English enterprise of colonization, was well put by Ciaran Brady: "How could the principal poet of the English Renaissance not merely tolerate or even defend, but actually celebrate the use of merciless and unrestrained violence against large numbers of his fellow men?"[56] While this may be a late twentieth-century take on a late sixteenth-century problem, it does reflect the inherent tensions between the broadly and deeply held moral purposes and the unpleasant necessities of the Elizabethan and later Anglo-American imperial project. As we have seen already and will see again, these tensions were particularly acute for the colonials themselves.

An independent analysis of Spenser's verse is beyond the competence of this study, and *The Faerie Queene* is especially boggy ground, made even more so by the fact that Spenser was a hugely but indirectly self-referential writer and the direct record of his life is extremely sparse. Uncertainties surround his birth, his death, and many of the years in between. As with Shakespeare, this is a mischievous combination that results in speculation as to whether Spenser authored all the works attributed to him, including *View*. There is, however, general scholarly accord that Ireland and the English attempt to colonize it provided a consistent framework for most of his later work. "One can no more speak of 'Spenser and Ireland' as a distinct topic," wrote Benjamin P. Myers, "than of, say, 'Walt Whitman and America.'"[57]

Spenser moved to Ireland in 1580, in the midst of the second Desmond Rebellion, taking a post as secretary to Arthur, Lord Grey de Wilton, who had been recommended by Sir Henry Sidney for the post of lord deputy and to suppress the revolt. Sir Walter Ralegh was also among Grey's reinforcements; in sum, the aggressive Protestant faction at court took command of Irish policy. The rebellion had begun the year previously, when James FitzMaurice FitzGerald had landed on the Dingle Peninsula with a small band of Spanish-supplied "papal" troops and with cleric Mateo de Oviedo—who twenty years on would be the driving force behind Spanish intervention in the Tyrone Rebellion—in tow. This second Desmond Rebellion also presaged the Tyrone war in that the FitzGeralds framed it as a Catholic crusade, whereas the first contest, fought in the 1560s, was a struggle between two "Old English" families, the FitzGeralds, and the Butlers, the earls of Ormond, for power in Munster. Thomas Butler, 10th Earl of Ormond, was also a distant cousin of Queen Elizabeth and an agent and beneficiary of encroaching Tudor authority in Ireland. Grey's mission was to pacify, govern, and ultimately people Munster with an English plantation. As Andrew Hadfield puts it in his biography of the poet: "Spenser was probably made an offer he could not refuse, and, although it may not have been quite what he wanted, Ireland was a land in which fortunes large and small could be made, higher standards of living could be enjoyed, and there was access to property for those without any obvious means of obtaining it in England."[58]

Spenser was a man on the make and on the rise. *The Shepheard's Calendar* had come out the year previously and sensationally established his literary reputation. And, as Hadfield convincingly demonstrates, it served as a kind of advertisement of his employability. Even more than the figures profiled previously, Spenser was a man of the "middling" sort whose wits and hard work took him from east London to a stellar career at Cambridge. His mentor and closest friend there was Gabriel Harvey, and it is not unlikely that Spenser attended Thomas Smith's Hill Hall colloquium on colonization described above. Spenser had already been secretary to John Young, the bishop of Rochester, and spent some time working for and perhaps in the household of the Earl of Leicester. He moved in a literary-political circle that included Sir Philip Sidney.

One of Spenser's first duties in Ireland would have been to accompany Grey on his initial campaign southward from Dublin into the Wicklow Mountains to suppress the O'Byrne clan, who were supporting the Munster rebels from their fastness in Leinster. Marching his heavily armored column of about three thousand men up in pursuit up the gorge of Glenmalure, Grey's men became strung out. A passage in *Holinshed's Chronicles* vividly describes the military terrain as ideal ambush country: "boggy and soft, and full of great stones and slippery rocks, very hard and evil to pass through; the sides are full of great and mighty trees upon the sides of the hills and full of bushments and underwoods."[59] The result was perhaps predictable. While the casualty claims are even more unreliable than usual, Grey lost heavily, not only among his infantry but among his officers, including the leader of the detachment, Colonel George Moore, and Peter Carew, brother of George.

But within a few months, Grey had his revenge. Pope Gregory sent additional forces, both Italian and Spanish, to Dingle to support the Irish rebels. Thanks to a rapid concentration ordered by Grey, they were trapped near Smerwick by the English navy and Grey's army, now reinforced by Ormond's troops. The papal troops hastily erected earthworks on a headland inside Smerwick harbor—a position remarkably similar, though on a smaller scale, to Kinsale—but the siege was brief, just three days. The papal commanders were spared, but Grey's troops, some under Sir Walter Ralegh, massacred the six hundred left in the ranks. Absent outside support, the rebellion collapsed, although it took the better part of three years, during which time Grey and Ormond adopted the scorched-earth approach that Mountjoy was to follow in the aftermath of Kinsale to run Desmond to ground. Perhaps as much as a third of the Munster population perished from the famine that followed in the wake of the fighting.

With Desmond dispatched and his abandoned lands confiscated by the crown, Munster was a kind of political, economic, and military vacuum. It seemed, in short and by contrast to the wastes of Ulster, the ideal laboratory for a large-scale "plantation" of English society in Ireland. In 1584, Sir Valentine Brown began an extensive survey with a view to allocating the holdings to "undertakers," settlers of means who, in return for sizeable tracts, would import tenants to cultivate the land in the English manner and establish market towns that would also serve as points of defense, a kind of garrison. After Grey returned to London, Spenser entered the employ of Munster president Sir John Norris and his brother Thomas, with whom he would have worked on the plans for the Munster plantation. In reward for his work, Spenser would receive in 1589 the lucrative, three-thousand-acre estate of Kilcoman about twenty-five miles due north of Cork; the Norris home at Mallow was halfway between the city and Kilcoman. The poet-undertaker spent most of the rest of his life in Ireland, returning to England just three times: twice on substantial trips that coincided with the publishing of the two editions of The Faerie Queene and once, briefly, at the end of his life when he had fled Kilcoman at the peak of the Tyrone Rebellion.

The first two of these return trips to England must have had a strong effect on Spenser, for arguments advanced in View presented the problems of colonization as a combination of difficulties at the periphery and neglect or misunderstanding at the center. The first trip, from mid-1589 to 1590, is of particular interest. Politically, much had changed in London and at court in the decade Spenser had been away. The leaders of the assertive Protestant faction, the supporters of "forward" strategies both for Europe and Ireland, were passing from the scene. Most notably, the Earl of Leicester, Robert Dudley, had died in 1588, shortly after the crisis of the Gran Armada, but also after his failure in the Netherlands and disgrace at Elizabeth's direction. Sir Philip Sidney had been killed in 1586, and Sir Francis Walsingham died while Spenser was in England. Lord Treasurer Burghley, now seventy, stood alone as the queen's strategic adviser and was grooming his son Robert as his successor. Only the young Essex, stolen away on the Portugal expedition, had the lineage and charisma to inherit the Leicester mantle.

The publication of the first books of *The Faerie Queene*, Spenser's first task in London, reestablished his reputation as the foremost poet of the time, but the poem also was rife with criticisms of the queen, the court, and Elizabethan policy, especially for Ireland. Burghley and his patronage networks appeared to Spenser as corrupt, the source and manifestation of a rot that infected the entire political order. The success of *The Faerie Queene* earned Spenser a fifty-pound-per-year grant from Elizabeth, but the ink was barely dry on the pension—and Spenser back in Ireland—when the publication of *Complaints*, a compilation of nine "sundrie small poemes of the world's vanitie" caused "a major international scandal in the English-speaking world."[60] The contents of *Complaints* are indeed sundry in style, but what binds them together is that they represent the most direct attack in what Bruce Danner describes (in the very title of his 2001 book) as *Edmund Spenser's War on Lord Bughley*.[61] No aspect of the lord treasurer's life was spared; he was allegorized as a deceitful fox, his grand house Theobald described as the product of bribery, even his son Robert's hunchback mocked. In *Mother Hubberd's Tale*, the best-known of the poems, the court was painted as a swamp of corruption:

> For nothing there is done without a fee:
> The Courtier needs must recompensed bee
> With a Benevolence, or have in gage the Primitias of your
>   Parsonage:
> Scarce can a Bishopric forpas them by,
> But that it must be gelt in privitie.
> Doo not therefore seeke a living there.[62]

Though Spenser has frequently been caricatured as a man who wished, like Ralegh, to become a courtier, the evidence is that he had few experiences of court and was repulsed by those he did have. Certainly he wished to live comfortably, but the poet was, like his friend Daniel Harvey, a hopeless contrarian, pursuing fame as a writer rather than social recognition. This return trip to London confirmed to Spenser his outsider status, and he returned to Ireland to "seeke a living there," more than ever tied to his frontier, colonial, and deeply Protestant "New English" identity.

This identity can only have been solidified through the period of the early 1590s. In 1594, Spenser married—it was his second marriage—Elizabeth Boyle, a relative of Sir Richard Boyle, an ambitious New English planter and a political rising star; he would later be named the first Earl of Cork and privy councillor for Ireland. Shortly after Spenser died, Sir Richard acquired Ralegh's sprawling Irish estates for a bargain-basement price. Having committed himself to a career in Ireland, Spenser, too, set about building his estate, achieving a level of success that permitted him the leisure to write. The period was as productive as any for the poet. Among other efforts, he published a sequence of sonnets and a long work, *Colin Clouts Come Home Againe*, satirizing the English court and transferring the English pastoral framework of the early books of *The Faerie Queene* explicitly to Ireland; he also added the material for the second edition of *The Faerie Queene*. Yet Spenser's prospects were clouded by the looming and growing threat of the Tyrone Rebellion; though it was centered in Ulster, it created an increasing danger to the new and small English plantation in Munster, where the numbers and military organization of settler society had failed to fulfill plans or expectations. Spenser's home at Kilcolman was a tiny English island in a churning Gaelic sea.

Spenser returned to London again in 1596, as the second edition of *The Faerie Queene* was published. Again, the poem garnered acclaim and provoked controversy, having a "polemical urgency," as Andrew Hadfield observes, derived from Spenser's worries about Ireland. "The poem displays a terrifying vision of English civilization, which had been in a fragile and semi-formed state at the start of the poem, engulfed by hostile forces it is unable to repel."[63] The anxieties overshadowed the aspirations. The second edition also angered James VI of Scotland, the likely heir to the English throne, for its portrayal of his mother, Mary, Queen of Scots; it made James so livid that he spent two years trying to commission a book "answering" Spenser. It is also probable that, while in England, Spenser completed a draft of *View of the Present State of Ireland*. When, in 1597, it was set for printing, it was refused a license; not only was it a bold statement on a controversial subject—Tyrone was nearing the peak of his power and in the throes of negotiating his alliance with the Spanish—but it gave details of military strategy and tactics that would prove highly accurate. At the same time, Spenser's knowledgeable assessment and topicality assured that *View* received wide circulation in manuscript; more than twenty copies remain extant. Hadfield argues that the work "was intended to persuade those in high office to adopt its political strategies, and not an attempt to impress a widespread audience."[64] At the same time, *View* was hardly written in the style of Richard Hakluyt's *Discourses of Western Planting*. If *Discourses* was a measured memorandum, *View* was a screed disguised as a dialogue.

In the context of this study, *View* looms not only as an expression of the ambitions and anxieties of the "New English" in Ireland but very much foreshadows the challenges of the New English in America. It more than repays a close reading. The British imperial project originated in the minds of Renaissance humanists. Colonization, civilization, and reformed Christianity had become and would long remain inseparably linked, but the contradictions inherent—between the effective exercise of power; the necessity for stability, order, and justice; and realizing God's design for humanity—are likewise on open display in *View*.

The full title of the work is *A View of the Present State of Ireland, Discoursed by Way of a Dialogue between Eudoxus and Irenius*. Eudoxus is the voice of Renaissance humanism, the well-educated Englishman, but no mere "straight man." Irenius (a masculine form of Irena, one of Spenser's personifications of Ireland in *The Faerie Queene*) speaks with the voice of colonial experience. Eudoxus opens the dialogue by enquiring why "no course is taken for the turning thereof to good uses and reducing that savage nation to better government and civility."[65] After all, the Anglo-Normans had first conquered Ireland in the twelfth century and the Tudor reforms initiated in the 1540s, yet five decades later Ireland was in open rebellion and about to enlist Spain, the greatest power of the age, to its cause. The failures of the British imperial project could hardly be more manifest. Irenius responds that the underlying problems are fundamental: "The evils which seem to be most hurtful to the common weal of that land . . . are of three kinds: the first is in the laws, the second in customs, the last in religion."[66] The Irish are badly governed, their culture is barbaric, and, despite being nominally Catholic, they remained pagan and had yet to become truly Christian.

The Gaelic order, enshrined in the practice of "Brehon" law and, in particular, succession by tanistry is inherently chaotic and corrupt, argues Irenius. Gaelic lords are absolute, and the law has no independent meaning or value outside the power of the clan or sept leader. And even where English law is followed in form, it is subverted in practice, even in trial by jury. "All the freeholders"—and thus all those who may serve on juries—"of that realm are Irish," says Irenius, "which, when the cause shall fall between an Englishman and in Irish, or between the Queen and any freeholder of that country, they make no more scruple to pass against the Englishman or the Queen, though it be to strain their oath, than to drink milk unstrained, so that before the jury go together, it is all to nothing what their verdict will be."[67]

But it should be no surprise that Gaelic law is corrupt, argues Irenius, for Irish culture is barbaric and the Irish have never been civilized. Here is the core of Spenser's analysis, and the following cultural critique was widely shared, not only for its diagnoses but also in its proposed remedies. As they encountered exotic peoples, and North Americans in particular, Europeans sought to make sense of the experience through reference to classical and biblical texts, comparing the practices and customs of Indians and, in Spenser's case, the Irish, to those described by the ancients.[68] The bywords for barbarians were *Tartar*—Englishmen and others who had opened the sea trade with Russia had picked up and corrupted the word *Tatar*—and, even more commonly, *Scythian*, relating both to the story of the ten tribes of Israel. This tribe was believed to have spread northward then both eastward and westward across Eurasia, and was, in the 1610 assessment of Giles Fletcher the Elder, "The Most Vile and Barbarous Nation of All the World."[69]

As the Scythians, in Irenius's telling, "overflowed all Christendom" in their northern migrations, they touched down in Ulster. The most obvious manifestation of the Scythian influence of Ireland was "booleying," the "transhumanence" or following of cattle herds described above. Nothing was more inimical to the New English concept of civilized life; not only did this promote cattle rustling and other forms of thievery, but more generally, "the people that live thus in these *bollies* grow thereby more barbarous and live more licentious than they would in towns, using what means they list and practicing what mischiefs and villainies they will, either against the government there generally by their combination, or against private men whom they malign by stealing their goods or murdering themselves; for they think themselves half-exempted from law and obedience, and having once tasted freedom do, like steer that hath been long out of his yoke, grudge and repine ever after to come under rule again."[70]

Irenius goes on to describe a variety of other Scythian customs prevalent among the Irish, including a host of military customs—war cries, weapons, the lack of armor, and preference for ambush. Irish religious and social ceremonies reveal Scythian roots, he claims, citing Lucian, the rhetorician and satirist whom Spenser consciously emulated. In sum, Irenius believes that he can "reasonably conclude that the Irish are descended from Sythians," and that they suffered from "the most loathly and barbarous traditions of any people I think under heaven, for from the time that they enter into that course [of military service] they do use all the beastly behavior that may be to oppress all men: they spoil as well the subject as the enemy; they steal; they are cruel and bloody, full of revenge and delighting in deadly execution, licentious swearers and blasphemers, common ravishers of women and murderers of children."[71]

Indeed, this barbarity was so pervasive that it caused the "Old English" to degenerate to a like level of instability and incivility. Their natures "grew wild," with the most noble—notably the "the Butlers and the Gerldines"—becoming the worst. "They grew insolent and bent both that regal authority and also their private powers, one against another, to the utter subversion of themselves and strengthening of the [Gaelic] Irish again." Exchange among the Old English and Irish did not advance civility but was destroying it. "Fostering and marrying with the Irish . . . are two most dangerous infections."[72]

Irish incivility even cast its shadow across what might seem to be the confessional divide. For though the Irish "are all papists by their profession," they are "so blindly and brutishly informed for the most part, as that ye would rather think them atheists or infidels; but not one amongst a hundred knoweth any ground of religion and article of his faith, but can perhaps say his *pater noster* or his *ave Maria* without any knowledge or understanding of what one word thereof meaneth."[73]

In Irenius's telling, the colonial and imperial project in Ireland was collapsing comprehensively. The conquest had never been properly complete. As a result, proper civility and order could not take root and, indeed, the Old English had become degenerate and a big part of the problem. Where there was no civility, there could be no Christianity, let alone a prospect for Protestant reform. In Spenser's poetical imagination, Ireland had supplanted England as a pastoral dream; the land was rich and lovely, ripe for civilizing development. But in Irenius's view, Irish culture—and, in particular, its political culture—was inherently hostile, evil, and, in the form of the Tyrone Rebellion, an increasingly present danger.

What was to be done? Asks Eudoxus: "How then do ye think is the reformation thereof to be begun, if not by laws and ordinances?"

Only a reconquest will suffice, replies Irenius:

> Even by the sword, for all those evils must first be cut away by a strong hand before any good can be planted, like as the corrupt branches and unwholesome boughs are first to be pruned and the foul moss cleansed and scraped away before the tree can bring forth any good fruit.

> EUDOXUS: Is not the sword the most violent redress that may be used for any evil?

> IRENIUS: It is so, but yet where no other remedy may be devised, nor hope of recovery had, there must needs this violent means be used. . . . The first thing must be to send over into the realm such a strong power of men as should perforce bring in all that rebellious rout of loose people which either do now stand out in open arms, or in wandering companies do keep the woods, spoiling and infesting the good subject.[74]

Eudoxus, ever the prudent realist and no fan of open-ended military commitments, complains that such an effort would result in

> an infinite charge to Her Majesty to send over such an army as should tred down all that standeth before them on foot and lay on the ground all the stiff-necked people of that land, for there is now but one outlaw of any great reckoning, to wit, the Earl of Tyrone, abroad in arms, against whom ye see what huge charges she hath been at this last year in sending of men, providing of victuals and making head against him; yet there is little or nothing at all done, but the Queen's treasure spent, her people wasted, the poor country troubled and the enemy nevertheless brought into no more subjection than he was . . . which in effect is none, but rather a scorn of her power, an emboldening of a proud rebel and an encouragement unto all like lewd-disposed traitors that shall dare lift up their heel against their sovereign Lady.[75]

"How many men then would you require to the finishing of this which ye take in hand? And how long space would you have them

entertained?"[76] asks Eudoxus. Irenius advises a kind of "inkspot" counterinsurgency approach, a clear-and-hold campaign:

> Verily, not above ten thousand footmen and one thousand
> horsemen, and all those not above the space of one-year-
> and-a-half . . . for it is well-known that he is a flying enemy,
> hiding himself in woods and bogs from whence he will not
> draw forth but into some strait passage or perilous ford where
> he knows the army must needs pass. . . . Therefore, to seek
> him out that still flitteth and follow him that can hardly be
> found were vain and bootless, but I would divide my men
> in garrison upon his country. . . . I doubt not but upon the
> settling of these garrison, such a terror and near consideration
> of their perilous state will be stricken into most of [the rebels]
> that they will covet to draw away from their leaders.[77]

The campaigning must be year-round, lest the Irish replenish their
strength: "In Ireland the wintertime yieldeth the best services, for then
the tress are bare and naked, which use both to clothe and hide the
kern; the ground is cold and wet, which useth to be his bedding; the air
is sharp and bitter to blow through his naked sides and legs; the kine
are barren and without milk."[78]

In sum, the purpose of "the sword" was to drive Tyrone's rebels
to the point where they could not protect nor rely upon the economic
system upon which Irish society and the power of the Gaelic lords rested.
Having experienced Munster in the aftermath of the second Desmond
revolt, Spenser had no illusions about what the result would be.

> Although there should none of them fall by the sword, nor be
> slain by the soldier, yet thus being kept from manuarnce, and
> their cattle from coming abroad, by this hard restraint they
> would quickly consume themselves and devour one another,
> the proof whereof I saw sufficiently ensampled in those late
> wars of Munster: for notwithstanding that the same was a
> most rich and plentiful country, full of corn and cattle, that
> ye would have thought they could have been able to stand
> long, yet ere one-year-and-a-half they were brought to so
> wonderful wretchedness, as that any heart would have rued
> the same. Out of every corner of the woods and glens they

came creeping forth upon their hands, for their legs could not bear them. They looked like anatomies of death. They spake like ghosts crying out of their graves. They did eat the dead carrions, happy where they could find them, yea, and one another soon after, insomuch as the very carcasses they spared not to scrape out of their graves. . . . In short space there were almost none left, and a most populous and plentiful country suddenly left void of man or beast.[79]

This passage ends with a dry-eyed assessment: "Yet sure in all that war there perished not many by the sword, but all by the extremity if famine, which they themselves had wrought." To civilize the Irish, to separate the insurgents from their sources of sustainment, this kind of hard war was "very necessity."[80]

Spenser did not live to see Lord Mountjoy, in the aftermath of Kinsale, make use of those methods to crush the Tyrone revolt. By the autumn of 1598, it was plain that the O'More clan would lead a general uprising to attack the Munster plantation, and it is likely that Spenser and his family evacuated Kilcoman—which, though centered on a tower house, could hardly withstand a large raid—shortly before it was burned in late October. The poet and his family took refuge in Cork. As English reinforcements poured into the port city, Spenser took ship for London one last time, carrying the official cries of the New English rulers of Munster to Queen Elizabeth and her counselors. As a pamphlet of the times, the piteous yet bloodcurdling tract titled *The Supplication of the blood of the English, most lamentably murdred in Ireland, Cryeing our of the yearth for revenge*, put it:

To the high and mightie Princesse, ELIZABETH, by the grace of god Queene of Englande, ffrance, and Irlande, defender of the faith etc. ffrom the face of that disloyall and rebellious yearthe of Irland, Crieth the bloode of yo^{re} Ma:^{ties} subjects, whose bodies dismembered by the tyranie of traytors, devowered by the merciless laws of ravenous wolves, humblie Craveth at the hands of yo^{re} sacre Ma:^{tie} (unto whom god hath committed the sword of Iustice to punishe the offender, and upon whom he hath imposed a care and charge for the maintain[a]nce and defense of the innocent) To revenge the monstrous rapes of many poore forlorne widowes, and the bloody murders of many yore faithful subjects.[81]

Edmund Spenser died shortly after arriving in London, early in the new year of 1599. Modernity has come to remember him as "a morally flawed, self-interested sycophant, complicit with a brutal policy of extermination that he articulated with great skill in order to protect what he had gained as a colonist in Ireland." Karl Marx called him "Elizabeths archkissende" that is, arse-kissing, "poet."[82] "When Spenser wrote of Ireland," lamented William Butler Yeats, "he wrote as an official, and out of thoughts and emotions that had been organised by the State. He was the first of many Englishmen to see nothing but what he was desired to see. Could he have gone there as a poet merely, he might have found among its poets more wonderful imaginations than even those islands of Phaedria and Acrasia."[83]

Writers of our current postcolonial, anti-imperial age have been less willing to forgive. Critic Edward Said found that those "who study the great sixteenth-century poet Edmund Spenser, for example, do not connect his bloodthirsty plans for Ireland, where he imagined a British army virtually exterminating the native inhabitants, with his poetic achievement."[84] That is a too-tidy and trite complaint. To the degree it is exemplary rather than unique, Spenser's voice speaks for the British colonist who would carve utopia from a howling wilderness, begging, from the frontier to the imperial city, for protection and fearing abandonment. It is a voice we will hear again and again.

POSTSCRIPT

A Personality of Power

What, to paraphrase George Kennan, was the political personality of Elizabethan power?

To work backward from the Spenserian coda, it was a personality that reflected both anxieties and ambitions. The anxieties ranged from fears of barbarian peoples just outside the garden walls to being torn between France and Spain to internal subversion. But these anxieties were not simply an expression of political paranoia; they were firmly grounded in political reality: the Tudor regime had been on shaky ground for decades and Elizabeth left no heir; dealing with the Irish and Roanokes invariably introduced new levels of complexity and contradiction for her subjects on the scene; France made neither a reliable ally nor an obvious enemy; Spain, and the Habsburg dynasties together, sailed the most profitable colonies, bestrode most of continental Europe and represented an existential threat.

But the true form of British strategy-making was cast by its ambitions. These, too, were many, grand and wide-ranging. There was an ambition for power, grounded in a broadly shared cultural memory and reading of history as well as a keen appreciation of the global balance and sources of power of the day. But there was equally a larger ideological ambition to create a liberty for Protestant worship as well as a kind of justice in international affairs as the best guarantee of confessional and civil liberties. In sum, the Elizabethans looked at the world through a complex and compound set of strategic lenses.

The world in view was complex as well. To begin with, the Elizabethan view was a fully global field of regard; even the Pacific weighed in the frame. In particular, what went on in America did not stay there but, in the English assessment, had tipped the European balance of power profoundly in Spain's direction; to thrive or even survive, the English had not only to disrupt the flow of Hapsburg treasure but also to enter the colonial contest itself. To match an empire, England had to create an empire. In this, it could not replicate New Spain or New France as machines for resource extraction; what was yet unoccupied in America did not run rich with gold or silver or beaver pelts; despite their hopes, few shared Walter Ralegh's dream of *El Dorado*. The creation of New Englands would take more time, effort, and investment, first to secure and then to develop as a larger commonwealth. It required good "use" by zealous and hardworking colonists. In the meantime, securing the "near abroad" throughout the British Isles and, most critical of all, defending the coastal European "counterscarp" made an immediate imperative.

To have any hope of success, Elizabeth needed not only to secure the Tudor dynasty but to strengthen the Tudor state, especially its finances and its military, as well. Henry VIII had begun the process, but that was paid for by pillaging the properties of the English church; it was a one-time windfall. His daughter faced a tougher task of domestic reform and domestic persuasion. Simply to win the votes in parliament to finance her armies and navies, the queen needed to convince, not simply command, and the only way to do so was through fomenting a common view of international politics and power and England's role in the world.

Over the course of Elizabeth's reign, English strategists and the larger political nation groped their way toward a consensus. Because the challenges were so many and the military and financial resources so rarely adequate, the path toward consensus was marked by constant crisis and left the debate between maritime "offshore" and continental "onshore" postures unresolved. But Elizabethan strategy was not simply reactive; even the changeable queen and the cautious Burghley shared a basic geopolitical understanding with the aggressive Protestants like Leicester, Walsingham, and Essex.

But, like any cultural construct, the Elizabethan imperial consensus had its discontents. The Stuart monarchs—both those who succeeded Elizabeth and those restored to the throne in 1660—were chief among them, and in reaction they produced civil wars, an overtly republican commonwealth and Cromwellian protectorate, and, finally a Dutch invasion that derived its true glory by reclaiming the Elizabethan essentials while revolutionizing their imperial manifestation. George III found himself mightily discontented by the unforeseen consequences of the project, forcing his North American subjects to wrest their imperial inheritance from his grasp.

NOTES

PREFACE

1. Leslie H. Gelb, "Quelling the Teacup Wars," *Foreign Affairs*, November/December 1994, https://www.foreignaffairs.com/articles/1994-11-01/quelling-teacup-wars-new-worlds-constant-challenge.

INTRODUCTION

1. George Kennan, "The Sources of Soviet Conduct," *Foreign Affairs*, July 1947, https://www.foreignaffairs.com/articles/russian-federation/1947-07-01/sources-soviet-conduct.

2. Carl von Clausewitz, *On War*, ed. Michael Howard and Peter Paret (Princeton, New Jersey: Princeton University Press, 1976), 128.

3. "Department of Defense Dictionary of Military and Associated Terms," Joint Publication 1-02, United States Department of Defense, Washington, DC, November 10, 2010, as amended through February 15, 2016, https://irp.fas.org/doddir/dod/jp1_02.pdf.

4. *Merriam-Webster*, s.v. "culture," http://www.m-w.com/dictionary/culture.

5. Alastair Iain Johnston, *Cultural Realism: Strategic Culture and Grand Strategy in Chinese History* (Princeton, New Jersey: Princeton University Press, 1995), 1.

6. Jack L. Snyder, "The Soviet Strategic Culture: Implications for Limited Nuclear Operations," RAND R-2154-AF (RAND Corporation, 1977), https://www.rand.org/content/dam/rand/pubs/reports/2005/R2154.pdf.

7. My understanding of the various strains of thought about strategic culture owes much to Johnston's analyses in Johnston, *Cultural Realism*, 6.

8. Colin Gray, "National Styles in Strategy: The American Example," *International Security* 6, no. 2 (1981): 21–47. Gray's work, looking deep into history in search of the roots of American strategic culture, has much to recommend it and is indeed a similar approach to the one employed in this work.

9. Forrest E. Morgan, *Compellence and the Strategic Culture of Japan: Implications for Coercive Diplomacy in the Twenty-First Century* (Westport, Connecticut: Praeger, 2003), 28.

10. George F. Kennan, *American Diplomacy, 1900–1950* (Chicago: Chicago University Press, 1951), 66–69.

11. John Bew, *Realpolitik: A History* (Oxford: Oxford University Press, 2016), 218.

12. Chalmers Johnson, *The Sorrows of Empire: Militarism, Secrecy, and the End of the Republic* (New York: Owl Books, 2004), 284.

13. Reginald C. Stuart, *War and American Thought: From the Revolution to the Monroe Doctrine* (Kent, Ohio: Kent State University Press, 1982).

14. Stuart, *War and American Thought*, ix.

15. Stuart, *War and American Thought*, 20.

16. Stuart, *War and American Thought*, 182–185.

17. Nicole Hannah-Jones et al, *The 1619 Project: A New Origin Story* (New York: One World Books, 2021).

18. "Thomas Jefferson to James Madison," National Archives and Records Administration, April 27, 1809, https://founders.archives.gov/documents/Jefferson/03-01-02-0140.

19. David Armitage, *The Ideological Origins of the British Empire* (Cambridge: Cambridge University Press, 2000), 15.

20. Stephen Alford, *The Early Elizabethan Polity: William Cecil and the British Succession Crisis, 1558–1569* (Cambridge: Cambridge University Press, 1989).

CHAPTER 1

1. Samuel Bawlf, *The Secret Voyage of Sir Frances Drake 1577–1580* (New York: Walker, 2003), 192.

2. Paul Kennedy, *The Rise and Fall of the Great Powers: Economic Change and Military Conflict From 1500 to 2000* (New York: Random House, 1987), 31.

3. John R. Fisher, *The Economic Aspects of Spanish Imperialism in America, 1492–1810* (Liverpool: Liverpool University Press, 1997), 59; John Sudgen, *Sir Francis Drake* (New York: Henry Holt, 1990), 148–149.

4. For Spanish revenues, see Fisher, *The Economic Aspects of Spanish Imperialism*, 12–24; for Elizabethan income, see Sudgen, *Sir Francis Drake*, 148–149.

5. Sudgen, *Sir Francis Drake*, 52.

6. Sudgen, *Sir Francis Drake*, 73.

7. Wallace T. MacCaffrey. *Queen Elizabeth and the Making of Policy, 1572–1588* (Princeton, New Jersey: Princeton University Press, 1981), 164–216.

8. Kenneth R. Andrews, *Drake's Voyages* (New York: Scribner's, 1967), 46–53.

9. E. G. R. Taylor, "The Missing Draft Project of Drake's Voyage of 1577–1580," *The Geographical Journal* 75, no. 1 (January 1930): 46–47; Sudgen, *Sir Francis Drake*, 97.

10. For a definitive discussion, see K. R. Andrews, "The Aims of Drake's Expedition of 1577–1580," *The American Historical Review* 73, no. 3 (February 1968): 724–741.

11. Sudgen, *Sir Francis Drake*, 98.

12. Sudgen, *Sir Francis Drake*, 98; Derek Wilson, *The World Encompassed: Drake's Great Voyage 1577–1580* (London: Allison and Busby, 1977); Harry Kelsey, *Sir Francis Drake: The Queen's Pirate* (New Haven: Yale University Press, 1998); John Cummins, *Francis Drake: The Lives of a Hero* (London: Palgrave MacMillian, 1996); Bawlf, *The Secret Voyage of Sir Frances Drake*.

13. Wilson, *The World Encompassed*, 106–107.

14. Sudgen, *Sir Francis Drake*, 140.

15. Sudgen, *Sir Francis Drake*, 145.

CHAPTER 2

1. D. B. Quinn and A. N. Ryan, *England's Sea Empire, 1550–1642* (London: George Allen & Unwin, 1983), 70.

2. Paul E. J. Hammer, *Elizabeth's Wars: War, Government and Society in Tudor England, 1544–1604* (New York: Palgrave MacMillan, 2003).

3. Hammer, *Elizabeth's Wars*, 51.

4. Alford, *The Early Elizabethan Polity*.

5. Brendan Simms, *Three Victories and a Defeat: The Rise and Fall of the First British Empire* (New York: Basic Books, 2007).

6. R. B. Wernham, ed., *The Expedition of Sir John Norris and Sir Francis Drake to Spain and Portugal, 1589* (Aldershot: Temple Smith, 1988), 7.

7. Richard Hakluyt, "A Discourse Concerning Western Planting (1584)," Swarthmore College website, http://www.swarthmore.edu/SocSci/bdorsey1/41docs/03-hak.html.

8. John Knox, *The First Blast of the Trumpet against the monstrous regiment of Women*, ed. Edward Arber (Southgate, London: DB Publishing, 1558).

9. "Elizabeth's Tilbury Speech, July 1588," The British Library, https://www.bl.uk/learning/timeline/item102878.html.

10. Derek Wilson, *Sir Francis Walsingham: A Courtier in an Age of Terror* (New York: Carroll & Graf, 2007), 1–3, 61–85.

11. MacCaffrey, *Queen Elizabeth and the Making of Policy*, 173.

12. MacCaffrey, *Queen Elizabeth and the Making of Policy*, 446.

13. Wallace T. MacCaffrey, *Elizabeth I, War and Politics 1588–1603* (Princeton, New Jersey: Princeton University Press, 1992), 453–536.

14. Alford, *The Early Elizabethan Polity*, 17–23.

15. Alford, *The Early Elizabethan Polity*, 20–21.

16. Alford, *The Early Elizabethan Polity*, 61.

17. Alford, *The Early Elizabethan Polity*, 61.

18. Peter Lake and Steve Pincus, "Rethinking the Public Sphere in Early Modern England," *Journal of British Studies* 45, no. 2 (April 2006): 274.

19. J. E. Neale, *Elizabeth I and Her Parliaments* (London: Norton, 1953).

20. K. J. Kesselring, *The Northern Rebellion of 1569: Faith, Politics and Protest in Elizabethan England* (New York: Palgrave MacMillian, 2007).

21. Hammer, *Elizabeth's Wars*, 236–264.

CHAPTER 3

1. Kesselring, *The Northern Rebellion of 1569*, 98–99.

2. Patrick Collinson, *Archbishop Grindal, 1519–1583: The Struggle for a Reformed Church* (Berkeley: University of California Press, 1979), 231.

3. Conyers Read, *Mr. Secretary Cecil and Queen Elizabeth* (New York: Alfred A. Knopf, 1961), 431.

4. Michael Questier, "Practical Antipapistry during the Reign of Elizabeth I," *Journal of British Studies* 36, no. 4 (October 1997): 372.

5. Christopher Kitching, "The Durham Palatinate and the Courts of Westminster under the Tudors," in *The Last Principality: Politics, Religion and Society in the Bishopric of Durham, 1494–1660*, ed. David Marcombe (Loughborough: Echo Press, 1987), 49.

6. David Marcombe, "A Rude and Heady People: The Local Community and the Rebellion of the Northern Earls," in Marcombe, *The Last Principality*, 117.

7. David Marcombe, "A Rude and Heady People: The Local Community and the Rebellion of the Northern Earls," in Marcombe, *The Last Principality*, 117.

8. Kesselring, *The Northern Rebellion of 1569*, 22.

9. Marcombe, "A Rude and Heady People," 121.

10. David Marcombe, "A Rude and Heady People," 127–128.

11. Wallace T. MacCaffrey, *The Shaping of the Elizabethan Regime: Elizabethan Politics, 1558–1572* (Princeton, New Jersey: Princeton University Press, 1964).

12. MacCaffrey, *The Shaping of the Elizabethan Regime*.

13. MacCaffrey, *The Shaping of the Elizabethan Regime*, 262, 268–290; R. B. Wernham, *The Making of Elizabethan Foreign Policy, 1558–1603* (Berkeley: University of California Press, 1980), 37–39; Read, *Mr. Secretary Cecil and Queen Elizabeth*.

14. Neville Williams, *Thomas Howard Fourth Duke of Norfolk* (New York: E. P. Dutton, 1965), 127.

15. Williams, *Thomas Howard Fourth Duke of Norfolk*, 138.

16. Williams, *Thomas Howard Fourth Duke of Norfolk*, 141.

17. Alan Kendall, *Robert Dudley, Earl of Leicester* (London: Cassell, 1980), 117.

18. Williams, *Thomas Howard Fourth Duke of Norfolk*, 156–157.

19. Williams, *Thomas Howard Fourth Duke of Norfolk*, 162.

20. Williams, *Thomas Howard Fourth Duke of Norfolk*, 158–159.

21. Williams, *Thomas Howard Fourth Duke of Norfolk*, 161.

22. Kesselring, *The Northern Rebellion of 1569*, 54.

23. Kesselring, *The Northern Rebellion of 1569*, 58–59.

24. Kesselring, *The Northern Rebellion of 1569*, 68.

25. Kesselring, *The Northern Rebellion of 1569*, 74–90.

26. Kesselring, *The Northern Rebellion of 1569*, 83.

27. Kesselring, *The Northern Rebellion of 1569*, 91–117; Hammer, *Elizabeth's Wars*, 83–85.

28. Kesselring, *The Northern Rebellion of 1569*, 94.

29. Kesselring, *The Northern Rebellion of 1569*, 104.

30. Kesselring, *The Northern Rebellion of 1569*, 107.

31. Kesselring, *The Northern Rebellion of 1569*, 95.

32. *A Discourse Touching the Pretended Matche betweene the D[uke] of Norfolk and the Queene of Scots*, quoted in Anne McLaren, "Gender, Religion, and Early Modern Nationalism: Elizabeth I, Mary Queen of Scots, and the Genesis of English Anti-Catholicism," *The American Historical Review* 107, no. 3 (June 2003): 757; Williams, *Thomas Howard Fourth Duke of Norfolk*, 167–169.

33. Collinson, *Archbishop Grindal, 1519–1583*, 188.

34. Michael Questier, "Practical Antipapistry during the Reign of Elizabeth I": 373.

35. Collinson, *Archbishop Grindal, 1519–1583*, 189.

36. Richard L. Greaves, "Concepts of Political Obedience in Late Tudor England: Conflicting Perspectives," *Journal of British Studies* 22, no. 1 (Autumn 1982): 30.

37. Elizabeth Evenden and Thomas S. Freeman, "Print, Profit and Propaganda: The Elizabethan Privy Council and the 1570 Edition of Foxe's 'Book of Martyrs,'" *The English Historical Review* 199, no. 484 (November 2004): 1292.

38. Evenden and Freeman, "Print, Profit and Propaganda": 1301.

39. Kesselring, *The Northern Rebellion of 1569*, 156.

40. K. J. Kesselring, "'A Cold Pye for Papistes': Constructing and Containing the Northern Uprising of 1569," *Journal of British Studies* 43, no. 4 (October 2004): 440.

CHAPTER 4

1. Henry Kamen, *The Duke of Alba* (New Haven: Yale University Press, 2004), 112.

2. Wallace MacCaffrey, *Elizabeth I* (London: Edward Arnold, 1993), 166.

3. MacCaffrey, *Elizabeth I*, 190.

4. MacCaffrey, *Elizabeth I*, 74–75.

5. MacCaffrey, *Elizabeth I*, 191–197.

6. R. B. Wernham, *Before the Armada: The Emergence of the English Nation*, 1485–1588 (New York: Harcourt, Brace & World, 1966), 357.

7. Wernham, *Before the Armada*, 356–358.

8. Wernham, *Before the Armada*, 369.

9. R.B. Wernham, *Before the Armada*, 369.

10. Elizabeth, Queen of England, Declaration of the Causes Moving the Queene of England to Give Aide to the Defence of the People Afflicted and Oppressed in the Lowe Countries, ed. Christopher Barker (London, 1585).

11. Hammer, *Elizabeth's Wars*, 126.

12. J. E. Neale, "Elizabeth and the Netherlands, 1586–87," *The English Historical Review* 45, no. 197 (July 1930): 375.

13. Hammer, *Elizabeth's Wars*, 129.

14. Burghley to Walsingham, August 9, 1588, *State Papers Domestic*, ccxii, number 66, reprinted in Wernham, *The Expedition of Sir John Norris and Sir Francis Drake*, 4.

15. Luis Gorrochategui Santos, *The English Armada: The Greatest Naval Disaster in English History* (London: Bloomsbury Academic 2018).

16. Wernham, *The Expedition of Sir John Norris and Sir Francis Drake*, xiv–xv.

17. "A proportion to be furnished by Her Majesty of all sorts of provisions fit for the enterprise of Portugal," *State Papers Domestic*, ccxvii, number 79, in Wernham, *The Expedition of Sir John Norris and Sir Francis Drake*, 8–10.

18. "A proportion to be furnished by Her Majesty of all sorts of provisions fit for the enterprise of Portugal," xviii.

19. Lord Willoughby to the Privy Council, October 28, 1588, *State Papers Holland*, xxvii, folio 196, in Wernham, *The Expedition of Sir John Norris and Sir Francis Drake*, 36.

20. Sir John Norris to Walsingham, October 29, 1588, *State Papers Holland*, xvii, folio 212, in Wernham, *The Expedition of Sir John Norris and Sir Francis Drake*, 36–37.

21. Sir John Norris to Walsingham, October 29, 1588, xxii.

22. Instruction from Sir John Norris and Sir Francis Drake, February 23, 1589, *State Papers Domestic*, ccxxii, number 90, in Wernham, *The Expedition of Sir John Norris and Sir Francis Drake*, 82–88.

23. Instruction from Sir John Norris and Sir Francis Drake, February 23, 1589, 82–88.

24. Burghley to Anthony Ashley, March 4, 1589, *Bodleian Library Lansdowne MSS*, ciii, folio 93, in Wernham, *The Expedition of Sir John Norris and Sir Francis Drake*, 102–103.

25. Hammer, *Elizabeth's Wars*, 157.

26. Wernham, *The Expedition of Sir John Norris and Sir Francis Drake*, xxxv.

27. The Earl of Essex to Francis Knollys, April 1, 1589, in Wernham, *The Expedition of Sir John Norris and Sir Francis Drake*, 133.

28. The Earl of Essex's Apology written to Mr. Anthony Bacon, 1598, in Wernham, *The Expedition of Sir John Norris and Sir Francis Drake*, 137–138.

29. Drake and Norris to the Privy Council, April 6, 1589, *State Papers Hamburg and Hanse Towns*, iii, folio 63, in Wernham, *The Expedition of Sir John Norris and Sir Francis Drake*, 141–142.

30. William Fenner to Anthony Bacon, 1589, in Wernham, *The Expedition of Sir John Norris and Sir Francis Drake*, 237.

31. nthony Wingfield's discourse, August 30, 1589, Richard Hackluyt, *Principal Navigations, etc.*, vi, 470–527, all in Wernham, *The Expedition of Sir John Norris and Sir Francis Drake*, 150.

32. Norris to Burghley, May 8, 1589, in Wernham, *The Expedition of Sir John Norris and Sir Francis Drake*, 152–153.

33. The Queen to Norris and Drake, May 20, 1589, *State Papers Domestic*, ccxxiv, number 53, all in Wernham, *The Expedition of Sir John Norris and Sir Francis Drake*, 164–168.

34. A letter to Burghley, June 25, 1589, in Wernham, *The Expedition of Sir John Norris and Sir Francis Drake*, 193.

35. Wernham, *The Expedition of Sir John Norris and Sir Francis Drake*, xlix.

36. Anthony Wingfield's discourse, August 30, 1589, Richard Hackluyt, *Principal Navigations, etc.*, VI, inWernham, *The Expedition of Sir John Norris and Sir Francis Drake*, 246–290.

37. Sir John Norris to Walsingham, July 4, 1589, *State Papers Domestic*, ccxxv, Number 5, in Wernham, *The Expedition of Sir John Norris and Sir Francis Drake*, 199–200.

38. Gorrochategui Santos, *The English Armada*, 237–252.

CHAPTER 5

1. Lorcan Ó Mearáin, "The Battle of Clontibret," *Clogher Record* 1, no. 4 (1956): 12–13.

2. Ó Mearáin, "The Battle of Clontibret," 10.

3. Ó Mearáin, "The Battle of Clontibret," 10.

4. Ó Mearáin, "The Battle of Clontibret," 18.

5. Ó Mearáin, "The Battle of Clontibret," 19.

6. Ó Mearáin, "The Battle of Clontibret," 21.

7. Ó Mearáin, "The Battle of Clontibret," 26–27.

8. Ó Mearáin, "The Battle of Clontibret," 27.

9. MacCaffrey, *Elizabeth I, War and Politics*, 332–333.

10. James P. Myers, ed., *Elizabethan Ireland: A Selection of Writing by Elizabethan Writers on Ireland* (Hamden, Conneticut: Arhon Books, 1983), 6.

11. Jane H. Ohlmeyer, "'Civilizing of Those Rude Partes': Colonization within Britain and Ireland, 1580s–1640s," in *The Origins of Empire: British Overseas Enterprise to the Close of the Seventeenth Century*, ed. Nicholas Canny (Oxford: Oxford University Press, 2001), 124–147.

12. Hiram Morgan, *Tyrone's Rebellion: The Outbreak of the Nine Years War in Tudor Ireland* (Woodbridge, Suffolk: Boydell & Brewster, 1999), 29–30.

13. Morgan, *Tyrone's Rebellion*, 55–81.

14. Morgan, *Tyrone's Rebellion*, 85–135.

15. Morgan, *Tyrone's Rebellion*, 172.

16. R. B. Wernham, *The Return of the Armadas: The Last Years of the Elizabethan War against Spain, 1595–1603* (Oxford: Oxford University Press, 1994), 45–54; Hammer, *Elizabeth's Wars*, 191–192.

17. Wernham, *The Return of the Armadas*, 55.

18. Wernham, *The Return of the Armadas*, 82–140.

19. John Silke, *Kinsale: The Spanish Intervention in Ireland at the End of the Elizabethan Wars* (New York, New York: 1970), 29–32.

20. Marc Caball, "Faith, Culture and Sovereignty: Irish Nationality and Its Development, 1558–1625," in *British Consciousness and Identity: The Making of Britain, 1533–1707*, ed. Brendan Bradshaw and Peter Roberts (Cambridge: Cambridge University Press, 1998).

21. Cyril Falls, *Elizabeth's Irish Wars* (London: Constable and Company, 1996), 203.

22. Falls, *Elizabeth's Irish Wars*, 207.

23. Falls, *Elizabeth's Irish Wars*, 213.

24. Falls, *Elizabeth's Irish Wars*, 215–219.

25. Falls, *Elizabeth's Irish Wars*, 223–224.

26. Falls, *Elizabeth's Irish Wars*, 221.

27. Falls, *Elizabeth's Irish Wars*, 222.

28. Falls, *Elizabeth's Irish Wars*, 228.

29. Falls, *Elizabeth's Irish Wars*, 229.

30. Wernham, *The Return of the Armadas*, 299.

31. Wernham, *The Return of the Armadas*, 300.

32. Wernham, *The Return of the Armadas*, 304.

33. Wernham, *The Return of the Armadas*, 305.

34. Wernham, *The Return of the Armadas*, 312.

35. Wernham, *The Return of the Armadas*, 312.

36. Wernham, *The Return of the Armadas*, 312.

37. Wernham, *The Return of the Armadas*, 313.

38. Wernham, *The Return of the Armadas*, 315.

39. Wernham, *The Return of the Armadas*, 316.

40. Wernham, *The Return of the Armadas*, 316–317.

41. Wernham, *The Return of the Armadas*, 318.

42. John Silke, *Kinsale*, 60.

43. Thomas O'Connor, "Hugh O'Neill: Free Spirit, Religious Chameleon or Ardent Catholic?" in *The Battle of Kinsale*, ed. Hiram Morgan (Wicklow: Wordwell, 2004), 71.

44. Patrick Williams, *The Great Favourite: The Duke of Lerma and the Court and Government of Philip III of Spain, 1598–1621* (Manchester: Manchester University Press, 2006).

45. Silke, *Kinsale*, 75.

46. Silke, *Kinsale*, 79.

47. Cyril Falls, *Mountjoy: Elizabethan General* (London: Odhams Press Limited, 1955); Morgan, *The Battle of Kinsale*; Cyril Falls, *Elizabeth's Irish Wars* (London: Constable and Company, 1996), 253–267.

48. Falls, *Elizabeth's Irish Wars*, 271.

49. Falls, *Mountjoy*, 148.

50. Wernham, *The Return of the Armadas*, 345.

51. Wernham, *The Return of the Armadas*, 346.

52. Enrique García Hernán, "Philip II's Forgotten Armada," in Morgan, *The Battle of Kinsale*, 45–58.

53. Silke, *Kinsale*, 81–82.

54. Silke, *Kinsale*, 92–104.

55. Archivo General de Simancas, Guerra Antiqua 3144, translated and summarized in Silke, *Kinsale*, 107.

56. Silke, *Kinsale*, 111.

57. Silke, *Kinsale*, 160–165.

58. Silke, *Kinsale*, 165–166.

59. Silke, *Kinsale*, 166.

60. Falls, *Elizabeth's Irish Wars*, 292–296; Hiram Morgan, "The Historiography and Heritage of the Battle of Kinsale," in Morgan, *The Battle of Kinsale*, 9–44.

61. Hiram Morgan, "Disaster at Kinsale," in Morgan, *The Battle of Kinsale*, 102.

62. Lughaidh Ó Clérigh, *Beatha Ruaidh Uí Dhomhnaill: The Life of Red Hugh O'Donnell, Prince of Tyrconnell*, ed. Dennis Murphy (Dublin, 1893), 299, quoted in Morgan, "Disaster at Kinsale," 106–107.

63. Ó Clérigh, *Beatha Ruaidh Uí Dhomhnaill*, in Morgan, "Disaster at Kinsale," 107.

64. Ó Clérigh, *Beatha Ruaidh Uí Dhomhnaill*, in Morgan, "Disaster at Kinsale," 108.

65. John McGurk, "English Naval Operations at Kinsale," in Morgan, *The Battle of Kinsale*, 147–160.

66. Morgan, "Disaster at Kinsale," 116.

67. Morgan, "Disaster at Kinsale," 120.

68. Morgan, "Disaster at Kinsale," 121.

69. Óscar Recio Morales, "Spanish Army Attitudes to the Irish at Kinsale," in Morgan, *The Battle of Kinsale*, 121.

70. Morgan, "Disaster at Kinsale," 122.

71. Morgan, "Disaster at Kinsale," 127.

72. Morgan, "Disaster at Kinsale," 129.

73. Morgan, "Disaster at Kinsale," 129.

74. Morgan, "Disaster at Kinsale," 134.

75. Morgan, "Disaster at Kinsale," 133.

76. Ralph Birkenshaw, "Discourse occasioned upon the defeat, given to the Arch-rebels, Tyrone and Odonnell, by the right Honourable the Lord Mountjoy, Lord Deputie of Ireland, the 24. Of December, 1601, being Christs Eave: And the yielding up of Kinsale shortly after by Don John to his lordshippe," in Hiram Morgan, "Birchensha's Choice," in Morgan, *The Battle of Kinsale*, 391–407.

77. Vincent Carey, "What Pen Can Paint or Tears Atone? Mountjoy's Scorched Earth Campaign," in Morgan, *The Battle of Kinsale*, 209.

78. Falls, *Elizabeth's Irish Wars*, 334.

CHAPTER 6

1. "31 March 1588: The Privy Council to Sir Richard Grenville," *Acts of the Privy Council, 1588*, 7; in *The Roanoke Voyages 1584–90*, vol. 2, ed. David Beers Quinn (Mineola, New York: Dover Publications, 1991), 560–561.

2. Kenneth R. Andrews, *Trade, Plunder and Settlement: Maritime Enterprise and the Genesis of the British Empire, 1480–1630* (Cambridge: Cambridge University Press, 1984), 218.

3. D. B. Quinn, *Ralegh and the British Empire* (New York: Collier Books, 1962), 134.

4. Quinn, *Ralegh and the British Empire*, 134.

5. Lord Alfred Tennyson, "The Revenge: A Ballad of the Fleet," The Literature Network, http://www.online-literature.com/tennyson/726/.

6. "Letter Patent to Sir Humfrey Gilberte June 11, 1578," in *Sir Humfrey Glylberte and His Enterprise of Colonization in America*, ed. Rev. Carlos Shatter (Boston: The Prince Society, 1903), 95–102.

7. David Beers Quinn, *Set Fair for Roanoke: Voyages and Colonies, 1584–1606* (Chapel Hill, North Carolina: The University of North Carolina Press, 1985), 3.

8. Walsingham to Hakluyt, March 11, 1582, in *The Writings and Correspondence of the Two Richard Hakluyts*, vol. 2, ed. E. G. R. Taylor (London:

Hakluyt Society, 1935), 76; Peter C. Mancall, *Hakluyt's Promise: An Elizabethan's Obsesssion for an English America* (New Haven: Yale University Press, 2007), 102.

9. Hakluyt to Walsingham, January 7, 1584, in Taylor, *The Writings and Correspondence of the Two Richard Hakluyts*, 2:128.

10. Mancall, *Hakluyt's Promise: An Elizabethan's Obsesssion for an English America*, 129.

11. Richard Hakluyt, *A Particuler Discourse Concerning the Great Necessitie and Manifolde Commodyties That Are Likely to Growe to This Realme of Englande by the Westerne Discoveries Lately Attempted* (London: Hakluyt Society, London, 1993), 239–240.

12. Hakluyt, *Discourse*, 142–145.

13. Hakluyt, *Discourse*, 146.

14. Hakluyt, *Discourse*, 147–148.

15. Hakluyt, *Discourse*, 44, 147.

16. Hakluyt, *Discourse*, 154.

17. Arthur Barlowe, "Arthur Barlowe's Narrative of the 1584 Voyage," in *The First Colonists: Documents on the Planting of the First English Settlements in North America, 1584–90*, ed. David B. Quinn and Alison M. Quinn (Ralegh: North Carolina Department of Cultural Resources, 1985), 5.

18. For an insightful understanding of the strategic perspective of the coastal Algonkian peoples, see Michael Leroy Oberg, *The Head in Edward Nugent's Hand: Roanoke's Forgotten Indians* (Philadelphia: University of Pennsylvania Press, 2008).

19. Barlowe, "Arthur Barlowe's Narrative of the 1584 Voyage," 8.

20. Quinn, *Set Fair for Roanoke*, 40–42.

21. Michael R. Lynn, "Review: Thomas Harriot, An Elizabethan Man of Science," *The Sixteenth Century Journal* 33, no. 1 (Spring 2002): 207–208.

22. Quinn, *Set Fair for Roanoke*, 50.

23. Quinn, *Set Fair for Roanoke*, 52–54; Karen Ordahl Kupperman, *Roanoke: The Abandoned Colony* (Savage, Maryland: Rowman and Littlefield, 1984), 18.

24. Quinn, *Set Fair for Roanoke*, 57.

25. Kupperman, *Roanoke*, 19–22.

26. Quinn, *Set Fair for Roanoke*, 63.

27. Oberg, *The Head in Edward Nugent's Hand*, 64–65.

28. "Ralph Lane to Richard Hakluyt the Elder and Master H——— of the Middle Temple, 3 September 1585," in Quinn and Quinn, *The First Colonists*, 22–23.

29. "Ralph Lane to Richard Hakluyt the Elder and Master H——— of the Middle Temple, 3 September 1585," 22.

30. Thomas Harriot, "A Briefe and True Report of the New Found Land of Virginia," in Quinn and Quinn, *The First Colonists*, 46.

31. Oberg, *The Head in Edward Nugent's Hand*, 73.

32. Quinn, *Set Fair for Roanoke*, 85.

33. Oberg, *The Head in Edward Nugent's Hand*, 81.

34. Ralph Lane, "Ralph Lane's Narrative of the Settlement," in Quinn and Quinn, *The First Colonists*, 109; Kupperman, *Roanoke*, 77.

35. Lane, "Ralph Lane's Narrative of the Settlement," 31.

36. Oberg, *The Head in Edward Nugent's Hand*, 87.

37. Oberg, *The Head in Edward Nugent's Hand*, 88.

38. Oberg, *The Head in Edward Nugent's Hand*, 90; for Oberg's analysis of the situation, see p. 91.

39. Oberg, *The Head in Edward Nugent's Hand*, 95.

40. Oberg, *The Head in Edward Nugent's Hand*, 96.

41. Oberg, *The Head in Edward Nugent's Hand*, 98, quoting David Beers Quinn, ed., *The Roanoke Voyages, 1584–1590* (London: Hakluyt Society, 1955), 265.

42. Andrew Thomas Powell, *Grenville and the Lost Colony of Roanoke* (Leicester: Troubador Publishing, 2011), 99.

43. Kupperman, *Roanoke*, 93.

44. Oberg, *The Head in Edward Nugent's Hand*, 100.

45. Oberg, *The Head in Edward Nugent's Hand*, 102.

46. Quinn, *Set Fair for Roanoke*, 250.

47. Kupperman, *Roanoke*, 104.

48. "John White's Narrative of His Voyage," in Quinn, *The Roanoke Voyages, 1584–1590*, 515–538.

49. "John White's Narrative of His Voyage," 517.

50. "John White's Narrative of His Voyage," 517–518.

51. "John White's Narrative of His Voyage," 522.

52. "John White's Narrative of His Voyage," 522–524.

53. Kupperman, *Roanoke*, 115; Oberg, *The Head in Edward Nugent's Hand*, 113–114.

54. "John White's Narrative of His Voyage," 525–526.

55. "John White's Narrative of His Voyage," 530.

56. "John White's Narrative of His Voyage," 532.

57. "John White's Narrative of His Voyage," 534.

58. "John White's Narrative of His Voyage," 536–537.

59. "7 March 1589: Agreement between Sir Walter Ralegh, Thomas Smythe Etc., and John White Etc. for the Continuance of the City of Ralegh Venture," in Quinn, *The Roanoke Voyages, 1584–1590*, 569–576.

60. "John White's Narrative of the 1590 Voyage to Virginia," 612–613.

61. Kupperman, *Roanoke*, 138–139.

62. Peter C. Mancall, ed., *Envisioning America: English Plans for the Colonization of North America, 1580–1640* (Boston, Massachusetts: Bedford Books, 1995), 16.

63. Thomas Harriot, "A Briefe and True Report of the New Found Land of Virginia," in Quinn and Quinn, *The First Colonists*, 47–48.

64. Harriot, "A Briefe and True Report of the New Found Land of Virginia," 49.

65. Harriot, "A Briefe and True Report of the New Found Land of Virginia," 67–68.

66. Harriot, "A Briefe and True Report of the New Found Land of Virginia," 67.

67. Harriot, "A Briefe and True Report of the New Found Land of Virginia," 68.

68. Harriot, 68–70.

69. Harriot, "A Briefe and True Report of the New Found Land of Virginia," 70–71.

CHAPTER 7

1. Glyn Parry, *The Arch-Conjuror of England, John Dee* (New Haven: Yale University Press, 2001), 108.

2. Parry, *The Arch-Conjuror of England, John Dee*, xi.

3. Parry, *The Arch-Conjuror of England, John Dee*, 94.

4. Glyn Parry, "John Dee and the Elizabethan British Empire in its European Context," *The Historical Journal* 49, no. 3 (2006): 661.

5. Armitage, *The Ideological Origins of the British Empire*, 106.

6. Parry, *The Arch-Conjuror of England, John Dee*, 107.

7. Parry, *The Arch-Conjuror of England, John Dee*, 116.

8. Parry, *The Arch-Conjuror of England, John Dee*, 116.

9. William Sherman, *John Dee: The Politics of Reading and Writing in the English Renaissance* (Amherst, Massachusetts: University of Massachusetts Press, 1995), 158.

10. Sherman, *John Dee*, 165.

11. Sherman, *John Dee*, 180.

12. Sherman, *John Dee*, 181.

13. Sherman, *John Dee*, 185.

14. Sherman, *John Dee*, 182.

15. Parry, *The Arch-Conjuror of England, John Dee*, 141–144; Sherman, *John Dee*, 182–185.

16. Parry, *The Arch-Conjuror of England, John Dee*, 143.

17. Mary Dewar, *Sir Thomas Smith: A Tudor Intellectual in Office* (London: University of London Athlone Press, 1964), 12–25.

18. Anne McLaren, "Reading Sir Thomas Smith's *De Republica Anglorum* as Protestant Apologetic," *The Historical Journal* 42, no. 4 (1999): 915.

19. Andrew Hadfield, *Edmund Spenser: A Life* (Oxford: Oxford University Press 2012), 65.

20. Lisa Jardine, "Encountering Ireland: Gabriel Harvey, Edmund Spenser and English Colonial Ventures," in *Representing Ireland: Literature and the Origins of Conflict, 1534–1660*, ed. Brendan Bradshaw, Andrew Hadfield, and Willey Malley (Cambridge: Cambridge University Press, 1993), 63.

21. Dewar, *Sir Thomas Smith*, 88–114.

22. McLaren, "Reading Sir Thomas Smith's De Republica Anglorum as Protestant Apologetic," 911–939.

23. Sir Thomas Smith, *De Republica Anglorum: a Discourse on the Commonwealth of England*, ed. Mary Dewar (Cambridge: Cambridge University Press, 1982), 57, 76.

24. Dewar, *Sir Thomas Smith*, 156–157.

25. Dewar, *Sir Thomas Smith*, 157.

26. Hiram Morgan, *Tyrone's Rebellion: The Outbreak of the Nine Years War in Tudor Ireland* (Woodbridge, Suffolk: Boydell & Brewster, 1999), 268, 270.

27. Morgan, *Tyrone's Rebellion*, 277, 278, 272.

28. Dewar, *Sir Thomas Smith*, 164.

29. Dewar, *Sir Thomas Smith*, 166.

30. Dewar, *Sir Thomas Smith*, 165.

31. John S. Nolan, *Sir John Norreys and the Elizabethan Military World* (Exeter: University of Exeter Press, 1997), 242.

32. Nolan, *Sir John Norreys and the Elizabethan Military World*, 242.

33. See Stephen Saunders Webb, *The Governors-General: The English Army and the Definition of Empire, 1569–1681* (Chapel Hill: University of North Carolina Press, 1979).

34. John S. Nolan, "The Militarization of the Elizabethan State," *The Journal of Military History* 58, no. 3 (July 1994): 401.

35. Webb, *The Governors-General*, 4.

36. See Nolan, *Sir John Norreys and the Elizabethan Military World*.

37. Wernham, *The Expedition of Sir John Norris and Sir Francis Drake*, xxiii.

38. Nolan, *Sir John Norreys and the Elizabethan Military World*, 15.

39. Nolan, *Sir John Norreys and the Elizabethan Military World*, 16.

40. Nolan, *Sir John Norreys and the Elizabethan Military World*, 244, 245.

41. Nolan, *Sir John Norreys and the Elizabethan Military World*, 246.

42. Nolan, *Sir John Norreys and the Elizabethan Military World*, 27.

43. Nolan, *Sir John Norreys and the Elizabethan Military World*, 27.

44. Nolan, *Sir John Norreys and the Elizabethan Military World*, 26–27.

45. Nolan, *Sir John Norreys and the Elizabethan Military World*, 29.

46. Nolan, *Sir John Norreys and the Elizabethan Military World*, 29.

47. Michael MacCarthy-Morrough, *The Munster Plantation: English Migration to Southern Ireland, 1583–1641* (Oxford: Clarendon Press, 1986).

48. Nolan, *Sir John Norreys and the Elizabethan Military World*, 69.

49. Nolan, *Sir John Norreys and the Elizabethan Military World*, 106.

50. MacCaffrey, *Elizabeth I, War and Politics*, 158.

51. Nolan, *Sir John Norreys and the Elizabethan Military World*, 202.

52. Nolan, *Sir John Norreys and the Elizabethan Military World*, 221.

53. Nolan, *Sir John Norreys and the Elizabethan Military World*, 242.

54. Richard Hofstadter, "The Paranoid Style in American Politics," *Harper's Magazine*, November 1964, https://harpers.org/archive/1964/11/the-paranoid-style-in-american-politics/.

55. Hofstadter, "The Paranoid Style in American Politics."

56. Ciaran Brady, "Spenser's Irish Crisis: Humanism and Experience in the 1590s," *Past & Present*, no. 111 (May 1986): 18.

57. Benjamin P. Myers, "The Green and Golden World: Spenser's Rewriting of the Munster Plantation," *English Literary History* 76, no. 2 (Summer 2009): 473.

58. Hadfield, *Edmund Spenser*, 155.

59. Falls, *Elizabeth's Irish Wars*, 136.

60. Hadfield, *Edmund Spenser*, 265.

61. Bruce Danner, *Edmund Spenser's War on Lord Burghley* (London: Palgrave MacMillan, 2001).

62. Danner, *Edmund Spenser's War on Lord Burghley*, 177.

63. Hadfield, *Edmund Spenser*, 333.

64. Andrew Hadfield, *Spenser's Irish Experience: Wilde Fruit and Salvage Soil* (Oxford: Clarendon Press, 1997), 84.

65. Edmund Spenser, *A View of the Present State of Ireland*, as reprinted in *Elizabethan Ireland*, ed. James P. Myers (Hamden, Connecticut: Archon Books, 1983), 60–108.

66. Spenser, A View of the Present State of Ireland, 63.

67. Spenser, A View of the Present State of Ireland, 74.

68. Richard W. Cogley, "'Some Other Kinde of Being and Condition': The Controversy in Mid-Seventeenth Century England over the Peopling of Ancient America," *Journal of the History of Ideas* 68, no. 1 (January 2007): 35–56.

69. Richard W. Cogley, "'The Most Vile and Barbarous Nation of all the World': Giles Fletcher the Elder's *The Tartars Or, Ten Tribes*," *Renaissance Quarterly* 58, no. 3 (Fall 2005): 781–814.

70. Spenser, A View of the Present State of Ireland, 80.

71. Spenser, A View of the Present State of Ireland, 87, 101.

72. Spenser, A View of the Present State of Ireland, 92.

73. Spenser, A View of the Present State of Ireland, 107.

74. Spenser, A View of the Present State of Ireland, 108.

75. Spenser, A View of the Present State of Ireland, 109–110.

76. Spenser, A View of the Present State of Ireland, 111.

77. Spenser, A View of the Present State of Ireland, 115–116.

78. Spenser, A View of the Present State of Ireland, 112.

79. Spenser, A View of the Present State of Ireland, 115–116.

80. Spenser, A View of the Present State of Ireland, 116.

81. Hadfield, *Edmund Spenser*, 388.

82. See Russ Leo, "The Species-Life of Wordlings," *Spenser Studies: A Renaissance Poetry Annual*, University of Chicago Press Journals, Volume 30, 2015, at https://www.journals.uchicago.edu/doi/epdf/10.7756/spst.030.013.201-27.

83. William Butler Yeats, *The Complete Works of William Butler Yeats (Vol. 1–8): Complete Edition of Works in Verse and Prose* (Good Press, 2020).

84. Willy Malley, *Salvaging Spenser: Colonialism, Culture and Identity* (Palgrave MacMillan, 1997), 3.

INDEX

Note: Page numbers followed by *f* indicate material in figures.